[illegible] the Age of AI

Literacies in the Age of AI

Teaching and Learning in the Digital Era

Gabriela C. Zapata
Bill Cope
Mary Kalantzis

WILEY

Published by John Wiley & Sons, Inc., Hoboken, New Jersey.

Library of Congress Cataloging-in-Publication Data
Names: Zapata, Gabriela C., author. | Cope, Bill, author. | Kalantzis, Mary, author.
Title: Literacies in the age of AI : teaching and learning in the digital era / Gabriela C. Zapata, Bill Cope, Mary Kalantzis.
Description: First edition. | Hoboken : Wiley, 2026. | Includes index.
Identifiers: LCCN 2025033030 (print) | LCCN 2025033031 (ebook) | ISBN 9781394338627 (paperback) | ISBN 9781394338641 (adobe pdf) | ISBN 9781394338634 (epub)
Subjects: LCSH: Computers and literacy. | Literacy–Study and teaching. | Artificial intelligence.
Classification: LCC LC149.5 .Z37 2026 (print) | LCC LC149.5 (ebook)
LC record available at https://lccn.loc.gov/2025033030
LC ebook record available at https://lccn.loc.gov/2025033031

Cover Design: Wiley
Cover Image: © Yuichiro Chino/Getty Images

Set in 11.5/14 pts STIXTwoText by Straive, Pondicherry, India

Printed and bound by CPI Group (UK) Ltd, Croydon, CR0 4YY

C9781394338627_120126

Contents

List of Figures

List of Tables

List of Appendices

Preface

This book explores literacy's evolution—from early human communication without formal writing systems to the digital era's multimodal landscapes and the recent integration of generative artificial intelligence (GenAI)—revealing how diverse meaning forms, including text, sound, image, space, and gesture, interact to shape the way we communicate, teach, and learn. By highlighting the interplay of these meaning forms and their functions in contemporary communication, we broaden the very definition of literacy, examining not only traditional reading and writing but also more fluid, interconnected literacy practices.

Across eight chapters, we explore various literacy pedagogies, proposing a reflexive instructional framework that synthesizes didactic, authentic, functional, and critical aspects. Reflexive pedagogy recognizes that learners, educators, and communities co-construct knowledge through continuous dialogue, reflecting on diverse social realities, emergent technologies, and ethical imperatives. The book also offers a comprehensive view of the complexities of digital and AI literacies, tackling pressing challenges such as algorithmic bias, fabricated or misleading content, and concerns about privacy and surveillance. At the same time, we advocate for responsible GenAI use, with detailed discussions of how these technologies can transform personalized learning, inclusive assessment, and research, and how these transformations might shape education's future.

In **Chapter 1**, we trace the historical arc of literacy from its beginnings in pre-writing cultures to the pivotal moments of invention—writing systems, the printing press, and now GenAI—each reshaping our modes of creating, interpreting, and circulating meaning.

Chapter 2 explores the inherently multimodal character of human communication. Through discussion and examples, we show how text, image, space, object, body, sound, and speech all converge in a complex yet seamless interplay of meanings that are essential for contemporary literacies.

Chapter 3 shifts toward the examination of the functional and transformative facets of literacy. In this chapter, we discuss the evolution of grammar studies, the concept of design as an integral part of meaning-making, and the social participation that undergirds literacy. Additionally, we emphasize the importance of interpreting literacy in a social context—particularly relevant as GenAI-generated content becomes more prevalent.

In **Chapter 4**, we offer a critical survey of historical and current approaches to literacy education. For instance, we describe the principles and tenets of didactic, authentic, functional, and critical frameworks, illustrating how each of these pedagogies has contributed unique insights and practices. Building on these traditions, we advocate for a reflexive approach that brings together the strengths of various pedagogical perspectives while remaining flexible to the digital transformations characterizing modern classrooms to incorporate diverse learner identities and answer their unique personal and academic needs.

Chapter 5 focuses on the profound ways in which digital technologies and GenAI have influenced traditional understandings of literacy. From social media and participatory culture to GenAI's potential for streamlining or personalizing meaning-making, the chapter offers both cautionary tales about data privacy, surveillance, or content fabrication and a forward-looking view of how GenAI might power new modes of teaching and learning. In this chapter, we also offer key definitions of AI literacy and what it means for literacy education.

In **Chapter 6**, we examine how literacy evolves in tandem with cognitive growth and social development. Drawing on key theoretical perspectives, this chapter delves into how children progress from basic conceptual understandings to more abstract, symbolic literacies. We also discuss how GenAI-powered tools can enhance or challenge this developmental arc, underscoring the need for careful pedagogical design and ethically grounded technology use based on the needs of specific educational contexts. Additionally, we highlight the need for the plural conceptualization of *literacies*, establishing connections with both multimodal communication and AI literacy development.

In **Chapter 7**, we explore inclusive education and assessment, emphasizing the importance of embracing and responding to material, embodied, and symbolic differences among learners as well as the uniqueness of each student's lifeworld. We discuss how culturally responsive literacy practices and thoughtful use of GenAI can support personalized learning paths, offering diverse, individualized assessment formats that promote equity, inclusion, and learner agency.

Chapter 8 surveys new horizons in literacy scholarship, foregrounding the expanded role of education in addressing contemporary crises and championing equity. In this chapter, we envision how educators can position themselves as researchers, harnessing GenAI alongside socially grounded methods to design learning ecologies that respond to rapidly changing realities.

We hope that the chapters in this volume will offer a roadmap for educators to empower students as critical thinkers, effective communicators, and responsible digital citizens—active participants in a world where literacy is increasingly multimodal, interactive, and entwined with human–machine collaboration. We trust our volume will deepen readers' engagement with the possibilities for GenAI-supported, transformative, and, more importantly, inclusive literacies instruction, inspiring new questions and creative, locally responsive solutions for the pressing challenges in education we currently face.

AI Disclosure

In this volume, DALL·E 3.0., accessed via OpenAI's ChatGPT 4.0, was employed to generate images in Chapters 1, 2, 3, and 5 in order to illustrate the affordances and limitations of Generative AI and its possible uses in educational contexts. All image generation adhered to OpenAI's sharing and publication guidelines (https://openai.com/policies/sharing-publication-policy/). Additionally, content related to Generative AI was discussed in all chapters, but was not generated by AI.

Chapter 1
What Is Literacy?

Introduction

In this chapter, we present an account of the evolution of the concept of literacy in human history. We examine the concept in connection with three major historical periods involving social processes over approximately our 100,000 years of existence as a species (Kalantzis & Cope, 2006). First, we explore how humans communicated before the advent of writing as we know it. Next, we consider the profound effects that the development of writing and print literacy exercised on human societies, including the establishment of standardized meanings and the emergence of hierarchical social structures. This is followed by an exploration of the digital age, where electronic technologies for creating and distributing meaning—most recently exemplified by generative artificial intelligence (henceforth, GenAI)—have revolutionized traditional understandings of literacy, highlighting the capacity to produce and interpret meaning across diverse formats. The goal is to illuminate how understandings of communication and literacy have consistently adapted to technological advancements and societal

Literacies in the Age of AI: Teaching and Learning in the Digital Era,
First Edition. Gabriela C. Zapata, Bill Cope, and Mary Kalantzis.

shifts, shaping the ways in which people make meaning, learn, and interact with the world. The chapter ends with a glossary of terms useful for the understanding of GenAI, as well as suggestions for further research, reflection, and action.

Before Writing: First Languages

Human beings are inherently global creatures. From the moment we emerged as a species, we became the first sentient beings to inhabit virtually every part of the Earth. This expansion occurred during the first 95,000 years of our existence and was driven by the speakers of what we call *first languages*—Indigenous languages (and cultures) that originally represented and communicated meanings without an alphabetical or character-based writing system. Starting from sub-Saharan Africa, an initially small population eventually spread across the globe. We then evolved into different peoples with different languages, largely due to the relative isolation of one tribe from another, resulting in language divergence over time (Figure 1.1).

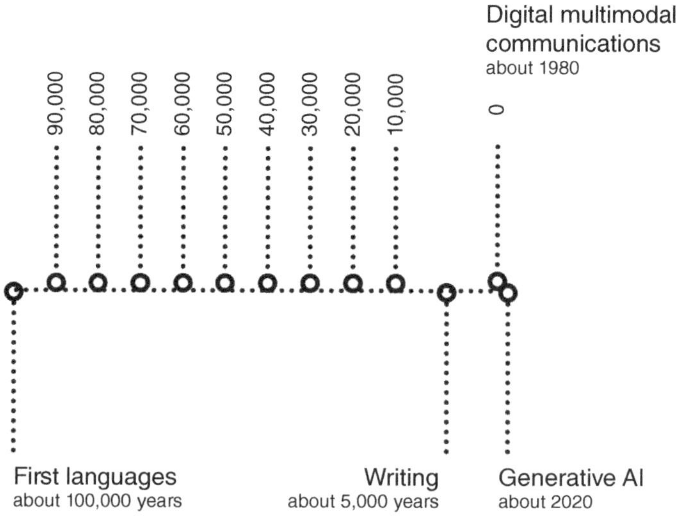

Figure 1.1 A timeline of human systems of meaning.

However, this divergence is only part of the story. We suggest that the differentiation of languages during this period of human history was a more integral and systematic process than merely the result of accidental drift and isolation. First languages, we argue, were specially designed to differ, often in ways that are difficult for us to understand today. The result was an enormous number of languages for a species that, until recently, had a relatively small population.

Indeed, the diversity of language forms among first languages is nothing short of staggering, demonstrating the vast capacity of humans to invent meanings. The rich, sophisticated character of these first systems of oral and multimodal communication can still be observed today in Indigenous communities around the world. Consider, for example, *Yolŋu Matha*, a first language of northeastern Australia. Among its thousand or so speakers, people speak various forms of language, including baby language, adult language, women's language, old men's sacred language, as well as dialects of different clans or family groups. These differences are intentional, as they convey information about individuals and their place in the world. For instance, what you call a place or a person provides insights into your relationship with that place or person. The same word may also represent a totem (a sacred animal), a location, or a living person because these elements are so closely linked in the cosmology and epistemology (i.e., the way of knowing) of Yolŋu Matha speakers. Additionally, you may name a place differently from someone else, depending on your unique ownership relationship to it. When a person dies, their name can no longer be spoken, and the world must be renamed in response, including its places and totems, as a sign of respect.

This example illustrates the dynamism and flexibility of first languages in their oral form (Christie, 1993) that continues to be seen today. These systems encompass sophisticated, graphical, and *multimodal* ways of conveying meaning, involving an overlay of diverse forms of communication such as word, image, gesture, sound, and space. When considering these aspects of first languages, we can define *literacy* as inherently multimodal, blending oral traditions, visual representations, bodily gestures, and rituals to communicate meaning (Glowczewski, 2019; Kalantzis & Cope, 2006). These integrated forms of communication are highly adaptable and accessible across different communities. The interplay of diverse forms of communication expresses rich, shared meanings and offers evidence for both the complexity of first languages and the fundamentally multimodal nature of human communication from its earliest origins (see Chapter 2 for an in-depth discussion of different forms of meaning-making) (Figure 1.2).

Figure 1.2 Multimodal communication: Yolŋu Garma Festival, Yirrkala, Northern Australia.

The ancestral homes of these first languages are found today in many regions of the world—for example, in Australia, Melanesia, the Americas, Siberia, and Arctic Europe. Unfortunately, many of these rich systems of communication are rapidly disappearing. This process has been ongoing for millennia now, as first languages have been replaced by those introduced by the evolution of farming societies which used writing as a tool of elite control, including religious hierarchy, bureaucratic regulation, and privileged knowledge. The process of decline began with the Indo-European and Celtic languages brought to Europe by invading farmers, the Greek and Latin languages in Europe, the African kingdoms' languages (like the Bantu languages), the Mesoamerican languages of the Maya, Aztecs, Olmecs, and Incas, and the Chinese languages and their derivatives in East Asia (Figure 1.3). More recently, industrial societies have used "standard" or national forms of their languages as a tool for mass citizenship. In the following section, we explore the coming of writing that resulted in the decline of first languages and its ascent as the most valued medium of communication.

Figure 1.3 The birthplaces of the first writing.

The Coming of Writing and Print Literacy

Writing as we understand it today emerged as regularized systems of repeatable, symbolic graphemes (i.e., the smallest units of a writing system that represent a meaningful sound or symbol). Some languages used alphabetical symbols (such as English), while others employed character-based symbols (such as Chinese) to record language. Writing first developed in Mesopotamia about five thousand years ago and later emerged independently in India, China, and Mesoamerica (Christin, 2002). Initially, this new technology served as a tool for maintaining inventories of ownership and wealth, functioning primarily as an instrument of state bureaucracy to manage and redistribute surpluses. Over time, it became a source of religious authority, reinforcing social order and addressing the deep social tensions caused by inequality (Goody, 1986).

In modern societies, we have come to refer to the birth of writing as "the beginning of history" or "the dawn of civilization." The long preceding period is often called "prehistory," inhabited by "uncivilized" peoples. By adopting this view, we forget most of the history of human presence as a species. This moment marked the beginning of a different kind of history. With these new societies came inequalities never experienced before. Farming brought opportunities for accumulating wealth and using surpluses for projects beyond the immediate needs of daily life. The monumental ruins of ancient civilizations testify to the magnitude of this inequality, and writing played a significant role in this social transformation.

These societal differences were amplified with the mechanization of writing, which began in 1039 and advanced significantly in 1450. Pi Sheng's invention of movable type in China in 1039, while innovative, did not extend beyond his workshop (Tsien & Needham, 1985). Gutenberg's printing press of 1450, however, became the prototype for modern systems of modularization, repetition, and division of labor (Eisenstein, 1979). As the first true industrial technology, the printing press revolutionized communication, but it also perpetuated social divisions (Figure 1.4).

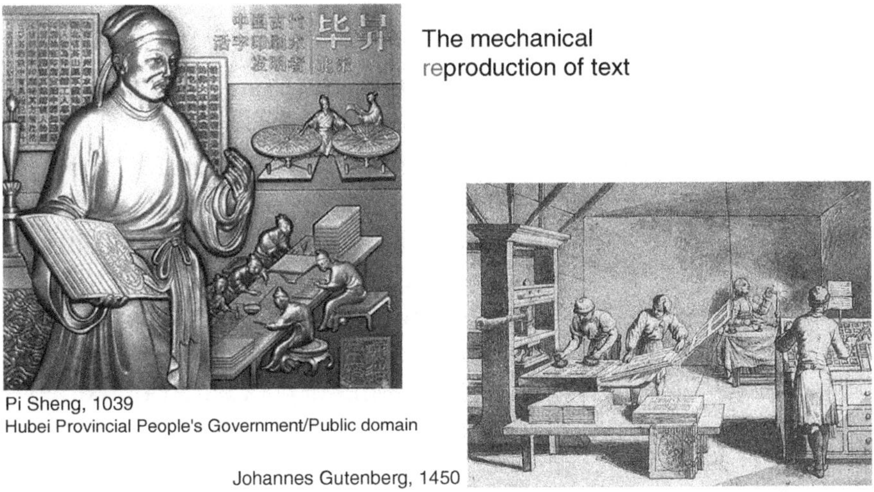

Pi Sheng, 1039
Hubei Provincial People's Government/Public domain

Johannes Gutenberg, 1450
Daniel Nikolaus Chodowiecki/Wikimedia Commons/Public Domain

Figure 1.4 The mechanization of writing.

Indeed, in its early centuries, the printing press reinforced the impact of writing by facilitating its rise as a tool of power and exclusion. As a consequence, *literacy* was now understood as the ability to read and write, and it consolidated the authority of the ruling class, who relied on elite knowledge of printed laws, administrative memos, and financial ledgers. In Europe, the ruling class communicated in Latin, an inaccessible language for most (Waquet, 2001). Gutenberg's *Bible* was printed in Latin, requiring priests, their chants, and the grandeur of church architecture to mediate between the mystically inaccessible text and the masses. Thus, this new *literacy*, unlike the meaning-making that had predominated during the realm of first languages, drew stark social divides, remaining a privilege of the elite. Books were costly, literacy rates stayed low, and literacy itself perpetuated gender inequalities—favoring men—and colonialism, from overt administrative domination to subtler "development" programs (Street, 1995).

Universal literacy did not become a societal goal until the 19th and 20th centuries, coinciding with mass-institutionalized education. As industrialization drew parents away from the home, the state assumed the role of socializing children. Yet for most students, education's aims were minimal—teaching the basic "three Rs" (reading, writing, and arithmetic) at a level sufficient for the demands of industrial capitalism (Bowles & Gintis, 1976). Graff (1987) notes that beyond functionality, during this period, literacy was a medium for moral instruction, shaping workers to embody qualities such as punctuality, discipline, and subordination, creating a "controllable, docile, [and] respectful workforce" (p. 261).

As the "universal" literacy goal expanded, it adopted new mechanisms for regulating inequality. The ideology of opportunity promised basic literacy for all but maintained unequal outcomes through school results. This stratification culminated in the scientific justification of inequality using the "normal" distribution curve, which labeled only a few as "genius" or "above average" while relegating most to "average" or worse (e.g., labels like "moron," "imbecile," or "idiot") (Goddard, 1920). This curve often failed to account for the social realities of literacy, rationalizing inequality as natural when it was shaped largely by external conditions (Fischer et al., 1996).

Exclusions became even starker for marginalized groups. Black/African American descendants of slaves faced systemic barriers (Anderson, 1988), while Indigenous and immigrant children, such as those belonging to Hispanic/Latinx populations in the United States, were stripped of their home languages (Phillipson, 1992). Efforts to standardize literacy thus aimed to erase linguistic and cultural diversity, creating an "imagined community" of linguistic homogeneity to bolster nationalism (Anderson, 1991). Nevertheless, rather than resolving differences, these efforts often created new forms of exclusion, such as disjunctions between school literacy and working-class speech (Bernstein, 1971), the rejection of English dialects such as Black English (Labov, 1972), and the exclusion of minoritized languages (Lo Bianco, 2014). Although standardized literacy, where writing reigned supreme, was intended to equalize opportunity, it often fell short, reinforcing social divisions more than bridging them.

In the last part of the 20th century and the first part of the 21st, however, significant changes in the way we humans communicate challenged the seemingly fixed, absolute power of writing and standardized literacy. These changes involved shifts in communication technologies, the balance of text and other forms of meaning, and the broad accessibility of new communication media. In the following section, we explore this new era of human history.

Writing in the Digital Era

The 20th century saw a series of transformations in the ways that print meanings were produced and reproduced. These were influenced by new technologies associated with photography, followed by lithographic printing, film, and analog television, which brought image and text closer together. The pace of change accelerated with the widespread adoption of digital technologies for communication from the last quarter of the 20th century into the early 21st century.

After five millennia in which the written word was a source of power in many societies, and half a millennium in which this power had been amplified by the printing press, photographic means of representation began to restore power to the image. Starting from the third quarter of the 20th century, digital technology further accelerated this shift by reducing the elementary modular unit of textual meaning from the character to the pixel. But before we explore the radical changes that these new innovations brought to the ways in which we communicate, and subsequently, to our conceptualization of *literacy*, let's consider the transformations that writing has undergone in the digital era.

Written text is defined as the work of scribing graphemes into a two-dimensional spatial array. Traditionally, much of writing is linear or one-dimensional, but a second dimension comes into play in various forms such as lists, tables, headings, diagrams, and page or screen layouts. In the digital era, even one-dimensional text has adopted multilinear characteristics, as computer-mediated keystrokes have replaced hand scribing. Writers can now draft, edit, and refine texts without the difficulties of crossing out handwritten words or the burden of re-scribing untidy passages. The word processor allows a writer's cursor to jump seamlessly backward and forward between the words of a sentence, and across a page or screen layout, ensuring careful design both in terms of language and visual presentation. Writing, in sum, has become a process of spatial, two-dimensional design (Olmanson et al., 2016).

The constituent components of written text have also changed in the digital age. Text is now defined as a system of conventional graphemes recorded for the digital era in the universal scripting system known as Unicode. This system has standardized text representation across digital devices, making almost every digitized text accessible anywhere. The current version of Unicode, Version 16.0.0 (released in September 2024), catalogs 154,998 encoded characters, or graphemes, and covers 168 scripts. A small portion of these graphemes represent spoken sounds, or phonemes, such as "a," "ض," or "ŋ." However, most represent ideas or ideographs, such as numerals ("8"), symbols ("+", "@"), Chinese characters ("知"), or emojis ("☺"). Widely adopted across platforms, Unicode plays a critical role in enabling seamless communication and data processing in a multilingual digital world (Figure 1.5).

Indeed, nearly every grapheme that captures regularized aspects of the human experience is found in Unicode, from ancient symbols of lost and still-unintelligible languages to emojis and icons that have only recently entered our digital cultures. The

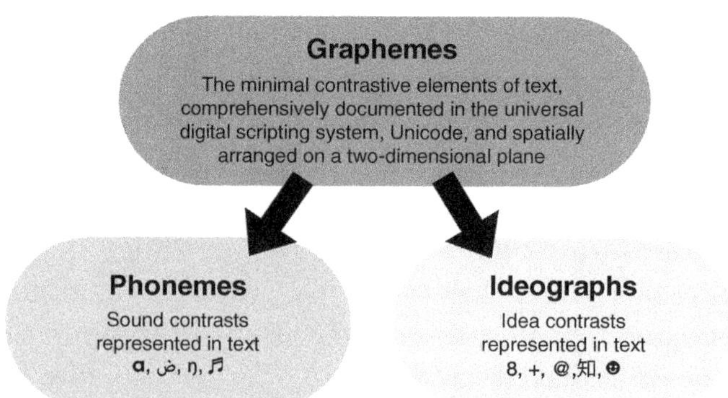

Figure 1.5 Text: Graphemes arranged in space.

appearance of these graphemes may vary slightly across devices or fonts, but their meaning is standardized through Unicode (Cope & Kalantzis, 2020). In fact, even handwritten text, when digitized, is converted into Unicode, which has become ubiquitous in all forms of digital text.

Unicode characters are composed of both phonemes, which represent sounds in alphabetic literacies (e.g., Arabic script, shown in Figure 1.6), and ideographs, which convey ideas, such as numerals, Chinese characters, and emojis. The majority of these characters are ideographs, which are being used with increasing frequency in the digital age, seen in functional icons, emoticons, navigation symbols, and representations of both quantity (countable entities) and quality (measurable attributes). Late in his life, the renowned anthropologist of literacy Jack Goody, in a display of his characteristic wit, remarked, "We're all turning Chinese"—suggesting that even in the domain of text, we are experiencing a drift away from phonemic representations toward more ideographic forms of writing (Kalantzis & Cope, 2020). This shift in textual practice underscores a broader transformation in how we understand and use written text in the digital age. We examine the implications of this shift in the following section.

The Rise of Multimodality

In the digital era, the transformations that have challenged the status of writing as the reigning medium of communication have originated in the diverse meaning-making affordances offered by new technologies. For example, we have witnessed a return to the aural and oral. New combinations of oral and written meaning forms have emerged, such as email and text messaging, which more closely resemble the fluidity of speaking compared to earlier literate forms like letters and memoranda. This marks a return to *multimodality*. Writing has lost its privileged status as the most effective means to convey meanings across time and space, as other technologies are now available to record and transmit oral,

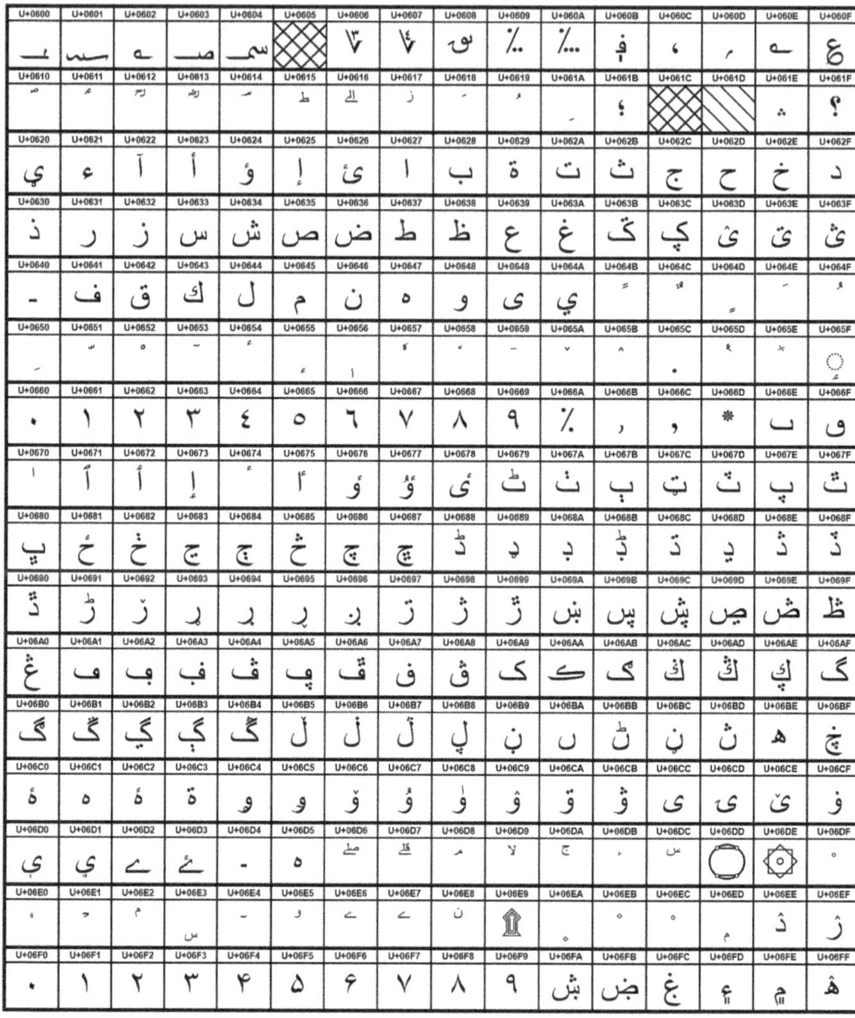

Figure 1.6 Graphic board for Arabic Unicode
(SOURCE: Antonsusi/Wikipedia/CC BY 3.0/).

audio, visual, and gestural meanings. As a result, we find ourselves constantly switching meaning forms.

Digital communication technologies have also made media production and distribution more accessible, allowing more people to create and share content. The internet and digital platforms have enabled a return to some aspects of the diversity of the first languages we discussed in the first section of this chapter, with new forms of English and other languages diverging into distinct varieties influenced by subcultures, communities, and peer groups. Language differences have become important again, with different dialects, sociolects, and regional variations flourishing in online communities and digital spaces.

The rise of multimodality has also influenced education, as educators increasingly recognize the need to teach students how to navigate and create content across multiple forms of communication as well as to critically understand and effectively employ different types of digital technologies. This shift reflects a broader understanding of literacy. In this digital, diverse world where multimodal communication is the norm, the traditional concept of *literacy*, tied to the printed medium and "a single, official, or standard form of language" (Cope & Kalantzis, 2015, p. 1), is clearly no longer adequate. *Literacy* now involves the ability to interpret and produce meaning using a range of meaning forms, tools, and technologies (Jewitt, 2008; Kress, 2009).

So here we are, 5,000 years after the invention of writing. The historical narrative we have recounted so far is a story of a partial return to multimodality, divergence, multilingualism, and deep diversity. But in many ways, it is not a return at all—it is something new in human history, with unpredictable consequences. One thing is certain: the future will be unlike any of our pasts, particularly when we consider perhaps the most important technological development of this era, GenAI.

GenAI as a Multimodal Literacy Technology

The development of GenAI represents a new phase in the evolution of multimodal communication and a major step in the history of artificial intelligence (AI). But what exactly does this term refer to, and how did it originate? Before we discuss GenAI, let's learn more about AI.

The term "artificial intelligence" was first coined in 1955 by computer scientist John McCarthy to attract funding for a workshop held at Dartmouth College, gathering a small group of influential figures in computing. In the workshop proposal, AI was defined as the ability to "mak[e] a machine behave in ways that would be called intelligent if a human were so behaving" (McCarthy et al., 2006, p. 12). Years earlier, British computing pioneer Alan Turing had described a similar concept, which he had called "mechanical intelligence" (Turing, 1950) (Figure 1.7).

For many decades, the promise of AI remained largely unrealized, at least on a practical or widely applicable scale. The first generation of AI was characterized by symbolic-logical approaches, which attempted to encapsulate generalizable patterns of human behavior and cognition within software code. However, these expert-created, rules-based systems were ultimately unable to address the complexities of the real world, leading to the so-called "AI winter," a period when the field experienced a significant decline in interest and investment (Nilsson, 2009).

Despite these setbacks, there were promising but limited applications of expert systems, such as the PLATO computer learning system introduced in 1949 (Cope & Kalantzis, 2023; Dear, 2017) and subsequent intelligent tutoring systems (Graesser et al., 2001). These early educational systems included applications in literacy,

Figure 1.7 Artificial intelligence: The very idea.

focusing primarily on formal language features and text comprehension (Vojak et al., 2011).

From the beginning of the 21st century, a second generation of AI emerged, characterized by data-driven development. This phase revolved around the use of large datasets and machine learning, both supervised (involving annotated data to identify statistical patterns) and unsupervised (identifying inherent patterns in the data). A prominent example of AI's application to literacy during this phase was automated essay assessment, where a sample of student texts was graded by human examiners, and machine learning algorithms graded new texts by statistically evaluating their similarities using natural language processing techniques (Cope et al., 2011; Shermis, 2014; Warschauer & Grimes, 2008).

The emergence of GenAI marks the third, and probably most consequential, paradigm shift in the evolution of AI. While this new iteration of AI retains the data-driven, statistical approach of the second generation, it introduces a new technique called "self-supervised learning." GenAI combines two key technologies: a *chatbot* (Weizenbaum, 1966) and a corpus of text known as a *large language model* (LLM). The chatbot enables a human user to interact with the text by providing a *prompt*—a specific input or query designed to elicit a relevant response from the model. This interaction results in the creation of a uniquely reconstituted digital artifact, which could be in the form of text, image, sound, or a multimodal combination.

The LLM operates on *tokens* as its fundamental unit of analysis. A token can sometimes represent a whole word, but for words with composite meanings, a token may consist of less than a word. Tokens are reduced to binary notation, abstracted by the machine in an identical and, for analytical purposes, meaningless form. Their variation lies solely in the quantified weight of their proximity to other tokens (*vectors*) within written textual corpora. Any meaningful relationship between tokens is incidental, as the statistical mechanisms of analysis deliberately avoid any theoretical framework of meaning. That is, the machine learns by masking the next word in a sentence and then determining whether its prediction was correct (reinforcement) or incorrect (Christian, 2020).

Behaviorist learning processes that were once thought to be overly mechanistic for humans have proven to be ideal for machines, albeit through inscrutable and recursive calculations. Additionally, *Reinforcement Learning from Human Feedback* is employed to further refine the system's behavior, as human users adjust the model to avoid producing undesirable outputs (Ouyang et al., 2022).

The implications of this paradigm shift for literacy are profound. While technologies such as those created by Pi Sheng and Johannes Gutenberg mechanized the reproduction of written text, GenAI is the first technology to mechanize the production of original written text, along with derivative multimodal meanings. Before the advent of GenAI, humans had exclusively controlled the creation of represented meaning. Machines could reproduce meaning, but they could not generate new meanings. GenAI has changed this dynamic, ushering in a new era of literacy production and multimodal communication.

Let's have a look at an example, focusing on the verb "bathe." GenAI finds the verb "bathe" in many different relations to surrounding words, such as "John bathes" (Figure 1.8), "John bathes his doll" (Figure 1.9), or "John is bathed by the fall sunlight" (Figure 1.10).

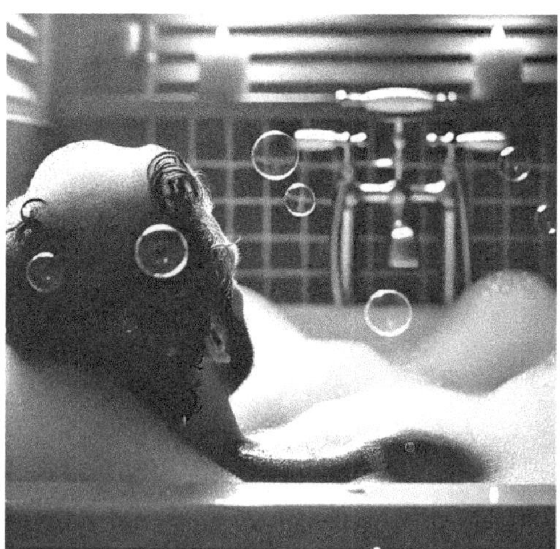

Figure 1.8 John bathes
(SOURCE: Generated with AI using DALL·E 3.0. - OpenAI).

Figure 1.9 John bathes his doll
(SOURCE: Generated with AI using DALL·E 3.0. - OpenAI).

Figure 1.10 John is bathed by the fall sunlight
(SOURCE: Generated with AI using DALL·E 3.0. - OpenAI).

These instances create different "bathe" tokens because the words near each "bathe" are different. The differences between the kinds of "bathe" (i.e., intransitive versus transitive versus figurative/passive) are defined by weights or the probability of one kind of "bathe" being connected to certain kinds of surrounding words. The *parameters* in an LLM are the number of surrounding words that are examined and thus the number of potential variations of "bathe." Then, in its design of responses, the AI takes its cue from human prompts.

This is how LLMs come to have a vocabulary of sorts numbering in the billions of words and trillions of parameters or word-to-word relations. However, it is crucial to note that LLMs do not create or understand tokens. These tokens have been crafted by humans who have placed spaces between the words. Linguists and technicians manually "stem" words that consist of more than one token, a process first proposed by Michael Halliday and colleagues in the early days of language computing (Richens & Halliday, 1957).

That is, the LLM can never truly know the meaning of intransitive, transitive, or figurative/passive "bathe." It simply treats language as a meaningless "bag of words," a phrase coined by linguist Noam Chomsky's dissertation advisor (Harris, 1954, p. 156). Computers do not derive meaning beyond binary notation—zero or one. Instead, they calculate by textual transposition: recorded Unicode > chunked into tokens > binary notation > calculation of the probability of the next token > token > human-readable Unicode. These calculations are executed through self-supervised learning of a low-level behaviorist kind, processed through a filter of statistical significance called a *transformer* (Vaswani et al., 2017), hence the "T" in OpenAI's GenAI platform ChatGPT. The complexity of these calculations is so vast and dull in its zero-and-one nature that it is impossible to trace exactly how the next word has been calculated, leading to the concept of the "black box"—a term first applied to computing by one of the founders of cybernetics (Ashby, 1956, p. 86). There's a ghost in the machine, so to speak.

GenAI relies on the universal graphemic symbology of Unicode, which, as discussed in the previous section, supports the representation of both natural and formal languages. This means that AI can handle not only natural language text but also mathematical symbols and computer code, treating them all as sequences of characters. The ability of AI to work across different forms of meaning highlights the growing importance of multimodality in digital communication.

GenAI has also made it possible to create and manipulate content in ways that were previously unimaginable. AI-generated images, like the ones presented in Figures 1.8–1.10, as well as videos and music, have opened up new possibilities for creative expression. And of course, due to its affordances, including ubiquity and user-friendly customization tools, AI is transforming education. In this volume, we seek to explore this new landscape in human history and education.

Conclusion

In this chapter, we have examined the evolution of literacy, from the diverse and flexible first languages of early human societies, through the standardization brought about by writing and print literacy, to the dynamic and multimodal forms of communication enabled by digital technologies and, more recently, GenAI. As we have seen in this chapter, our conceptualization of literacy has continually evolved, adapting to technological advancements and changing societal needs. Each historical phase has redefined what it means to be literate, expanding our understanding of how we create, share, and interpret meaning.

The rest of the book will build on these foundational ideas, presenting the different dimensions of literacy in the digital age. We will explore how literacy extends beyond text to include images, sounds, gestures, and spaces, and how these elements can be combined to create richer forms of meaning. We will also examine the practical applications of literacy in education, focusing on pedagogical approaches that integrate digital and AI technologies to support diverse learners. Additionally, we will address the ethical challenges posed by new technologies, such as AI bias and privacy concerns, and discuss strategies for fostering inclusive and responsible literacy practices. Ultimately, this book aims to provide a comprehensive understanding of literacy in an era of rapid change, preparing readers to navigate and shape the future of communication and learning.

Glossary of Terms

In this section, we offer a glossary of key AI terms, with a focus on GenAI. Some of these concepts were introduced earlier in the chapter, but here they are summarized, defined, and ordered alphabetically for clarity. We believe knowledge of these terms is crucial for the understanding of technology in the GenAI era. We will make reference to them throughout the book.

- **AI Agents:** These are instructions directed to an LLM from multiple perspectives or "agents," each adopting different roles, like participants in a debate team (Li et al., 2024). This approach allows GenAI to simulate multiple perspectives and their interrelations.
- **AI Bias:** This refers to the prejudice that may be embedded in LLMs, resulting from the sexism, racism, violence, profanity, and other societal biases found in the training data. GenAI scrapes from the web without discrimination, which might result in outputs that may reflect these biases. This aspect highlights the historical biases embedded in written texts (Bender et al., 2021; Magee et al., 2021).
- **Binary Notation:** This is a system used by computers to name and calculate relationships using zeros and ones. It represents all information in base-two format and forms the foundation of digital processing.
- **Black Box:** This term refers to the opaque nature of GenAI models. It is difficult, if not impossible, to determine exactly which sources or pathways led to a particular output from the model. The statistical relationships formed during unsupervised reinforcement learning are intricate and cannot

be fully traced, effectively making the machine a "black box" (Ashby, 1956, p. 86).

- **Chatbot:** This refers to a program that enables users to interact with computers using natural language. Originally, this was done through preprogrammed dialogs (Weizenbaum, 1966), but modern chatbots are integrated with LLMs to enable more dynamic and contextual interactions.
- **Contextual AI:** This involves records of real-time interactions with computing devices, including geolocation, time stamps, clickstream data, and body sensor readings. This information enables AI systems to use contextual data to improve the quality of user interactions.
- **Context Window:** This involves the amount of text that an LLM can process within the instructions it receives. It refers to the span of tokens that can be considered in the generation of a response. A larger context window allows for more coherence in lengthy conversations or complex texts.
- **Fine-Tuning:** This is the process of enhancing a generic or foundational LLM by providing it with supplementary specialized text. This text can include verified scientific knowledge or other domain-specific data. *Retrieval augmented generation* (more commonly known as RAG) is often used in this context, where trusted text is uploaded into a vector database, allowing the model to improve its domain-specific knowledge (Lewis et al., 2020).
- **Filters:** These are mechanisms that mitigate AI bias by removing or preventing the expression of prejudiced views. LLMs achieve this by covering or excluding offensive responses through supervised machine learning. Ironically, these filters can introduce their own biases, often in favor of certain ideological views or ethnic/racial groups in visual representations (Buyl et al., 2024).
- **Hallucination:** This refers to a phenomenon in which GenAI produces information that appears factual but is fabricated. Since the AI is only trained to form coherent sentences based on statistical probabilities, it lacks the ability to verify content, leading to "hallucinations" (Klein, 2023; Munn et al., 2023).

- **Jailbreak:** This indicates a specially crafted prompt that bypasses the AI's filters, allowing it to produce otherwise restricted content (Shen et al., 2023).
- **Large Language Model (LLM):** This encompasses a corpus of text scraped from the web, comprising billions of words. An LLM is pretrained by calculating the statistical likelihood of a specific token following another. LLMs are the foundation for GenAI.
- **Machine Learning:** This refers to the process by which an LLM learns to understand and generate human-like responses. Machine learning occurs during the training phases, and there are two main types, supervised and unsupervised learning.
- **Multimodal AI:** This type of AI is capable of creating content in various forms, such as images, videos, or sounds. GenAI does this based on text labels of sources and written prompts (Cope & Kalantzis, 2023; Zhang et al., 2023). It treats software, mathematics, and audiovisual elements as forms of written text.
- **Parameters:** These are the metrics that define the LLM's capabilities, such as the number of tokens it processes, the extent of its context window, and the range of actions it can perform. LLMs typically have billions or trillions of parameters, determining their ability to perform complex tasks.
- **Prompt**: This refers to an input or query provided to an LLM that guides the generation of a response. It can be a question, statement, or any piece of text intended to elicit a specific output from the model. Prompts are crucial for effective interaction with LLMs, as they shape the nature and quality of the generated content.
- **Prompt Engineering:** This is the practice of crafting effective prompts to elicit useful responses from an LLM. A well-designed prompt functions similarly to a classroom essay prompt, guiding the AI toward the desired type of response (Schulhoff et al., 2024).
- **Supervised Machine Learning, or Reinforcement Learning from Human Feedback:** This refers to a machine learning technique in which humans help train the system to behave appropriately, often by applying "filters" to manage AI biases and ensure responsible output.

- **Temperature:** This is a setting that controls the randomness of token selection when generating text. Higher temperature values result in more diverse and creative responses, while lower values make the output more predictable and robotic.
- **Token:** A token refers to the smallest meaningful unit of analysis in an LLM. A token can be a complete word or a part of a word. Tokens are sequences of Unicode characters used by the LLM to predict and generate language.
- **Unicode:** This refers to the universal character set used for encoding text in computers. Each character has a unique representation in binary notation, allowing for consistent interpretation across different systems and platforms (see Figure 1.6 on page 12, for an example).
- **Unsupervised, Reinforcement Learning:** In unsupervised reinforcement learning, the LLM parses vast quantities of text and predicts the most likely next word based on existing patterns. This repetitive process refines probability calculations, though it lacks any theoretical framework for meaning. It is akin to behaviorist psychology on a massive scale, where learning is achieved through repeated pattern recognition.
- **Vector:** A vector is a numerical value representing the proximity of one token to another. These vectors define the relationships between tokens, such as various shades of meaning (e.g., the different senses of the verb "bathe" in different contexts discussed on pages 16–18).
- **Weights:** Vectors create weightings for tokens, effectively forming a lexicon that represents grammatical relations. These weightings help the LLM establish semantic relationships between billions of morphemes.

Consolidate, Explore, Reflect, Do

We end this chapter with activities that will allow you to apply the concepts discussed in novel ways. Our goal is that these tasks will facilitate further exploration and reflection and will inspire your present and/or future teaching practice.

Task 1: What Is Literacy? Personal Connections

Step 1. Reflect on the different definitions of literacy presented in the chapter. Write your own definition of this concept and explain how it has evolved after reading the chapter. Compare your definition with a peer's and discuss any similarities or differences. Where do you think similarities and/or differences originate?
Step 2. Now choose a GenAI platform (e.g., OpenAI's *ChatGPT* or Google's *Gemini*). Write a prompt to ask the AI to define literacy (e.g., "define the concept of literacy"). Does the definition reflect aspects of standardized or new literacy? With the peer you worked with in **Step 1**, compare your and the AI's definitions. Reflect on similarities and differences.

Task 2: Literacy Throughout History

Step 1. Create a multimodal (e.g., using language, images, sound, etc.) timeline of literacy development, covering the three major historical phases we discussed in this chapter: First Languages, Print Literacy, and Digital Literacy, including the GenAI era. Use key events from the chapter and include illustrations/multimodal artifacts to depict each phase.
Step 2. Choose an image-generation GenAI platform (e.g., OpenAI's *DALL·E 3*). Write a prompt to ask the AI to create a visual representation of literacy. Analyze the resulting image. Does it reflect aspects of standardized or new literacy? Why do you think this is the case? What might the AI rely on to produce its output?
Step 3. Reflect on the image-generation process. Focus on the affordances you identified in the platform as well as its limitations. Consider how such platforms might facilitate (or limit) your teaching practice.

Task 3: Multimodality in Today's Indigenous Languages

This activity involves the analysis of a research study carried out by Kathy Mills and her colleagues (Mills et al., 2022) on the relationship between multimodality, Indigenous identity, and education in Australia.

Step 1. Read Mills et al.'s work, openly available through this link: https://www.tandfonline.com/doi/full/10.1080/15348458.2022.2149531.
Step 2. With three or four peers, identify and discuss examples of multimodal communication presented in the article. How do these multimodal activities foster Indigenous cultural identity? How would you define literacy when considering these examples?
Step 3. With the members of your group, create a multimodal, digital presentation to explain the role of totemic identity and multimodality in sustaining Indigenous knowledge (and education) based on the content of the article. The presentation should include visuals, videos, and/or audio. The meaning forms chosen should align with the multimodal approach discussed in the article.

Task 4: First Languages Today

As discussed in this chapter, there are many examples of first languages in our society. However, most of them are in danger of extinction. In this activity, we focus on them, encouraging you and your classmates to find out more about them.

Step 1. Choose a language to focus on. Here are some possible options (but you can also make your own choice):

- Africa: Gusilay, Hadza, N|uu
- The Americas: Chaná, Kawésqar, Pilagá, Pirahã, Tarahumara, Tehuelche, Yaghan, Yuuchi
- Asia: Great Andamanese, Jarawa, Koro, Onge, Sentinelese
- Australia: Martuthunira, Malyangapa, Ngardily, Warlpiri

Step 2. With three or four peers, collect as much information about your chosen language as possible. Include data on areas where it is spoken, numbers of speakers, linguistic characteristics, multimodal aspects of communication, efforts to document/preserve it,

and its role in education. Also, explore how this language conveys cultural meaning, identity, and relationships.
Step 3. Create a multimodal, digital presentation to share your findings. If possible, include audio/video samples.

Task 5: Literacy Throughout History: Comparison

Based on the content of this chapter, create a table to summarize and compare the characteristics of literacy as understood in the three periods discussed. Outline the benefits, challenges, and implications of each conceptualization, particularly in educational contexts. Also address embedded societal values and ideologies.

Task 6: Personal Literacy Timeline

Create a multimodal timeline of your own literacy development. Include phases such as learning to read and write, using technology for communication, and employing digital tools in your personal and professional life, including GenAI. Reflect on how these phases align with the evolution of literacy presented in this chapter, as well as on the role of your identities, sociocultural background (including values and ideologies), and educational context.

References

Anderson, B. (1991). *Imagined communities: Reflections on the origin and spread of nationalism*. Verso.

Anderson, J. D. (1988). *The education of blacks in the south, 1860-1935*. University of North Carolina Press.

Ashby, W. R. (1956). *An introduction to cybernetics*. Chapham & Hall.

Bender, E. M., Gebru, T., McMillan-Major, A., & Shmitchell, S. (2021). On the dangers of stochastic parrots: Can language models be too big? *In Proceedings of the 2021 ACM Conference on Fairness, Accountability, and Transparency* (pp. 610–623). https://doi.org/10.1145/3442188.3445922

Bernstein, B. (1971). *Class, codes and control: Theoretical studies towards a sociology of language*. Routledge & Kegan Paul.

Bowles, S. & Gintis, H. (1976). *Schooling in capitalist America: Education reform and the contradictions of economic life*. Basic Books Inc.

Buyl, M., Rogiers, A., Noels, S., Dominguez-Catena, I., Heiter, E., Romero, R., Johary, I., Mara, A.-C., Lijffijt, J., & De Bie, T. (2024). Large language models reflect the ideology of their creators. *arXiv*. https://doi.org/10.48550/arXiv.2410.18417

Christian, B. (2020). *The alignment problem: Machine learning and human values*. W.W. Norton.

Christie, M. (1993). Exploring aboriginal alternatives to western thinking. *Education Australia*, *22*, 6–8. https://search.informit.org/doi/10.3316/ielapa.940504209

Christin, A.-M. (2002). *A history of writing: From hieroglyph to multimedia*. Flamarrion.

Cope, B. & Kalantzis, M. (2015). The things you do to know: An introduction to the pedagogy of multiliteracies. In B. Cope & M. Kalantzis (Eds.), *A pedagogy of multiliteracies: Learning by design* (pp. 1–36). Palgrave Macmillan.

Cope, B. & Kalantzis, M. (2020). *Making sense: Reference, agency and structure in a grammar of multimodal meaning*. Cambridge University Press. https://doi.org/10.1017/9781316459645

Cope, B. & Kalantzis, M. (2023). A little history of e-learning: Finding new ways to learn in the PLATO computer education system, 1959-1976. *History of Education*, *52*(6), 905–936. https://doi.org/10.1080/0046760X.2022.2141353

Cope, B., Kalantzis, M., McCarthey, S. J., Vojak, C., & Kline, S. (2011). Technology-mediated writing assessments: Paradigms and principles. *Computers and Composition*, *28*(2), 79–96. https://doi.org/10.1016/j.compcom.2011.04.007

Dear, B. (2017). *The friendly orange glow: The untold story of the PLATO system and the dawn of cyberculture*. Pantheon Books.

Eisenstein, E. L. (1979). *The printing press as an agent of change: Communications and cultural transformation in early-modern Europe*. Cambridge University Press.

Fischer, C. S., Hout, M., Sanchez Jankowski, M., Lucas, S. R., Swindler, A., & Voss, K. (1996). *Inequality by design: Cracking the bell curve myth*. Princeton University Press.

Glowczewski, B. (2019). *Indigenising anthropology with Guattari and Deleuze*. Edinburgh University Press.

Goddard, H. H. (1920). *Human efficiency and levels of intelligence*. Princeton University Press.

Goody, J. (1986). *The logic of writing and the organization of society*. Cambridge University Press.

Graesser, A. C., VanLehn, K., Rosé, C. P., Jordan, P. W., & Harter, D. (2001). Intelligent tutoring systems with conversational dialogue. *AI Magazine*, *22*(4), 39–51. https://doi.org/10.1609/aimag.v22i4.1591

Graff, H. J. (1987). *The legacies of literacy: Continuities and contradictions in western culture and society*. Indiana University Press.

Harris, Z. S. (1954). Distributional structure. *Word*, *10*(2-3), 146–162. http://dx.doi.org/10.1080/00437956.1954.11659520

Jewitt, C. (2008). Multimodality and literacy in school classrooms. *Review of Research in Education*, *32*(1), 241–267. https://doi.org/10.3102/0091732X07310586

Kalantzis, M. & Cope, B. (2006). On globalisation and diversity. *Computers and Composition*, *31*(4), 402–411. https://doi.org/10.1016/j.compcom.2006.09.002

Kalantzis, M., & Cope, B. (2020). *Adding sense: Context and interest in a grammar of multimodal meaning*. Cambridge University Press. https://doi.org/10.1017/9781108862059

Klein, N. (2023, May 8). *AI machines aren't 'hallucinating,' but their makers are. The Guardian*. https://www.theguardian.com/commentisfree/2023/may/08/ai-machines-hallucinating-naomi-klein

Kress, G. (2009). *Multimodality: A social semiotic approach to contemporary communication*. Routledge.

Labov, W. (1972). *Language in the inner city: Studies in the Black English Vernacular*. University of Pennsylvania Press.

Lewis, P., Perez, E., Piktus, A., Petroni, F., Karpukhin, V., Goyal, N., Küttler, H., Lewis, M., Yih, W.-T., Rocktäschel, T., Riedel, S., & Kiela, D. (2020). Retrieval-augmented generation for knowledge-intensive NLP tasks. *arXiv*. https://doi.org/10.48550/arXiv.2005.11401

Li, J., Zhang, Q., Yu, Y., Fu, Q., & Ye, D. (2024). More agents is all you need. *arXiv*. https://doi.org/10.48550/arXiv.2402.05120

Lo Bianco, J. (2014). Domesticating the foreign: Globalization's effects on the place/s of languages. *The Modern Language Journal*, *98*(1), 312–325. https://www.jstor.org/stable/43651760

Magee, L., Ghahremanlou, L., Soldatic, K., & Robertson, S. (2021). Intersectional bias in causal language models. *arXiv*. https://doi.org/10.48550/arXiv.2107.07691

McCarthy, J., Minsky, M. L., Rochester, N., & Shannon, C. E. (2006). A proposal for the Dartmouth summer research project on artificial intelligence, August 31, 1955. *AI Magazine*, *27*(4), 12–14. https://doi.org/10.1609/aimag.v27i4.1904

Mills, K. A., Doyle, K., & Friend, L. (2022). Multimodal language rights and indigenous totemic identity: Cross-cultural participatory research. *Journal of Language, Identity & Education*, *24*(2), 1–19. https://doi.org/10.1080/15348458.2022.2149531

Munn, L., Magee, L., & Arora, V. (2023). Truth machines: Synthesizing veracity in AI language models. *AI & Society*, *39*, 2759–2773. https://doi.org/10.1007/s00146-023-01756-4

Nilsson, N. J. (2009). *The quest for artificial intelligence: A history of ideas and achievements*. Cambridge University Press.

Olmanson, J., Kennett, K., Magnifico, A., McCarthey, S., Searsmith, D., Cope, B., & Kalantzis, M. (2016). Visualizing revision: Leveraging student-generated between-draft diagramming data in support of academic writing development. *Technology, Knowledge and Learning: Learning Mathematics, Science and the Arts in the Context of Digital Technologies*, *21*(1), 99–123. https://doi.org/10.1007/s10758-015-9265-5

Ouyang, L., Wu, J., Jiang, X., Almeida, D., Wainwright, C. L., Mishkin, P., Zhang, C., Agarwal, S., Slama, K., Ray, A., Schulman, J., Hilton, J., Kelton, F., Miller, L., Simens, M., Askell, A., Welinder, P., Christiano, P., Leike, J., & Lowe, R. (2022). Training language models to follow instructions with human feedback. *arXiv*. https://doi.org/10.48550/arXiv.2203.02155

Phillipson, R. (1992). *Linguistic imperialism*. Oxford University Press.

Richens, R. H., & Halliday, M. A. K. (1957). Word decomposition for machine translation. Paper Presented at the *Eighth Annual Round Table Meeting on Linguistics and Language Studies*, Georgetown University, Washington, D.C.

Schulhoff, S., Ilie, M., Balepur, N., Kahadze, K., Liu, A., Si, C., Li, Y., Gupta, A., Han, H., Schulhoff, S., Dulepet, P. S., Vidyadhara, S., Ki, D., Agrawal, S., Pham, C., Kroiz, G., Li, F., Tao, H., Srivastava, A., Da Costa, H., Gupta, S., Rogers, M. L., Goncearenco, I., Sarli, G., Galynker, I., Peskoff, D., Carpuat, M., White, J., Anadkat, S., Hoyle, A., & Resnik, P. (2024). The prompt report: A systematic survey of prompting techniques. *arXiv*. https://doi.org/10.48550/arXiv.2406.06608

Shen, X., Chen, Z., Backes, M., Shen, Y., & Zhang, Y. (2023). "Do anything now": Characterizing and evaluating in-the-wild jailbreak prompts on large language models. *arXiv*. https://doi.org/10.48550/arXiv.2308.03825

Shermis, M. D. (2014). State-of-the-art automated essay scoring: Competition, results, and future directions from a United States demonstration. *Assessing Writing*, *20*, 53–76. https://doi.org/10.1016/j.asw.2013.04.001

Street, B. V. (1995). *Social literacies: Critical approaches to literacy in development, ethnography and education*. Longman.

Tsien, T.-H. & Needham, J. (1985). Science and civilization in China. In *Chemistry and chemical technology, Pt. I: Paper and printing* (Vol. 5). Cambridge University Press.

Turing, A. M. (1950). Computing machinery and intelligence. *Mind*, *59*, 433–460. https://www.cs.ox.ac.uk/activities/ieg/e-library/sources/t_article.pdf

Vaswani, A., Shazeer, N., Parmar, N., Uszkoreit, J., Jones, L., Gomez, A. N., Kaiser, L., & Polosukhin, I. (2017). Attention is all you need. *arXiv*. https://doi.org/10.48550/arXiv.1706.03762

Vojak, C., Kline, S., Cope, B., McCarthey, S. J., & Kalantzis, M. (2011). New spaces and old places: An analysis of writing assessment software. *Computers and Composition*, *28*(2), 97–111. https://doi.org/10.1016/j.compcom.2011.04.004

Waquet, F. (2001). *Latin, or the empire of the sign*. Verso.

Warschauer, M. & Grimes, D. (2008). Automated writing assessment in the classroom. *Pedagogies: An International Journal*, *3*(1), 22–36. https://doi.org/10.1080/15544800701771580

Weizenbaum, J. (1966). ELIZA—A computer program for the study of natural language communication between man and machine. *Communications of the ACM*, *9*(1), 36–45. https://web.stanford.edu/class/cs124/p36-weizenabaum.pdf

Zhang, Y., Gong, K., Zhang, K., Li, H., Qiao, Y., Ouyang, W., & Yue, X. (2023). Meta-transformer: A unified framework for multimodal learning. *arXiv*. https://doi.org/10.48550/arXiv.2307.10802

Chapter 2
Literacy and the Combination of Different Meaning Forms

Introduction

In this chapter, we build on the historical exploration of literacy introduced in Chapter 1, shifting our focus to the inherently multimodal nature of meaning-making. Specifically, we examine the diverse ways in which communication and understanding are facilitated through different meaning forms, including text, image, space, object and body, sound, and speech. This multimodal perspective reflects both the practices of early societies, as seen in the first languages covered in Chapter 1, and aligns with the rapid technological advancements that have reshaped how we create and interpret meaning today. By framing literacy as a dynamic, multimodal, and

Literacies in the Age of AI: Teaching and Learning in the Digital Era, First Edition. Gabriela C. Zapata, Bill Cope, and Mary Kalantzis.

evolving practice, we reveal its rich complexity and consider its implications for our interconnected, digital age. We conclude the chapter by offering suggestions for further research, reflection, and practical application, encouraging readers to deepen their engagement with the concepts introduced throughout our discussion

Meaning Forms

In this book, we call the constituent elements of multimodality *meaning forms* instead of modes,[1] and we define them as the materials and practices we use in creating meaning. This includes *text*, *image*, *space*, *object*, *body*, *sound*, and *speech*. Each form opens specific possibilities for meaning while also presenting constraints. That is, the employment of different forms of meaning both enable and limit meaning-making, highlighting the need for multimodality—the use (and combination) of multiple meaning forms to fully express ideas. Each form's affordances (i.e., the possibilities offered by its material properties [Gibson, 1977]) shape meaning in unique ways, making multimodality not just a choice but a practical necessity due to the inherent limitations of individual forms (Cope & Kalantzis, 2020). We make a distinction here between forms of meaning and the mediums[2] by means of which each form can be represented.

- **Text**: The two-dimensional arrangement of symbolic graphemes (phonemes representing sounds such as "a," "ض," or "ŋ" and ideographs such as numerals ("8"), symbols ("+", "@"), Chinese characters ("知"), or emojis ("☺"). The representations of this form of meaning can occur in a range of mediums including screen or page, and keyboarding or hand scribing.

[1] We have chosen this terminology because, while there is broad agreement in the literature that multimodality is essential for analysis (especially in the digital media era), there is little consensus as to how to conceptualize modes (for an in-depth discussion on this issue, see Kalantzis & Cope, 2020, pp. 4–7).

[2] We employ the term *mediums* instead of *media* to avoid confusion with *media*, which commonly describes platforms and technologies for sharing content (e.g., social media and mass media).

In the digital era, all textual meanings are represented in the universal scripting system, Unicode (see Chapter 1, page 10). As a consequence, mathematics and computer code should both now be considered literacies.

- **Image**: Indexical picturing of the realistic, abstract, or symbolic world arranged in a two-dimensional space. This form of meaning can be represented in mediums such as photographs, paintings, drawings, diagrams, and plans. In generative artificial intelligence (GenAI), images can be created with textual prompts.
- **Three-Dimensional (3D) Space**: The sense of our surroundings and move around in them. Mediums of this form of meaning might include architecture and landscape—the differences between being in a kitchen, a classroom, a café, or a forest for instance.
- **Object**: This takes the form of a meaningful, 3D, material thing. Mediums for such "object-ness" might include tools, things of beauty, nostalgic mementos, or dangerous instruments.
- **Body**: A form of meaning by means of which we feel and enact. Mediums include gesture, facial expression, kinesthetics, demeanor, and fashion.
- **Sound**: The form of audio representation, organized over time. Mediums might include music, alerts, and ambient sound.
- **Speech**: A kind of audio meaning which organizes the presentation of language over time. Mediums include for example, conversation, speeches, and verbal instructions.

The same things—mountains, love, and speed—can be meant in multiple forms and combined in different mediums. We call the process of moving between and combining different forms of meaning *transposition* (Cope & Kalantzis, 2020; Kalantzis & Cope, 2020, 2022; see also Chapter 3, page 88). The meanings are never quite the same in one form as another, which is why we extend and deepen our meanings by supplementing one form or medium with another, or by mixing forms of meaning and mediums. The capacities to create and communicate in any of these forms separately and in multimodal communication are now all-but universally available in digital devices that we carry on our persons.

Meaning forms are crafted from raw materials taken out of their original contexts. These materials become available resources, not only because of their mediums (such as writing) but also because of the inescapable materiality of the resources used to convey meaning through them (e.g., pens, paper, printing presses, books, or iPhones). Roland Barthes (1977) called mediums the "material substance of signifieds" (pp. 38–41). We extract meaning forms from their contexts and refashion them, creating meanings with a unique contextual and material manifestation. We also acknowledge that the materiality of mediums affects how meaning is experienced by audiences. That is, the qualities of a medium shape how people interact with it, what kinds of meanings are made possible, and how those meanings resonate with people on a cultural level (Kalantzis & Cope, 2020). This insight is crucial in understanding the roles that different meaning forms and their mediums play in shaping both individual and collective experiences.

In the following sections of this chapter, we explore the affordances and limitations of each meaning form and their mediums.

Text

Writing

Text, in its essence, is the representation of meaning through written symbols, resulting, as we saw in Chapter 1, in one of the most powerful and adaptable systems of communication in human history. For millennia, writing, as the medium of text, has provided the foundation for documenting, preserving, and disseminating knowledge across cultures and generations. This is achieved through the representation of meaning with visual symbols organized into systematic patterns, such as graphemes, words, and sentences. Alphabetic systems, like English, aim to approximate spoken sounds, whereas logographic systems, such as Chinese, encapsulate ideas and concepts directly.

Writing organizes meaning spatially, enabling reflection and analysis across time and contexts. Unlike speech, which exists within a fleeting temporal frame, text's spatiality allows it to remain fixed and revisited for deeper engagement. Writing also fosters abstraction, as it provides a means to articulate complex concepts that may be difficult to express orally. Furthermore, the inherent flexibility of text supports its integration with other forms of meaning, such as images, enriching the communicative experience.

Despite its affordances and its supreme status as a form of communication in society, writing can be a challenging and, in many ways, unnatural task. That is, writing using conventional spelling in English and other alphabetic systems is not natural. It demands learned and conscious understanding of the writing system and its meaningful symbols. English words, for instance, are constructed based on both sounds and meanings—it is a morphophonemic language (Adoniou, 2014). Conventional spelling involves knowledge of the following: phonology (how sounds are organized), orthography (letter sequences and grapheme choices, as English lacks simple phoneme–grapheme correspondence), morphology (word parts such as roots, prefixes, and suffixes), etymology (the origins of words, as English incorporates words from various languages), and visual recognition of word patterns.

Another "unnatural" aspect of writing is that it results in an artifact used for communication in which the writer and their audience may not be present in the same space or time. This artifact, therefore, must be comprehensible to those involved in the exchange of meaning, especially since the written artifact mediates this exchange and needs to be understood without immediate feedback or interaction. Even though it is common to think of writing as merely transcribing speech, it is far more complex. This transformation requires the author to "learn to hear and think about one's language in a new way" (Olson, 1998, p. 32). Writing and speaking also involve distinct mental processes.

Writing often begins with careful planning—outlining what to write in each section—and involves multiple revisions to ensure the right structure, tone, and wording. Writers aim to avoid unnecessary repetition, focusing on crafting a tightly structured text through a deliberate, multidirectional effort. Multiple drafts are often produced to refine the text. In contrast, speech is a linear, one-way flow, often messy, repetitive, and discursive, driven by the mind, voice, and emotions in the moment (Cope & Kalantzis, 2020; Kalantzis & Cope, 2020).

Since the late 20th century, technological advancements in writing tools have significantly transformed—and often simplified—the writing process. In the past, writing by hand or using a typewriter made revision cumbersome, requiring repeated rewrites to produce clean copies. By the 1980s, the advent of personal computers and word-processing software had rendered the process far more efficient. Revisions became as simple as deleting, retyping, or using cut-and-paste functions, allowing drafts to be refined easily. Modern digital tools now empower writers to revise texts without the limitations of earlier methods. Features like spell-check, grammar suggestions, thesauruses, templates, formatting styles, and collaboration tools have further streamlined the writing process.

Social media and digital communication tools have also given rise to new forms of writing, such as emails, text messages, and social media interactions or posts. These types of writing are often immediate and conversational, resembling speech while still maintaining elements of traditional writing. Additionally, they include predictive text and other enhancements that have made writing more fluid and accessible.

Yet, these advancements pale in comparison to the transformative impact of artificial intelligence (AI) on writing. GenAI has significantly transformed the writing process, introducing new avenues for creativity and enhancing cognitive engagement. These tools can assist in brainstorming ideas, generating creative content, and emulating specific writing styles, thereby expanding writers' perspectives and facilitating the exploration of novel approaches to meaning-making (Su et al., 2023). This has fundamentally shifted the creative process, making writing more dynamic and iterative (Wang, 2024).

Moreover, GenAI can foster deeper cognitive engagement by encouraging users to reflect on their writing choices (Kalantzis &

Cope, 2024). That is, beyond providing direct answers, GenAI can suggest diverse interpretations, enabling writers to explore various ways in which they can express their ideas. This interactive aspect allows for consideration of multiple perspectives, leading to refinements that align with the intended message and audience (Lin, 2024).

In sum, AI has transformed writing by enhancing efficiency, enabling new forms of creativity, and fostering deeper cognitive engagement. These advancements have made writing more interactive and reflective, fundamentally enriching the ways in which we create and share meaning. Of course, the implications of these transformation for education are extremely profound. We will not discuss them here, but we do so in Chapters 5–7. Now we turn to the other side of the text, reading.

Reading

Reading and writing are deeply interconnected forms of communication, as reading fundamentally involves decoding and interpreting meaning from written texts. These two meaning-making activities have evolved significantly over time, influenced by changes in societal practices, education, and technology.

Historically, literacy education emphasized reading as a process of decoding words to uncover meanings intended by authors. Phonics instruction helped translate speech sounds into written symbols (more on this in Section "Connecting Speech to Text: Phonics Controversies" of this chapter), and formal aspects of language, such as correct spelling and grammar, were prioritized. A standardized form of the national language, considered the "educated" or "proper" standard, was promoted through canonical texts and school readers (Afflerbach et al., 2008; Kalantzis & Cope, 2024). Literacy assessments measured students' proficiency in these conventions, while "good writing" was held up as an ideal to be appreciated. Reading, primarily viewed as a passive activity centered on comprehension, often took precedence over writing, which played a more limited role in everyday practices. For many, reading was a leisure activity, while writing served functional, utilitarian purposes.

With the advent of digital technologies, this dynamic began to shift. Reading and writing are now integrated into participatory practices that span social networking platforms, text messaging, and multimedia content creation. Platforms like Instagram, TikTok, and YouTube allow individuals to engage equally in consuming and producing content, breaking down traditional distinctions between these activities (Cope & Kalantzis, 2020; Kalantzis & Cope, 2020). Multimodal, image-rich online environments have expanded the scope of literacy, as texts now combine written language with visual and multimedia elements. Readers navigate hyperlinked structures, interact with content, and develop skills to locate, integrate, and evaluate diverse forms of information. Even print materials reflect these influences, blending visual and textual elements in ways that make reading and viewing inseparable.

This evolution has transformed reading from a passive act of comprehension to an active process of constructing meaning. Conceptualized as "design" (Table 2.1), modern reading reflects the complexity and dynamism of meaning-making (Kalantzis & Cope, 2024). Readers bring their "available designs," or mental models shaped by personal experiences, to their interpretations of texts. For instance, when encountering a sentence like, "the child walked into the classroom and sat at their desk...," a reader's interpretation will depend on their familiarity with different

Table 2.1 Reading as *"design"*

(Found) designs	Based on our experiences, identities, and lifeworlds, we recognize the word, phrase, or genre of text and understand its meaning, or at least we find enough clues to make sense of it, even if some parts are unfamiliar.
Designing	As we engage with the text, mental images conjured by its content guide us. We interpret its meaning in unique ways based on our lived experiences and perspectives.
The (re-) designed	We are left with our personal interpretation of the text, remembering its content and the way in which meaning has been conveyed. The text subtly reshapes our understanding of the world.

types of classrooms (e.g., based on the type of educational context they have been part of). Someone who associates classrooms with modern, technology-filled spaces might visualize desks arranged in small groups with interactive whiteboards, while another person, familiar with more traditional settings, might picture neatly aligned rows of desks and a blackboard at the front. These mental models, informed by lived experiences, enrich and expand our understanding, adding layers of meaning to texts.

GenAI has added yet another dimension to this process, leveraging advanced natural language processing to create personalized texts, summarize complex materials, and simulate interactive dialogs (Kalantzis & Cope, 2024). AI algorithms analyze user behaviors and suggest relevant content, fostering a collaborative relationship between readers and texts. This dynamic personalization exemplifies how reading has become an iterative, adaptive process, where meaning is co-constructed through engagement with AI-driven systems.

While these advancements have transformed how we read, nevertheless, the linear progression of text remains fundamental. Meaning still generally unfolds sequentially, shaping how readers engage with and interpret content. At the same time, digital tools enhance this process by offering interactivity and immediacy, enabling readers to navigate and synthesize information at their own pace.

As technology continues to shape literacy practices, the definition of reading itself has expanded. No longer confined to traditional practices of decoding and comprehension, reading now also encompasses the interplay of viewing and designing meaning across diverse mediums. These changes reflect the complexity of communication in the digital age, where multimodal texts are now the norm. In particular, the integration of images into texts has transformed how readers process and interpret information. Visual components, whether in digital or print-based formats, play a crucial role in meaning-making (Afflerbach et al., 2008; Cope & Kalantzis, 2020; Kalantzis & Cope, 2020, 2024). This shift underscores the importance of understanding how images function as a form of communication, a topic that we explore next.

Image

For centuries, text, as we have previously seen, was privileged as the form for meaning-making, a trend reinforced by the rise of print culture and the formalization of mass-institutionalized schooling. However, this dominance began to shift in the 20th century with the advent of new mediums, including photography, radio, and television. Each of these mediums offered alternative or supplementary ways of recording and communicating meaning, challenging the primacy of text.

These changes, however, also prompted concerns about the decline of reading and halted the rise of image for a while. For example, schools emphasized the superiority of text by moving children from picture books, considered suitable for early readers, to chapter books, where illustrations were deemed unnecessary. Comics, while popular, were also dismissed as frivolous and unacademic. Simultaneously, in some of the most influential academic theories of human communication and society, a parallel sentiment was expressed through the "language turn," in which language was taken to frame everything in our worlds of meaning and social interaction (Rorty, 1992). Yet, while language organizes meaning through categorization and syntax, visual mediums engage with meaning in distinctive, multifaceted ways (Cope & Kalantzis, 2020; Kalantzis & Cope, 2020).

Images are not merely static representations but dynamic tools for creating meaning, and they fall into two fundamentally different categories: *perceptual* and *mental* images. *Perceptual images* involve a direct, material, and bodily encounter with the world through our visual system (Figure 2.1). Light enters the eye, passing through the cornea and lens to project an inverted image onto the retina, where specialized photoreceptor cells process it. Signals travel via the optic nerve to the brain's visual cortex, where they are combined and recombined across various brain regions to form a unified percept. This process, known as "binding," results in the immediate recognition of an object, such as the ocean or a cat, in the present moment. Perceptual images are grounded in the here and now; they require

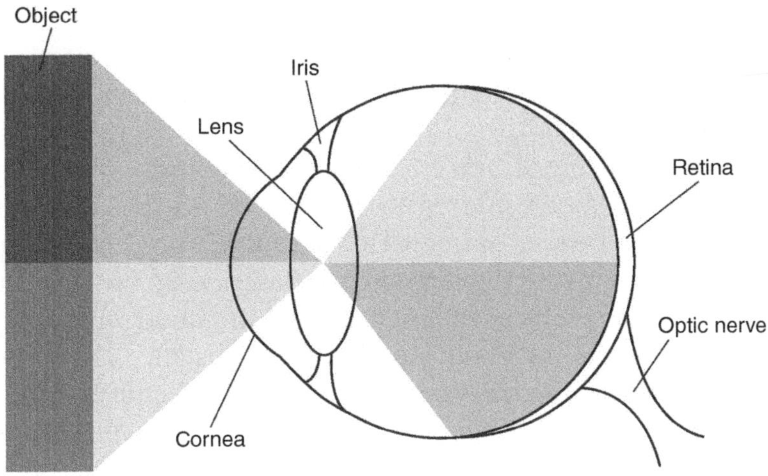

Figure 2.1 Human vision.

the physical presence of the object being seen. For instance, when viewing a cat, the cat must exist within the visual field for perception to occur (Koch, 2004).

In contrast, *mental images* are created in the absence of the physical object. These images are constructed from memory or imagination and allow us to recall past experiences or envision scenarios that do not exist in reality. Unlike perceptual images, which are dynamic and continuously discoverable as attention shifts to new details, mental images are static and limited to what the mind retains or constructs. They are inherently selective, reflecting only what the mind remembers or imagines. For example, we might visualize a cat we have seen before or imagine a fictional cat described in a story, such as the Cheshire Cat in Lewis Carroll's (2014 [1865]) *Alice's Adventures in Wonderland*. Mental images enable speculative thinking, offering the freedom to reanalyze, reinterpret, or envision entirely new constructs, such as imagining what this cat might look like based on the textual description offered in the book: "The Cheshire Cat only grinned when it saw Alice. It looked good-natured... still it had very long claws and a great many teeth"

(Carroll, 2014 [1865], p. 76). Thus, while perceptual images represent the immediate, material world, mental images engage with the absent or hypothetical, creating a bridge between reality and imagination (McGinn, 2004).

Cultural learning plays a critical role in shaping both perceptual and mental imagery. Children learn to recognize and understand objects such as cars or animals through direct perceptual experiences before acquiring the language to describe them. This underscores how vision precedes language in human cognition, laying the groundwork for symbolic and linguistic systems. For instance, children might recognize a car as a distinct object even when its defining features, such as wheels, are not visible from certain angles. This perceptual learning forms the basis for later mental imagery, where the concept of "carness" can be recalled or imagined even in the absence of an actual car. Classic perceptual puzzles, such as the vase-faces illusion (Figure 2.2), further demonstrate the role of cultural and cognitive frameworks in visual interpretation. These puzzles show how selective attention and prior knowledge influence what we perceive and how we interpret visual stimuli, highlighting how perceptual images are filtered and mental images are shaped by cultural context and personal experience (McGinn, 2004).

Figure 2.2 Representation of the vase-faces illusion.

GenAI has added a new dimension to the interplay between perceptual and mental images. Tools like *DALL-E*, *MidJourney*, and *Stable Diffusion* synthesize images from textual prompts, effectively transforming mental constructs into perceptual-like visual outputs. Thus, GenAI bridges the gap between these two categories by materializing imagined scenarios in a tangible, visual form. For example, a prompt containing a description of the Cheshire cat similar to that created by Carroll (2014 [1865]) can be converted into the image presented in Figure 2.3. The AI's rendering blends the speculative nature of mental imagery with the material presence of perceptual imagery, including details such as the purple color added to the prompt by one of this book's authors, whose mental image of the Cheshire cat has been influenced by Disney's representation of this character in the animated movie *Alice in Wonderland*.

By enabling individuals with no artistic training, like the author of this book who generated the Cheshire Cat image, to create intricate visuals, GenAI thus simplifies (and somehow "democratizes") visual creation. Additionally, this technology brings to the forefront

Figure 2.3 GenAI's rendering of the Cheshire Cat. (SOURCE: Generated with AI using DALL·E - 3.0 OpenAI).

the interconnectedness of text and image, as linguistic prompts guide the generation of visual outputs. By doing so, GenAI underscores the multimodal nature of communication and enriches the process of meaning-making, allowing for new ways to explore and express imagination (Kalantzis & Cope, 2024). We will deal with the profound implications of these affordances for education later in this book.

Human communication, however, is not just confined to text and image. Space also plays an equally significant role in how we perceive, communicate, and construct meaning. In the following section, we explore this form of meaning and its mediums in more depth.

Space

Space, in essence, is defined by what lies between objects, by the relationships created through their placement, and by the ways bodies and objects move within it. Space has long served as a fundamental form of communication, shaping how we interact with our surroundings and with one another. From the physical arrangement of objects that guide our movements, to the designed or natural environments that influence our activities, and now to the digital and virtual worlds we inhabit, space conveys meaning and prompts interpretation. It is not simply a backdrop against which human life unfolds but a dynamic interface that can be understood, designed, navigated, and represented through various modes of technology, culture, and cognition (Cope & Kalantzis, 2020).

Our spatial meanings arise from both the real and virtual places we inhabit, and from the ways we move through and engage with them. We do not merely see these environments; we also feel them, interact with them, and experience them in tactile and embodied ways (more on this in the following section of the chapter). Because we inhabit space physically and, increasingly, virtually, the meanings that emerge do so over time and through sequences that are spatially framed. The extent of our movement, in turn, is influenced by the ways in which spaces have been designed—either by human intention or, in the case of natural environments, by the cultural and intellectual values we attribute to them, such as appreciating their natural beauty or investigating their scientific significance.

Different locations serve different functions, whether they are houses, schools, supermarkets, libraries, offices, places of worship, factories, theaters, or even electronic screens. Each of these environments has its own internal and external designs, within which we follow distinct patterns—entering a lecture theater to sit and listen to a talk before leaving, or passing through a house as we move from room to room while cooking, working, or sleeping. These experiences lead us to create mental maps, conceptual frameworks, and itineraries. Some representations remain internalized, while others are drawn on paper or generated digitally (Cope & Kalantzis, 2020; Kalantzis & Cope, 2020).

New technological tools like geographic information systems (GIS) and global positioning systems (GPS) have further transformed our engagement with space, introducing novel ways to represent (and navigate) our environments. Virtual reality environments have also allowed us to simulate real-world places or craft entirely original spaces (Bailenson, 2018). With the recent rise of GenAI, our ability to communicate and interpret spatial meaning has even expanded in undoubtedly unprecedented ways. Now, we can employ GenAI tools to generate 3D spaces in a matter of seconds (Figure 2.4), offer context-aware digital maps, and create simulations that personalize the flow of people and objects based on user interactions. Also, AI-driven platforms can dynamically alter digital landscapes, guide our attention to certain objects or pathways, and inspire entirely new forms of exploration that transcend physical limitations.

As our communication through space becomes increasingly mediated by these advanced technologies, we enrich and complicate our spatial narratives, forging connections between presence and absence, inside and outside, local and global, natural and artificial, physical and virtual. In doing so, we continuously reshape spatial meaning and expand the horizon of what it means to inhabit and understand the spaces around us. Next, we examine object and body.

Figure 2.4 GenAI's 3D rendering of a prehistoric cave inspired by the Paleolithic Cueva de Altamira in Spain. (SOURCE: Generated with AI using DALL·E 3.0. – OpenAI).

Object and Body

Object and body are deeply intertwined as forms of meaning and their mediums of communication. Objects, with their tangible and usable forms, extend the capabilities of our bodies, acting as tools, symbols, and representations of our intentions and identities. Similarly, the body itself is an expressive meaning form, communicating through gestures, body postures, and sensory experiences. Together, objects and bodies do not merely coexist but function synergistically, creating, transmitting, and interpreting meaning across diverse contexts.

Objects are 3D, tangible, and usable things, often produced digitally in 3D renderings. Objects hold meaning for us and contribute to our understanding of the world through their presence and application. These can include utensils, tools, furniture, toys, and devices like pencils, phones, or computers, which allow us to create meanings across time and distance (Cope & Kalantzis, 2020).

We interact with objects through our senses—seeing, touching, smelling, and tasting. Through these sensations, we distinguish textures, temperatures, and chemical compositions. Taste integrates with tactile sensations, as the tongue perceives temperature, texture, and piquancy (e.g., chili-hot!). Smell adds layers of distinction, creating a complex interplay of meanings. Together, these senses form a rich tapestry of tactile experiences, shaping our language and metaphorical understanding (Lakoff & Johnson, 1980). Words like "hot," "cool," "rough," and "sweet" exemplify how sensory meanings permeate our cognitive frameworks.

From infancy, tactile experiences shape meaning. Babies explore the world by touching, holding, and moving objects, constructing foundational understandings of agency, interconnectedness, and subjectivity. Through objects, young children learn to design and redesign their immediate environments, developing basic capacities for meaning-making (Stern, 1985). These tactile interactions remain central to human cognition and communication, as evidenced by tools like Braille, which translate written language into tactile form for the sight-impaired.

Gestural meanings complement tactile ones, involving bodily movements, postures, and symbolic gestures. Gestures communicate meanings through body spacing, orientation, facial expressions, and hand movements (Kendon, 2004; McNeill, 1992, 2012). These meanings may be spontaneous, as in everyday interactions, or premeditated, as in role-playing, theater, or dance.

An example of this type of communication can be seen in Figure 2.5. This digital representation, created by one of the book's authors' 8-year-old daughter, illustrates the interplay of gestures and symbolism. The body movements, postures, and facial expressions of the two figures in the image vividly convey a message of love and happiness. Additionally, the child has used elements such as color, hair style, body size, and clothing to clearly identify the figures as herself and her mother, personalizing the message and deepening its emotional resonance. The artifact also plays a fundamental role

Figure 2.5 Digital representation relying on object, body, and image for communication.

as a digital object developed and employed by a child to express her love for her mother.

Through physical engagement, we also manipulate and use objects as extensions of ourselves. They become material and cognitive prostheses, serving ritualistic purposes and representing cultural or natural meanings based on their context (Cope & Kalantzis, 2022).

This dynamic has been further extended by GenAI through the novel possibilities it offers for interaction and meaning-making. For example, by synthesizing and interpreting multimodal data, GenAI systems have enhanced the ability of objects "to communicate." Wearable devices equipped with AI can now analyze bodily movements, gestures, and physiological signals, translating them into actionable insights or interactive responses (Taylor et al., 2020). Additionally, AI-powered objects, such as virtual assistants or augmented reality devices, can facilitate the seamless integration of physical and virtual spaces. These technologies have also enabled personalized, context-sensitive communication, further blurring the lines between the tangible and the digital (Dogan et al., 2024).

In sum, the interplay between objects and the body forms a foundational aspect of human communication, enabling the creation and interpretation of meaning through tangible and sensory experiences. This relationship, deeply rooted in our cognitive and cultural frameworks, continues to evolve with technological advancements, enhancing the communicative potential of objects through AI integration.

Our attention now turns to sound, which offers a distinct yet complementary channel for expressing and interpreting meaning. Let us explore its role in communication.

Sound

Audio meanings encompass a wide range of experiences, from the ambient or background sounds in our environment to symbolic sounds and the complex emotional and narrative representations found in music. Human hearing, which operates through the detection of air pressure waves, allows us to perceive sounds in terms of loudness (amplitude) and pitch (frequency). However, our auditory capacity is constrained by specific limits. Extremely loud sounds risk causing hearing damage, while low frequencies can sometimes be felt as vibrations rather than heard (Cope & Kalantzis, 2020; Kalantzis & Cope, 2020).

Sound perception begins in the inner ear, where signal processing occurs (Figure 2.6). This process can be affected by masking, in which one sound is obscured by a more prominent one. The ways by which we derive meaning from sounds are influenced by rhythm, pitch, volume, tempo, texture, and directionality, creating a foundation for interpreting everyday soundscapes, music, and speech. For example, a bell ringing, mood-setting music in a store, or a car horn all carry meanings that we learn to interpret. Similarly, we create sounds with intentional meanings, such as warning signals or music that evokes specific emotions (Ball, 2010).

The meanings derived from sound can be categorized into three overlapping types: *likeness*, *directedness*, and *abstraction*. *Likeness* refers to sounds that resemble their sources, such as a dog's bark

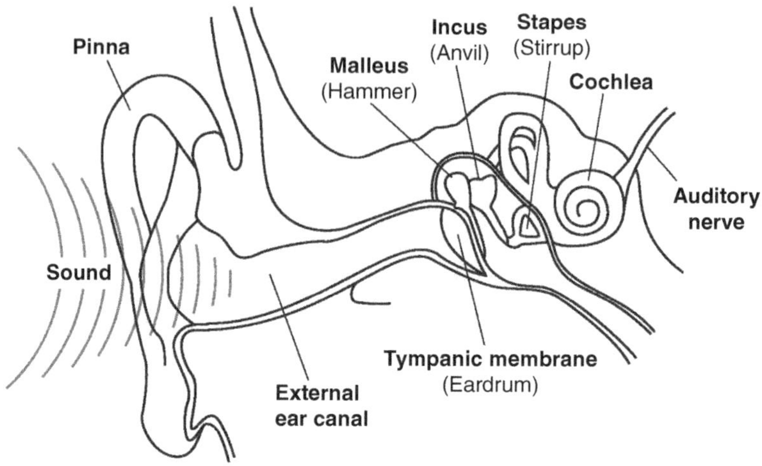

Figure 2.6 The ear.

indicating the presence of a dog. These sounds populate both natural and urban soundscapes (Krause, 2015; Thompson, 2002) and extend to musical representations like Rimsky-Korsakov's "Flight of the Bumblebee." *Directedness* involves sounds that point to something beyond themselves, such as sirens, bells, or train whistles, as well as human expressions like crying or laughing (Connor, 2014). *Abstraction* entails symbolic meanings developed through cultural and historical contexts, such as the association of organ music with churches or blues music with melancholy. These abstract meanings are often conventional, reinforced by lyrics that provide explicit interpretations, like the evocative phrases in songs such as "Summertime" or "God Save the King."

The distinctions between likeness, directedness, and abstraction are fluid; a sound initially resembling its source can evolve into a symbolic or warning sound. Silence, too, can carry meaning, as seen in the pauses between musical movements or John Cage's exploration of silence in his works (Cage, 2012). Background sounds, white noise, and dissonance also inhabit the edges of meaningful auditory experience.

GenAI has significantly transformed sound and communication, introducing new possibilities for representation, abstraction, and interaction. AI tools can now generate synthetic voices that closely resemble human speakers, enhancing applications in virtual assistants and automated announcements (Zhang et al., 2023). Additionally, AI systems are capable of composing music in specific styles or creating soundscapes that evoke particular cultural or emotional contexts, thereby redefining likeness by producing sounds that mimic natural or human-made phenomena (Zhu et al., 2023). Directedness is enhanced as GenAI tailors auditory cues to specific environments, such as personalized notifications or dynamically adaptive soundscapes in interactive media (Huang et al., 2023). Furthermore, AI's ability to invent new symbolic frameworks allows for the composition of music in traditional genres or the crafting of innovative soundscapes for media and immersive experiences, extending abstraction in creative domains (Xiong et al., 2023).

Sound differs fundamentally from other forms of communication, such as image. For example, sound unfolds over time, while images are arranged spatially. Yet, both forms can represent each other's characteristics, albeit imperfectly—for instance, recorded sound simulating spatial depth through stereophonic effects. Innovations in digital audio, such as the precedence effect, have enhanced the dimensionality of sound, creating impressions of space and echo (Kalantzis & Cope, 2020). GenAI has built upon these innovations, creating even more immersive auditory experiences by leveraging advanced modeling to simulate acoustics that feel authentic. For example, by generating 3D sound environments for virtual reality or physical spaces, AI amplifies the visceral and immersive qualities of sound (Ratnarajah & Manocha, 2023).

Moreover, in the broader cultural and communicative context, GenAI can be said to be redefining the relationship between sound and meaning, challenging traditional notions of creation, interpretation, and representation. By expanding the universe of audible meanings, GenAI is bridging human artifice, nature, and the synthetic (Agchar et al., 2024; Hernandez-Olivan et al., 2022). This evolution underscores the role of sound as a meaning form that connects the organic and artificial, the individual and collective, and the temporal and spatial. For instance, AI-driven streaming services like *Spotify* have introduced features such as AI-generated playlists (i.e., Spotify's AI DJ) and podcasts analyzing users' listening habits and thus enhancing personalized auditory experiences (Spotify, 2023). Also, AI technologies are being employed to recreate the voices of deceased musicians, exemplified by projects that simulate performances by artists like Amy Winehouse or Freddie Mercury (Molloy, 2023). As GenAI continues to innovate, it might reshape not only the materiality of sound but also its potential to evoke, direct, and symbolize meaning in increasingly complex and varied ways.

Sound, as a form of communication, finds its most intricate and versatile expression in speech. Speech builds upon the affordances of sound, transforming it into structured, symbolic language. As we transition from the realm of sound to the exploration of speech, in the following section, we examine how this meaning form extends the auditory experience, combining rhythm, tone, and abstraction to create a system of communication that is uniquely human and profoundly impactful.

Speech

Speech as a form of meaning can be defined as vocalized meanings conveyed through the medium of spoken language, following phonemic conventions, and capable of being digitally captured, transmitted, or reproduced using synthetic or sampled sound (Cope & Kalantzis, 2020). That is, oral communication manifests in two principal forms: listening, where meanings are interpreted from auditory input, and speaking, where individuals produce linguistic expressions for interpretation by others. In the spectrum of communication mediums, therefore, speech lies in its close alignment with sound. Speech also maintains a linguistic connection to text. Nevertheless, despite this connection, oral and written languages are distinct, necessitating separate consideration (Bezemer & Kress, 2016; Halliday, 2002; Kalantzis & Cope, 2022).

At a fundamental level, speech and writing differ in their sensory modes and their connection to time and space. Speech is transient, existing in the moment and unfolding through sound waves, while writing, as discussed in Section "Writing" of this chapter, is persistent, existing in visual symbols that can be revisited. The temporal nature of speech emphasizes immediacy and interaction, while the spatial nature of writing allows for reflection, organization, and permanence. Consequently, speech often depends on shared situational contexts, using pronouns and temporal markers like "I," "you," or "yesterday," whereas writing demands greater explicitness, naming entities and constructing internal reference systems to ensure clarity for distant or future audiences (Kalantzis & Cope, 2020).

Thus, the process of meaning-making in speech can be described as dynamic and interactive, reflecting its reliance on real-time communication. Hesitations, false starts, and self-corrections are typical, highlighting its iterative nature akin to "thinking aloud." In contrast, writing is deliberate and refined, with these iterative steps concealed in a polished final product. This refinement lends writing an aura of objectivity and detachment, whereas speech fosters personal connection and immediacy. Writing also often condenses complex ideas using nominalization and structured logic, creating a dense, compact form. Speech, however, is process-oriented, connecting ideas through simpler structures like "and" or "because" (Halliday, 2002). These distinctions reveal not only their formal differences but also their divergent cognitive and representational functions. In other words, writing does not simply transcribe speech, as it is often perceived, but instead reshapes meaning through its medium and cannot fully capture the richness of oral expression.

This remains the case even if recent advancements in GenAI have improved the ways in which speech is digitally captured. For instance, technologies such as OpenAI's *Whisper* (Graham & Roll, 2024) and Google's *DeepMind WaveNet* (van den Oord et al., 2016) have improved speech recognition and synthesis, enabling unprecedented accuracy and naturalness in audio processing. These innovations have facilitated real-time translation, context-aware virtual assistants, and tools for creating synthetic voices that preserve individual speaker identity.

Nevertheless, GenAI is fundamentally a writing technology as it primarily relies on source texts that were originally created as written material. While Large Language Model (LLM) corpora may include some transliterations of speech, these typically derive from structured or text-like speech forms, such as lectures, readings, or narrative scripts, rather than spontaneous conversations. As a result, key features of speech—such as prosody, dialect, gesticulation, embodied context, redundancy, hesitation, and circumlocution—are largely absent. Consequently, the grammar of written text dominates the functionality of GenAI (Cope & Kalantzis, 2024).

Clearly, as shown in this section, speech and text entail different ways of thinking and representing the world. Each meaning form is chosen based on its appropriateness for the intended meaning and context. These differences, however, have not always been reflected in our conception of literacy and the ways in which we have approached the teaching of both writing and reading. In the following section, we examine this topic.

Connecting Speech to Text: Phonics Controversies

Phonics, a foundational approach in traditional literacy instruction, is the method of teaching reading and writing by connecting spoken sounds (phonemes) to their written representations (graphemes). It is rooted in the principle that learning the systematic relationships between sounds and letters equips learners to decode unfamiliar words, building a pathway to literacy. Phonics instruction is commonly divided into *synthetic* and *analytic* methods. *Synthetic phonics* teaches students to blend individual sounds to form whole words, progressing from simple phonetic elements like consonants and short vowels to more complex patterns such as diphthongs and multisyllabic words. *Analytic* phonics, conversely, starts with whole words, breaking them down into their sound components to help learners infer phonetic patterns through repetition and exposure (Schoenfeld & Pearson, 2009). While these methods are highly structured, the role and effectiveness of phonics in literacy education remain contentious.

Proponents of phonics emphasize its value in providing early readers with a clear, systematic framework for decoding words. This approach gives learners tools to navigate unfamiliar words and build their reading fluency, especially in alphabetic languages like English, where grapheme–phoneme correspondences play a crucial role. However, English presents unique challenges to phonics instruction, with its irregular spelling rules, numerous exceptions, and dialectal variations, which complicate the learning process (Cope & Kalantzis, 2020).

Consider the following. In spoken English, there are approximately 5000 distinct syllables, each combining unique sounds and letters when represented in written form (Snow et al., 1998). Berdiansky et al. (1969) conducted an analysis of over 6,000 one- and two-syllable words from school reading materials aimed at children aged 6–9 years, identifying 69 grapheme units (e.g., "th") associated with 38 distinct sounds, connected in 211 different ways. Their study uncovered 166 rules—patterns of sound-to-letter correspondences that appeared in at least 10 words—and 45 exceptions, where such correspondences occurred only once or in very few instances. They also discovered that vowels alone could be pronounced in 79 different ways. Critics, such as psycholinguist Frank Smith, argue that these complexities can make phonics less intuitive and "too complicated to be taught" (Smith, 2004, p. 143). Furthermore, these critics caution that an excessive focus on phonics risks turning reading into a purely mechanical process, detracting from its greater purpose of cultivating comprehension and engagement with the text.

To counter phonics' limitations, alternative approaches to reading, such as the naturalistic or whole-language approach, have been proposed. *Whole language* focuses on immersing learners in meaningful, authentic texts to naturally develop their literacy skills. This method views reading as a cognitive and interpretive process, emphasizing the use of context, prior knowledge, and mental schemas to derive meaning (Smith, 2004). Advocates such as Goodman (1996, 2005) argue that phonics alone cannot capture the richness of reading, as some words, such as "yacht," defy phonetic decoding and require recognition as whole units. By prioritizing meaning-making over decoding, the whole-language approach aligns with the ultimate goal of literacy—to understand and interact with the world through text. However, this method is not without its critics.

Opponents of the whole-language approach highlight its lack of systematic structure, which can leave struggling learners without the foundational tools to decode unfamiliar words. Without explicit phonics instruction, some students may find it difficult to connect written words to their sounds, leading to gaps in literacy development (Anderson et al., 1985). Moreover, the approach may favor students who already possess strong literacy backgrounds, inadvertently disadvantaging those with less exposure to written language. These limitations have prompted educators to advocate for balanced or hybrid approaches that integrate the strengths of both phonics and whole-language methods.

Balanced literacy programs aim to bridge the divide by combining systematic phonics instruction with strategies that foster comprehension and engagement through authentic texts. This approach recognizes the diverse needs of learners, blending the mechanical skill of decoding with the cognitive process of meaning-making. For example, the *Four Resources Model* proposed by Freebody and Luke (1990) provides a comprehensive framework for literacy instruction relying on text communication. It encourages readers to act as codebreakers (decoding phonics), meaning-makers (understanding text), text users (applying knowledge), and text analysts (critically evaluating content). This model, summarized in Table 2.2, not only incorporates phonics but also situates reading within broader social and cultural contexts, fostering critical engagement with texts.

The controversies surrounding phonics underscore the complexity of the speech–text relationship as well as literacy education with a focus on reading and writing. Phonics provides an essential foundation for early readers by equipping them with the tools to decode written language. Yet its limitations, such as the irregularities of the English language and its focus on mechanical decoding, necessitate integration with approaches that emphasize comprehension and engagement. On the other hand, whole-language methods foster a deeper connection to texts but risk neglecting the structural skills

Table 2.2 The four resources model

Codebreaker *Coding competence:* to break the code of written texts by recognizing and using fundamental features and architecture, including alphabet, sounds in words, spelling, and structural conventions and patterns	Meaning-maker *Semantic competence:* to participate in understanding and composing meaningful written, visual, and spoken texts, taking into account each text's interior meaning systems in relation to the reader's available knowledge and their experiences of other cultural discourses, texts, and meaning systems
Text user *Pragmatic competence:* to use texts functionally by knowing about and acting on the different cultural and social functions that various texts perform inside and outside school and understanding that these functions shape the way texts are structured, their tone, their degree of formality, and their sequence of components	Text analyst *Critical competence:* to analyze critically and transform texts by acting on knowledge that texts are not ideologically natural or neutral; that they represent particular points of view while silencing others and influence people's ideas; and that their designs and discourses can be critiqued and redesigned in novel and hybrid ways

SOURCE: Adapted from Freebody (2007); Freebody and Luke (1990); Luke and Freebody (1997)

some learners need to succeed. A balanced approach that combines the systematic rigor of phonics with the experiential richness of whole-language strategies offers a more inclusive framework for literacy instruction.

In this section, we have shown that the debate over phonics and whole-language approaches reflects broader tensions in literacy education between structure and meaning and mechanics and interpretation. By integrating the strengths of both methods, educators can craft hybrid approaches that address the diverse needs of learners, ensuring that literacy instruction is both effective and meaningful. This balanced approach, which regards reading as design (see Section "Reading" in this chapter), equips students with the skills to decode language, comprehend its communicative and structural subtleties, and engage critically with the texts that shape their understanding of the world. We will continue exploring these issues in Chapter 4, when we address literacy pedagogies in more depth.

Conclusion

This chapter has explored the multimodal nature of literacy, emphasizing how meaning can be constructed and communicated through a variety of meaning forms, including text, image, space, object, body, sound, and speech. We explored the unique affordances and constraints of each form and their mediums, highlighting their interplay in meaning-making practices. By examining these diverse forms, we underscored that literacy extends far beyond traditional notions of reading and writing: It is a dynamic and evolving process shaped by technological advancements, cultural practices, and individual experiences. This multimodal perspective not only reflects the rich complexity of historical and contemporary communication but also challenges us to rethink how we approach literacy in an increasingly interconnected and digital world, where our patterns of meaning-making are being reshaped and reconceptualized by GenAI. As we move forward, it becomes clear that literacy must do much more than facilitate communication; it must serve as a critical tool for understanding, navigating, and transforming the world while effectively facing its challenges.

In the following chapter, we illuminate the functional dimensions of literacy—how it maps meaning and enables action in various contexts. By examining what literacy does, we deepen our understanding of its roles and implications in shaping our lives and societies.

Consolidate, Explore, Reflect, Do

We end this chapter with activities that will allow you to apply the concepts discussed in novel ways. Our goal is that these tasks will facilitate further exploration and reflection and will inspire your present and/or future teaching practice.

Task 1: Multimodal Portfolio Creation

In this task, you will design a digital portfolio that showcases your understanding of the different forms of communication discussed in this chapter. Each section should focus on one meaning form (text, image, sound, etc.). Develop or find artifacts that reflect the affordances and constraints of each form and their mediums. Complement the presentation of each artifact with reflective notes. For example

1. Explain how your artifact illustrates the affordances and limitations of the forms and mediums of focus.
2. Describe what communication contexts it would be ideal for and why this is the case.
3. Consider what other form(s) and medium(s) would complement the meaning conveyed and why this is the case.

Share your portfolio with a classmate and reflect on similarities and differences. Is your understanding of the different meaning forms and mediums the same or different? Where could similarities and differences originate? Consider identities as well as personal and educational experiences.

Task 2: Forms of Meaning Explained

Step 1. With two or three classmates, plan and design a digital infographic to represent a complex topic from the chapter, such as "The Affordances of Different Meaning Forms." Use at least three different forms to communicate the information effectively.

Step 2. Exchange your infographic with another group and critically examine your and their artifacts. Address the following:

1. Have you chosen the same topic? If so, what differences and similarities have you found in the information that is conveyed and the way(s) in which you have expressed your message? Is your understanding of the topic the same or different? Where could similarities and differences originate? Consider identities as well as personal and educational experiences.

2. If you have chosen a different topic, discuss what guided your choices. Why did your groups focus on the topic of choice? How is your choice connected to your identities, personal and educational experiences, and/or professional objectives?

Reflect on infographics as multimodal tools of communication. What are their affordances? What are their limitations? Which communication contexts are they appropriate/ideal for?

Task 3: Interactive Multimodal Museum Exhibit

To complete this task, you will work with three or four classmates to create a mock exhibit for a virtual or physical museum that explores a theme like "Communication Through the Ages." As a departure point, use the content of this chapter and the previous one. Plan on incorporating the following into your exhibit: text panels, graphs/images, audio guides, and interactive, multimodal elements. Use resources like historical articles, multimedia tools, and design platforms (e.g., Canva) to create engaging and informative content. Create a short video in which you explain your design choices, considering how they support the exhibit theme and facilitate audience engagement.

Task 4: Mapping Spatial Communication

In this task, you will work with three or four classmates to analyze how spatial arrangements communicate meaning in a physical or virtual space.

Step 1. Choose a space (e.g., a library, a website, a classroom). Observe the layout of objects and open spaces and create a visual or digital map to record your observations (you can choose tools like *Lucidchart* or *Canva*). You can also transform your observations into a prompt and ask GenAI (e.g., DALL-E) to generate a 3D map.
Step 2. Add annotations explaining how semiotic choices (e.g., signage, spatial organization, free spaces) communicate meaning. Consider how this space is employed, and critically examine whether spatial communication is effective in connection to both

its purpose and who it is used by. What are the ideologies embedded in the space?
Step 3. Present your map and analysis to the class. Consider similarities and differences among products, reflecting on where they might originate.
Step 4 (optional). If you used GenAI to generate your map, consider the affordances and limitations of the tools you chose. What worked? What is missing? What does this say about the tool and GenAI as a whole?

Task 5: Lesson Plan on Meaning Forms and Multimodality

To complete this task, you will develop a lesson plan for teaching what meaning forms are and how they can work together to younger students. You can focus on primary- or secondary-school students, depending on your professional interests.

Step 1. Identify the target age group and educational context. Articulate key objectives and outcomes. You can either choose to introduce a variety of related meaning forms, such as space, object, and body, or only one.
Step 2. Based on these objectives and outcomes, create activities that involve the use of the chosen meaning form(s). Structure your plan to work with these activities, thinking of ways in which you will guide your students' understanding of how these forms work. How will learners use these forms in their own meaning-making? Your plan should include both critical analysis and use.
Step 3. Develop a multimodal lesson plan. You should be able to explain how it integrates the concepts discussed in this chapter, and how you have designed ways in which you can introduce these concepts to your students. Also, reflect on the challenges you might face.

Task 6: Gesture and Movement Case Study

To complete this task, you will record how gestures and body language are used for communication in a specific setting (e.g., your classroom, a café, public transportation).

Step 1. Identify the setting on which you want to focus. Choose a place in the chosen environment where you can observe a variety of interactions.
Step 2. Document at least five different types of interaction using notes and sketches.
Step 3. Develop a multimodal (if possible) report on your observations. Analyze the gestures and body postures that contributed to meaning-making. Consider whether communication was always effective or not and why this was the case. When communication appeared to fail, were other meaning forms used to compensate for limitations? Were these forms appropriate for the social interactions expected in the context observed? Explain.
Step 4. Share your report with a classmate. Were your experiences similar or different? Discuss your experiences and summarize the affordances and limitations of the meaning forms of focus based on the information you gathered.

Task 7: Redesign of Educational Material

In this task, you will transform a text-based educational material into a multimodal resource.

Step 1. Select an educational resource (e.g., a worksheet, textbook excerpt).
Step 2. Redesign it to include images, interactive elements, or videos using tools like *Canva* or *ThingLink*.
Step 3. Develop a multimodal (if possible) rationale to explain your choices. For example, focus on the reasons why you have chosen specific meaning forms/mediums (connection to learners, instructional objective, outcomes, literacy) and how your redesign supports diverse learners.
Step 4. Share your resource and rationale with a classmate. Compare your works. Reflect on your experiences working with different meaning forms/mediums, creative challenges, and affordances offered by the forms/mediums chosen that were not present in the original artifact. Do your works reflect a similar understanding of

the concepts discussed in Chapter 2? If not, why do you think this might be the case? Tie your reflection to personal and educational experiences.

Task 8: Analysis of a Multimodal Artifact

To complete this task, you will collaborate with a classmate to analyze how different meaning forms work in a multimodal artifact.

Step 1. With your classmate, select 2–4 advertisements across different media (paper newspaper/magazine, video, digital) or social media posts (e.g., Instagram or TikTok).

Step 2. Analyze your chosen artifacts, focusing on the following (adapted from Zapata, pp. 156–158):

1. **Focus on the Message Conveyed**
   - **(a)** What is this artifact about?
   - **(b)** What purposes does it serve (what is its goal?)
   - **(c)** Who created it?
   - **(d)** Who is the artifact for (intended audience)?
2. **Focus on Meaning Forms**
   - **(a)** What meaning forms are present in the artifact? Which is/are the most salient? Why do you think this is the case? Tie your answer to the purpose and intended audience.
   - **(b)** What does each meaning form contribute to the meaning of the artifact? What information does each part of the artifact convey?
   - **(c)** Would the artifact have been the same if one of the meaning forms had not been used?

Step 3. Create a report to share the result of your analysis with your class. Based on your classmates' analysis as well as yours, how has your knowledge of the concepts discussed in this chapter broadened? What surprised you about the artifacts you analyzed?

Step 4. Go back to the personal definition of literacy you developed in Chapter 1 and modify it based on the contents of this chapter and your experience in this activity. What has changed? What remains the same? Why?

References

Adoniou, M. (2014). What should teachers know about spelling? *Literacy, 48*(3), 144–154. https://doi.org/10.1111/lit.12017

Afflerbach, P., Pearson, P. D., & Paris, S. G. (2008). Clarifying differences between reading skills and reading strategies. *The Reading Teacher, 61*(5), 364–373. https://doi.org/10.1598/RT.61.5.1

Agchar, I., Baumann, I., Braun, F., Perez-Toro, P. A., Riedhammer, K., Trump, S., & Ullrich, M. (2024). A survey of music generation in the context of interaction. *arXiv*. https://arxiv.org/abs/2402.15294

Anderson, R. C., Hiebert, E. H., Scott, J. A., & Wilkinson, I. A. G. (1985). *Becoming a nation of readers: The report of the national commission on reading*. National Academy of Education.

Bailenson, J. (2018). *Experience on demand: What virtual reality is, how it works, and what it can do*. WW Norton & Company.

Ball, P. (2010). *The music instinct: How music works and why we can't do without it*. Oxford University Press.

Barthes, R. (1977). *Elements of semiology*. Hill and Wang.

Berdiansky, B., Cronnell, B., & Koehler, J. (1969). *Spelling-sound relations and primary form-class descriptions for speech comprehension vocabularies of 6–9 year olds*. Southwest Regional Laboratory for Educational Research and Development.

Bezemer, J. & Kress, G. (2016). *Multimodality, learning and communication: A social semiotic frame*. Routledge.

Cage, J. (2012). *Silence: Lectures and writings*. Wesleyan University Press.

Carroll, L. (2014 [1865]). *Alice's adventures in Wonderland*. Macmillan Children's Books.

Connor, S. (2014). *Beyond words: Sobs, hums, stutters and other vocalizations*. Reaktion Books.

Cope, B. & Kalantzis, M. (2020). *Making sense: Reference, agency and structure in a grammar of multimodal meaning*. Cambridge University Press.

Cope, B. & Kalantzis, M. (2022). Artificial intelligence in the long view: From mechanical intelligence to cyber-social systems. *Discover Artificial Intelligence, 2*(1), 13. https://doi.org/10.1007/s44163-022-00029-1

Cope, B. & Kalantzis, M. (2024). A multimodal grammar of artificial intelligence: Measuring the gains and losses in generative AI. *Multimodality & Society, 4*(2), 123–152. https://doi.org/10.1177/26349795231221699

Dogan, M. D., Gonzalez, E. J., Ahuja, K., Du, R., Colaco, A., Lee, J., Gonzalez-Franco, M., & Kim, D. (2024). Augmented object intelligence: Making the analog world interactable with XR-Objects. *Proceedings of the 37th Annual*

ACM Symposium on User Interface Software and Technology. https://doi.org/10.1145/3654777.3676379

Freebody, P. (2007). *Literacy education in school research: Perspectives from the past, for the future*. ACER.

Freebody, P. & Luke, A. (1990). Literacy programs: Debates and demands in cultural context. *Prospect: An Australian Journal of TESOL*, *5*(3), 7–16. https://www.researchgate.net/publication/246704522_Literacies_programs_Debates_and_demands_in_cultural_context

Gibson, J. J. (1977). The theory of affordances. In R. Shaw & J. Bransford (Eds.), *Perceiving, acting, and knowing: Toward an ecological psychology* (pp. 67–82). Routledge.

Goodman, K. (1996). *On reading*. Heinemann.

Goodman, K. (2005). *What's whole in whole language*. RDR Books.

Graham, C. & Roll, N. (2024). Evaluating OpenAI's Whisper ASR: Performance analysis across diverse accents and speaker traits. *JASA Express Letters*, *4*(2), 025206. http://dx.doi.org/10.1121/10.0024876

Halliday, M. A. K. (2002). On grammar and grammatics. In J. J. Webster (Ed.), *On grammar: The collected works of M.A.K Halliday* (Vol. 1). Continuum.

Hernandez-Olivan, C., Hernandez-Olivan, J., & Beltran, J. R. (2022). A survey on artificial intelligence for music generation: Agents, domains and perspectives. *arXiv*. https://arxiv.org/abs/2210.13944

Huang, R., Li, M., Yang, D., Shi, J., Chang, X., Ye, Z., Wu, Y., Hong, Z., Huang, J., Liu, J., Ren, Y., Zhao, Z., & Watanabe, S. (2023). AudioGPT: Understanding and generating speech, music, sound, and talking head. *arXiv*. https://arxiv.org/abs/2304.12995

Kalantzis, M. & Cope, B. (2020). *Adding sense: Context and interest in a grammar of multimodal meaning*. Cambridge University Press.

Kalantzis, M. & Cope, B. (2022). After language: A grammar of multiform transposition. In C. Lütge (Ed.), *Foreign language learning in the digital age: Theory and pedagogy for developing literacies* (pp. 34–64). Routledge. https://doi.org/10.4324/9781003032083-4

Kalantzis, M., & Cope, B. (2024). Literacy in the time of artificial intelligence. *EdArXiv*. https://doi.org/10.35542/osf.io/es5kb

Kendon, A. (2004). *Gesture: Visible action as utterance*. Cambridge University Press.

Koch, C. (2004). *The quest for consciousness: A neurobiological approach*. Roberts and Company.

Krause, B. (2015). *Voices of the wild: Animal songs, human din, and the call to save natural soundscapes*. Yale University Press.

Lakoff, G. & Johnson, M. (1980). *Metaphors we live by*. University of Chicago Press.

Lin, Z. (2024). Techniques for supercharging academic writing with generative AI. *Nature Biomedical Engineering, 18*. https://doi.org/10.1038/s41551-024-01185-8

Luke, A. & Freebody, P. (1997). Shaping the social practices of reading. In S. Muspratt, A. Luke, & P. Freebody (Eds.), *Constructing critical literacies: Teaching and learning textual practice* (pp. 185–225). Hampton Press.

McGinn, C. (2004). *Mindsight: Image, dream, meaning*. Harvard University Press.

McNeill, D. (1992). *Hand and mind: What gestures reveal about thought*. University of Chicago Press.

McNeill, D. (2012). *How language began: Gesture and speech in human evolution*. Cambridge University Press.

Molloy, L. (2023, June 22). *Should we use AI to bring musicians back from the dead?* Dazed. https://www.dazeddigital.com/music/article/60168/1/artificial-intelligence-ai-bring-musicians-back-from-dead-grimes

Olson, D. R. (1998). *The world on paper: The conceptual and cognitive implications of writing and reading*. Cambridge University Press.

Ratnarajah, A., & Manocha, D. (2023). Listen2Scene: Interactive material-aware binaural sound propagation for reconstructed 3D scenes. *arXiv*. https://arxiv.org/abs/2302.02809

Rorty, R. (1992). *The linguistic turn: Essays in philosophical method*. Chicago University Press.

Schoenfeld, A. H. & Pearson, D. P. (2009). The reading and math wars. In G. Sykes, B. Schneider, & D. N. Plank (Eds.), *Handbook of education policy research* (pp. 560–580). Routledge.

Smith, F. (2004). *Understanding reading: A psycholinguistic analysis of reading and learning to read* (6th ed.). Lawrence Erlbaum.

Snow, C. E., Burns, S. M., & Griffin, P. (1998). *Preventing reading difficulties in young children*. National Academy Press.

Spotify (2023, February 22). Spotify debuts a new AI DJ, right in your pocket. https://newsroom.spotify.com/2023-02-22/spotify-debuts-a-new-ai-dj-right-in-your-pocket/

Stern, D. L. (1985). *The interpersonal world of the infant: A view from psychoanalysis and developmental psychology*. Basic Books.

Su, Y., Lin, Y., & Lai, C. (2023). Collaborating with ChatGPT in argumentative writing classrooms. *Assessing Writing, 57*, 100752. https://doi.org/10.1016/j.asw.2023.100752

Taylor, W., Shah, S. A., Dashtipour, K., Zahid, A., Abbasi, Q. H., & Imran, M. A. (2020). An intelligent non-invasive real-time human activity recognition system for next-generation healthcare. *Sensors, 20*(9), 2653. https://doi.org/10.3390/s20092653

Thompson, E. (2002). *The soundscape of modernity: Architectural acoustics and the culture of listening in America, 1900–1933.* MIT Press.

van den Oord, A., Dieleman, S, Zen, H., Simonyan, K., Vinyals, O., Graves, A., Kalchbrenner, N., Senior, A., & Kavukcuoglu, K. (2016). WaveNet: A generative model for raw audio. *arXiv.* https://doi.org/10.48550/arXiv.1609.03499

Wang, C. (2024). Exploring students' generative AI-assisted writing processes: Perceptions and experiences from native and nonnative English speakers. *Technology, Knowledge and Learning, 30.* https://doi.org/10.1007/s10758-024-09744-3

Xiong, Z., Wang, W., Yu, J., Lin, Y., & Wang, Z. (2023). A comprehensive survey for evaluation methodologies of AI-generated music. *arXiv.* https://arxiv.org/abs/2308.13736

Zapata, G. C. (2022). *Learning by Design and second language teaching: Theory, research, and practice.* Routledge. https://doi.org/10.4324/9781003106258

Zhang, C., Zhang, C., Zheng, S., Zhang, M., Qamar, M., Bae, S.-H., & Kweon, I. S. (2023). A survey on audio diffusion models: Text to speech synthesis and enhancement in generative AI. *arXiv.* https://arxiv.org/abs/2303.13336

Zhu, Y., Baca, J., Rekabdar, B., & Rawassizadeh, R. (2023). A survey of AI music generation tools and models. *arXiv.* https://arxiv.org/abs/2308.12982

Chapter 3
What Literacy Does: Mapping the Functions of Meaning

Introduction

Building on the groundwork laid in the first two chapters, Chapter 3 transitions from the historical and multimodal perspectives on literacy to a deeper examination of the functional and transformative dimensions of meaning-making. Chapter 1 introduced the evolution of literacy from early human communication through the digital age, emphasizing the shifts in how societies encode and interpret meaning. Chapter 2 expanded this discussion by framing literacy as inherently multimodal, integrating diverse meaning forms like text, image, space, object, body, sound, and speech. In Chapter 3, we advance this narrative by exploring the functions of meaning, including how grammar, design, and participation influence literacy practices. The chapter begins by analyzing the evolution of

Literacies in the Age of AI: Teaching and Learning in the Digital Era, First Edition. Gabriela C. Zapata, Bill Cope, and Mary Kalantzis.

grammar from traditional to contemporary frameworks, followed by an exploration of how these approaches have influenced and/or might inform literacy learning. We then examine the process of creating meaning through design, culminating in an analysis of how individuals and societies transform meaning through representation, communication, and interpretation.

Our discussion then extends to the implications of meaning-making in the digital age, particularly in distinguishing between human and artificial intelligence (AI)-generated meaning. By examining this distinction, we highlight the importance of socially situated, context-dependent meaning in literacy pedagogy and emphasize the need for critical engagement with AI as a tool rather than a replacement for human sense-making. Taken together, this chapter offers a comprehensive foundation for understanding the dynamic interplay between traditional, functional, and computational approaches to meaning, bridging theoretical insights with practical applications in literacy pedagogy and digital literacy—topics that will be explored in Chapters 4 and 5

Traditional School Grammar

Overview

A traditional (school) grammar can be defined as a theory of language that identifies parts of speech and the formal grammatical relationships among them in a sentence (*syntax*). In this type of grammar—such as a traditional grammar of English—words constitute the vocabulary available for writing, reading, speaking, and/or listening. Word forms can shift based on number, person, and tense—for example, "eats," "eaten," and "ate" are forms of the verb "to eat." Also, word order might play a crucial role in meaning; for instance, "Sean called Evie" conveys a different meaning than "Evie called Sean," even though both sentences use the same three words.

Each part of speech serves a specific purpose in a sentence. For example,

1. A **noun** is a word that identifies a person, place, object, or manner of being/emotional state ("baby," "beach," "computer," "anxiety").
2. A **pronoun** is a word that substitutes for a noun once that noun has already been introduced in the sentence or is implied in context ("she," "there," "it").
3. An **adjective** is a word that ascribes an attribute to a noun or pronoun ("blue," "fast," "six").
4. A **verb** is a word that denotes an action or state of being ("type," "walks," "is").
5. An **adverb** ascribes an attribute to a verb and other parts of speech, excluding nouns, providing an explanation of "how" ("slowly," "well," "very").
6. A **preposition** begins a small cluster of words to show connections within a sentence and in the real world ("in," "with," "for").
7. A **conjunction** links parts of text—words, phrases, clauses, or sentences ("and," "or," "however").
8. An **interjection** is a word that conveys emotion, often standing alone as a single-word sentence ("hello," "sorry," "oh").

These eight parts of speech can become more ambiguous and complex upon closer examination. Here is a more detailed account of traditional grammar, highlighting the subtler distinctions among the parts of speech and their interconnections:

- **Proper nouns** are written with a capital letter and refer to a specific person or place (Evie, London); **common nouns** are lowercased and refer to generic or non-specific things (girl, city).
- **Personal pronouns** refer to people and things ("she," "it"); **relative pronouns** connect people and things ("who," "that"); **interrogative pronouns** pose questions ("who?," "where?"); **demonstrative pronouns** indicate specific items ("these," "that"); **reflexive pronouns** refer back to an original subject ("itself," "myself"); **indefinite pronouns** refer to unspecific people or things ("you," "something").
- **Adjectives** can be in the **positive** ("good"), **comparative** ("better"), or **superlative** ("best") degrees. **Articles** are special adjectives that must accompany common nouns, either as

a **definite article** specifying something particular ("the") or as an **indefinite article** for a general instance ("a").

- **Verbs** may be **transitive**, linking an actor to something that is acted upon ("kicks" in "The girl kicks the ball"), or **intransitive** when the action occurs but does not directly act upon anything ("laughed" in "The boy laughed").
- **Adverbs** can also be in the **positive** ("fast"), **comparative** ("faster"), or **superlative** ("fastest") degrees.
- **Prepositions** perform so many crucial connective functions that their usage spans nearly every possible meaning or relation ("in," "of," "at," "behind").
- **Conjunctions** may be **coordinating** ("and," "but"), **subordinating** ("because," "while"), or **correlative** ("either... or"; "not only..., but...").

These parts of speech can be modified and recombined in countless ways to express an infinite array of meanings. Consider the following:

- A **morpheme** is the smallest unit of meaning. For example, "unbelievable" contains three morphemes: the prefix "un," the stem "believe," and the suffix "able."
- **Nouns** can appear as **singular** ("cat"), **plural** ("cats"), or **possessive** ("cat's/cats'").
- **Pronouns** change based on whether they are **first person** singular or plural ("I," "me," "we"), **second person** ("you"), or **third person** (masculine, feminine, or neuter, singular or plural, "he," "she," "it," "they"). They can also show **possession** ("my," "our," "your," "her," "his," "their").
- **Verbs** vary in tense: **past** ("ate"), **past continuous** ("was eating"), **past perfect** ("had eaten"), **present** ("eats"), **present continuous** ("is eating"), **future** ("will eat"), **future continuous** ("will be eating"), **future perfect** ("will have eaten"), or **infinitive**, which is not tied to a specific time ("to eat").
- **Verbs** also take different moods: **indicative** ("You are well"), **imperative** ("Be well!"), **interrogative** ("Are you well?"), and **subjunctive** ("If you were well...").
- Finally, verbs can be in the **active voice**, where the subject directly carries out the action ("Evie painted that picture"), or in

the **passive voice,** where focus is placed on the recipient of the action ("That picture was painted by Evie").

Another important aspect of traditional grammars is *syntax*—the arrangement of various parts of speech into **phrase**s, **clauses**, and **sentences**. The possibilities are vast—so much so that no two sequences of hundreds of newly formed words are ever entirely alike. Let's have a look at syntactic categories:

- A **phrase** is a group of words functioning as a single unit, such as a **noun phrase**, which acts like a noun ("the lazy cat"), a **prepositional** phrase, which starts with a preposition ("in the kitchen"), or a **verb phrase**, which functions like a verb ("run quickly").
- A **clause** requires a **subject** (a person or thing that acts) and a **finite verb** (the action itself); an **infinite** verb does not act, nor do certain verb forms like **past participles** ("eaten") or **gerunds** ("eating"). Often, a clause will include a **predicate**, which is the person or thing that the subject acts upon.
- A **sentence** is an **independent clause** that can stand alone ("The cat sat on the mat"). **Dependent clauses** connect with other sentence elements. **Noun clauses** act as nouns ("What I can see" in "What I can see is something large and green"); **adverbial clauses** modify a verb ("When the party was over" in "When the party was over, we went home"); **adjectival clauses** describe a noun ("that we went to" in "The party that we went to was fantastic").
- **Sentences** can be **declarative** statements ("The cat sat on the mat"), **imperative** commands ("Please sit on the mat"), **interrogative** questions ("Is the cat sitting on the mat?"), or **exclamatory** expressions of emotion ("Oh my goodness, the cat is sitting on the mat!").
- When putting sentences together, we must ensure that related words, whose forms can vary, are in **agreement** (which they are not in "The cat are sitting") and are arranged in a proper **order** (which they are not in "Sitting here are cat").

This is only the start. Traditional grammars can become significantly more intricate because creating meaning is inherently diverse, complex, and nuanced.

We have compiled this overview because those of us working in literacy education should be aware of these foundational concepts. They arise frequently, especially for individuals who learned to read and write under a *didactic literacy pedagogy* (more on this in the following section) or studied another language through a traditional method. Moreover, the ideas behind these terms might, from time to time, be advantageous to all readers and writers.

The Pedagogy of Traditional Grammars

Traditional grammar is both tied to the traditional notions of literacy we discussed in Chapters 1 and 2, as well as to *didactic* pedagogy. This type of pedagogy fosters direct instruction, where knowledge is transmitted from teacher to student in a largely one-way process. Within this approach, students engage in a communicative process that Aristotle would describe as *mimesis.* As he states, "the instinct of imitation is implanted in man from childhood, one difference between him and other animals being that he is the most imitative of living creatures, and through imitation learns his earliest lessons" (Aristotle, 350 BCE, part IV). For the learner, the most evident sign of mimesis in the realm of knowledge is the imperative to *memorize*, while the teacher's role is to impart information in a didactic manner that students can internalize and replicate mentally.

Opportunities for learners to speak within *didactic-mimetic* pedagogies are limited in both frequency and scope. One example is classroom discourse (Cazden, 2001), where a teacher poses a question, a single student responds on behalf of the group while the others listen silently, and the teacher then evaluates the answer—issuing responses like "yes, that's right" or "no, try again." Because only one student speaks at a time, there are few chances for active meaning-making; moreover, it is typically the self-important or overconfident who tend to speak (Cope & Kalantzis, 2017).

Several distinctive characteristics define this communication architecture. Notably, one of the parties—the learner—remains silent for most of the time, positioned as a passive recipient, a situation that often leads to disengagement and boredom. The setting is highly individualized and isolating: the solitary student in a lecture theater or at a classroom desk, prohibited from conversing with neighbors; the individual reader of the textbook; the lone test taker.

How is, then, traditional grammar approached in a didactic pedagogy classroom? Essentially, instructors present numerous rules, which students memorize, and are evaluated in a piece of writing in part by counting the number of "errors" it contains. Below are several old-style grammar rules, along with examples showing that an apparent mistake may not always truly be an error. (By the way, some of these are still useful to know, especially if you are writing for someone who may judge certain constructions as incorrect, even if they might not be.)

1. A sentence must contain a verb. (But not if it's a title, or a headline, or an advertising slogan, or if you simply wish to be emphatic.)
2. Always place the subject at the beginning of a sentence. (However, that is not always what happens—for instance, "It's me." Moreover, because "It is I" would be grammatically correct, you might only say "It is I" when you want to sound formal or old-fashioned. Typically, "It's me" will be "correct" in everyday usage.)
3. Never use a double negative. ("I ain't got no ..." is a common form in certain dialects of English.)
4. Never split an infinitive. ("To boldly go"—but this usage is now quite common.)
5. Never end a sentence with a preposition. ("That's what it's for!"—except when you want a specific style or emphasis.)
6. Don't mix mass and unit. ("Fewer oranges" and "less coffee" are considered correct; "less oranges" is traditionally deemed incorrect, but it is now heard so frequently that the old grammatical distinction is losing ground.)
7. "That" introduces essential clauses ("The wooden shed that Pat painted"), while "which" introduces non-essential clauses ("Pat

painted a wooden shed, which he put in the garden"). There is, however, considerable flexibility in using "that" and "which" interchangeably.

8. Use commas to separate phrases and semicolons to separate clauses. (But it is not always so straightforward.)

Most of these rules deal with small-scale details rather than stemming from the fundamental concepts of traditional grammar. In didactic literacy pedagogy, the typical approach to traditional grammar also involves identifying parts of speech and memorizing rules in order to show in one's writing and speaking that these rules are understood. Yet, mastering parts of speech and these rules requires significant effort while yielding a comparatively small contribution to one's overall writing ability.

Additionally, traditional grammar provides only limited insights into the structure of a written text beyond the sentence level. The primary goal of traditional grammar, therefore, is to cultivate a specific type of formalism common in school settings. It can help you become a recognizable "educated" speaker or writer of the language (Carter & McCarthy, 2006). Nevertheless, there has been extensive debate about how much this style of teaching actually aids in the practical process of learning to read and write.

Building upon the limitations of traditional grammar in explaining language beyond the sentence level, scholars have sought more comprehensive frameworks for understanding linguistic structures. One such approach, transformational-generative grammar, emerged as a response to these gaps, providing deeper insights into how meaning is structured and conveyed through language. In the following section, we explore this approach.

Transformational-Generative Grammar

Overview

Transformational-generative grammar was introduced in 1957 by linguist Noam Chomsky in his seminal work *Syntactic Structures*. Chomsky (1957 [2002]) argued that traditional grammar failed to explain how language operates on a deeper structural level. For example, traditional grammar does not distinguish between sentences that share the same grammatical structure but convey vastly different meanings. Consider these examples: "The leaves are falling in the garden" versus "The leaves are gathering in the garden." While both sentences have the same grammatical construction, the first describes leaves in motion, whereas the second suggests that the leaves are accumulating in one place. Similarly, traditional grammar does not account for ambiguous sentences like "Flying planes can be dangerous" or explain how two distinct sentences, such as "Jane Austen wrote the novel" and "The novel was written by Jane Austen," can express the same meaning (Herndon, 1970).

Chomsky posited that underlying every sentence is a *deep structure* that represents its meaning, while the sentence itself constitutes a *surface structure*. The process of converting deep structures into surface structures is what Chomsky defined as *transformational* or *generative*. In essence, an innate cognitive mechanism transforms thoughts into language, generating meaningful expressions. The aim of transformational-generative grammar is to uncover these deep structures and elucidate how they give rise to surface expressions in language.

To achieve this goal, like traditional grammar, Chomsky's (1957 [2002]) system analyzes sentences (S), but his approach goes further into the components of sentence structure. That is, instead of merely identifying subjects, verbs, and objects, Chomsky's analysis includes elements such as noun (N), noun phrase (NP), pronoun (Pron), auxiliary (Aux), determiner (D), and various verb types—transitive (Vt), intransitive (Vi), and linking verbs (Vl), such as "be." These components are organized into hierarchical structures, often visualized through *tree structures* called *phrase markers* (Figure 3.1).

Chomsky's objective was therefore to establish a set of general rules from which it would be possible to generate every grammatically correct sentence in a given language while excluding any grammatically incorrect ones. This method of representing linguistic meanings has its foundations in mathematics and formal logic. His purpose in developing these abstract tools was to illustrate how the structures of human thought are reflected in language. Each

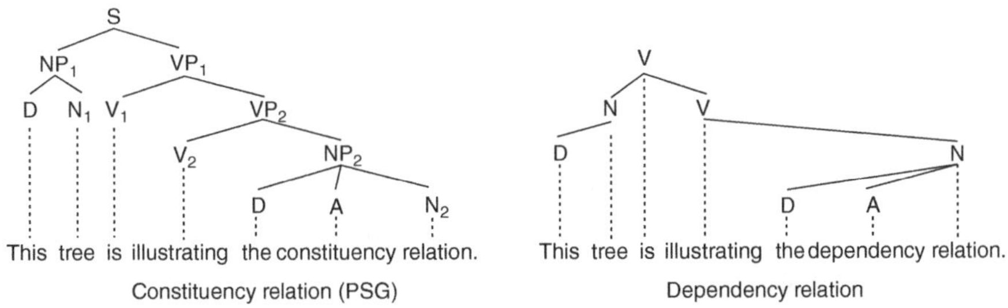

Figure 3.1 Example of tree structures. (SOURCE: Tjo3ya/Wikipedia/CC BY-SA).

unit of meaning, whether a word or phrase (a meaningful grouping of words), could be replaced with any relevant content. For instance, "apple" and "banana" are both nouns; swapping one for the other alters the specific meaning but does not affect the grammatical structure of a sentence. By applying generative rules, language users can form endless variations of grammatically valid sentences, even those never before spoken, such as "The glowing bicycle whispered softly through the silent mountains."

In sum, unlike traditional grammars, which emphasize memorization of words and sentence structures and in which it is valuable to label and learn single words, word order, and sentence structures, Chomsky's (1957 [2002]) model views language as a dynamic system of mental computations that generate grammatical utterances. This perspective shifts focus from static rules to the cognitive processes enabling linguistic creativity. In the following section, we examine the implications of this theory for our understanding of culture and learning.

The Chomskian View of Culture and Learning

Grounded in his theory, Chomsky (1957 [2002]) draws certain conclusions about culture and learning. When considering culture, he posits that all human languages share identical deep structures for generating meaning. In other words, the brains of all humans are wired in the same manner, even though the surface manifestations of these brain functions vary among languages. Put differently, the surface features of any given language (such as its vocabulary, word order, or grammar) may differ, but the underlying types of meaning units (nouns, verbs, etc.) and their logical interconnections remain constant across all human languages. This is why Chomsky and his followers frequently refer to their theory as *universal grammar*. Different languages may express words differently, but the fundamental underlying structures are always the same.

In terms of learning, Chomsky argues that the logical architecture of language is so elaborate that it could not be mastered in the relatively short time it takes a small child to acquire oral language skills. Notably, in a 1959 article (Chomsky, 2024 [1959]), he famously dismantled the learning theories of behaviorist psychology, which claimed that language was a behavior picked up by being immersed in an environment that supports the teaching and learning of that behavior. In contrast, Chomsky contended that there has to be some kind of language organ or innate set of ideas hardwired in the brain. A child then populates this built-in potential with the particular sounds that make up the words of the language they happen to be born into. The deep structures of universal grammar thus manifest themselves in the surface expressions of whichever language a child learns, by virtue of the group into which they were born.

We have included this concise overview of transformational-generative grammar in this chapter because it has become a central framework for understanding the capacity and processes of human meaning-making. However, it has not turned out to be especially useful in educational settings, and it was never designed to be. It may seem curious that a theory claiming to elucidate how language functions and is learned has not been readily applied in education. Yet the reasons for this are illuminating. They illustrate what not to do when examining the designs of meaning—at least, not if the aim is to enhance our theories of learning and our pedagogical methods.

First, the theory is abstract and formal. Its complexity grows the deeper it probes the nuances of language. Such complexity afflicts any system striving for exhaustive or universal rules. As details accumulate, the framework becomes increasingly convoluted. Indeed, not only has the transformational-generative model become more intricate over time, but some of its foundational ideas have proven inadequate and have been changed. For instance, the distinction between deep and surface structures was eventually found difficult to uphold and was replaced with notions like *logical form* and *phonetic form*, then with *internal* and *external* languages, and ultimately, any attempt at drawing this type of distinction was dropped. The concept of *rules* was also criticized for being too rigid and deterministic, and was therefore replaced with the more flexible notion of *principles*. Some scholars have even argued that a system this extensive inevitably collapses under the challenge of dealing with the human complexities of language (Searle, 2002).

Another issue is Chomsky's argument that language is innate, that it is part of an individual's natural abilities. If language is already embedded in a person's skill set, what does this imply for schools? How do we account for the variations in students' language use and proficiency? This question parallels, for instance, the debate around intelligence: If differences in learners' intelligence are innate, what can we do in schools? Such reasoning can lead to potentially problematic conclusions that label learners negatively or track them into ability groups too early in their education.

We do know that identity and social environments profoundly affect skills, knowledge, and ease with formal learning. Because we can shape these factors, we should. Concerning language, we must not make the mistake of thinking that one individual's "language organ" (if one exists at all, which is still up for debate) might appear to produce more powerful meanings than another's. Of course, Chomsky never meant to imply that. Yet this line of biological determinism can have unintended, disadvantageous outcomes.

We also observe that people's oral and literate abilities—and thus their capacity for thought and communication—can vary significantly, and that these differences can be explained by social context, personal history, motivation, and learning opportunities. Arguments invoking innateness cannot be verified and are of limited help in establishing a pedagogical framework. For these reasons, we should focus on what we can do to aid learners in broadening their meaning-making capacities and in thinking in more expansive, effective, and powerful ways.

In discussions of Chomsky's linguistics, individual and cultural differences also come to the forefront. Educators may view learners and their cultures in either of two ways. We might say that, at the end of the day, everyone fundamentally shares the same core of meaning-making but expresses it in superficially different ways—and thus dismiss learners' differences as "surface" matters. Alternatively, we can regard their differences as crucial, at least as significant as any similarities. Certainly, human beings and cultures share many notable similarities, but they also differ in important respects. There is no value in reducing every difference to a deeper sameness.

For instance, pronoun systems (expressing social relationships), tense systems (representing time), and transitivity (representing activities) can vary widely between languages. In Chapter 1, we noted examples of this variety in certain first languages. The same applies to each student's speaking or writing, the unique expression of their "voice" that emerges in the process of designing meaning, and even elements they write that, in Chomsky's system, might be considered "ungrammatical." There is potent meaning in these divergences, which we should not simply ignore as voice or label as error, nor should we reflexively subject them to deeper rules that automatically treat apparent differences as fundamentally the same.

Lastly, traditional and transformational-generative grammars share a few commonalities. Both include "parts of speech," which, as we have seen earlier in the chapter, present similar difficulties of definition and distinction. Knowing the label of a "part of speech" (noun, verb, preposition) does not necessarily reveal all the ways a specific instance of such a word contributes to making meaning. Moreover, both approaches seek universal grammatical rules for linking these parts of speech—covering matters like tense agreement, clauses, and connective devices. In both approaches, it is challenging to go beyond the sentence as the basic unit of meaning, and neither of them focuses much on the meanings formed at the level of whole texts, nor on the contexts that give these texts significance. Furthermore, both are heavily formal, involving technical names and analyzing abstract logics in ways that can quickly grow too unwieldy to be helpful in the practical task of enabling learners to use language and write more effectively.

While traditional and transformational-generative grammars have provided valuable insights into language structure, their focus on formal rules and sentence-level analysis leaves certain aspects of meaning unexplored. In the following section, we turn to systemic-functional grammar (SFG), a framework that shifts the emphasis from abstract grammatical structures to the ways language is used to create meaning in social contexts. This approach considers not only the rules governing language but also the choices speakers and writers make to communicate effectively within different situations.

Systemic-Functional Grammar

Overview

The central figure in *systemic-functional grammar* is M.A.K. Halliday (1975). Like traditional and transformational grammarians, Halliday was interested in how language operates as an integrated system of meaning. However, he also focused on what people do with language—that is, how they create and convey meaning through language in social interactions. Every time we speak or write, we are making choices among various ways to express meaning in order to achieve our communicative goals. Meaning always arises within specific settings or situations, and these meanings are sensible within their contexts because they are exchanged for particular communicative purposes, and not merely because there is an inherent internal logic, as might be assumed from the strict system focus in traditional and transformational grammars. Instead, the link between form and function is principled and oriented toward meaning.

Thus, Halliday describes grammar as "a resource for making meaning ... [and one that] embodies a theory of everyday life" for understanding our lived experiences (Halliday, 2009, p. 142). His *functional grammar* is a theory of language that examines how differences in language structure align with various social purposes or functions. In this approach, the grammatical choices we make serve three main functions or *metafunctions* of language (Halliday & Hasan, 1985, p. 12):

- **Ideational (Experiential) Metafunction**: Language used to express and connect ideas enables us to talk about objects, events, and our experiences in the world.
- **Interpersonal Metafunction**: Language used for interaction helps us establish and maintain social relationships and communicate our feelings and attitudes toward people and experiences.
- **Textual Metafunction**: Language used for organizing meaning allows us to create internal connections within a text and refer to aspects of the situation in which the text is produced, thereby generating coherent texts about the world and our relationships within it.

In any complete text—or even in a single sentence or clause—all three of these functions are at work simultaneously; as Halliday (2009, p. 265) puts it, "every act of meaning embodies all three metafunctional components." Let's now go deeper into the approach...

Meanings in a situation are realized in texts in three ways, as shown in Tables 3.1 and 3.2. These tables provide a simplified overview of Halliday's SFG. Like all grammatical frameworks, it becomes more complex and heavily qualified the more it is asked to account for the totality of language. Importantly, each of the three metafunctions is a perspective on meaning that applies to every clause, capturing all its subtlety and complexity. Even seemingly straightforward meanings in language are intricate because they are always serving all three functions simultaneously. And it is truly remarkable that human consciousness can attend to so many aspects of meaning at once—we instinctively focus on the most relevant aspects at any given moment, while other elements remain in the background or on the periphery.

Table 3.1 Three ways in which meanings in situations can be realized by texts

Meanings in a situation	Expressed through	Realized as meanings in a text
Field (what is going on)	Ideational metafunction	Experiential meanings
Tenor (how participants communicating are connected)	Interpersonal metafunction	Interpersonal meanings
Mode (the role of language)	Textual metafunction	Textual meanings

SOURCE: Adapted from Halliday and Hasan (1985).

Table 3.2 Summary of meaning and function in systemic-functional grammar

Metafunction	Definition and grammatical resources	Examples
Experiential meanings; ideational metafunction (influenced by the field of discourse)	• Concerned with participants (who is involved), processes (what is happening), and circumstances (where, when, how, and why it is happening). Meaning-making resources are structured around **transitivity**, which explains who or what does what to whom or what.	• **Participants:** Different roles include **actor** (e.g., "the cat" in *The cat chased the mouse*), **carrier** (*She is tall*), **sayer** (*He told a story*), **beneficiary** ("her" in *They sent her a letter*), and **goal** ("letter" in *They sent her a letter*). • **Processes:** These link participants through actions, including **material processes** (e.g., "build" in *They built a bridge*), **verbal processes** ("shout" in *She shouted for help*), **relational processes** ("own" in *They own a bakery*), and **mental processes** ("believe" in *I believe in science*). • **Circumstances:** Provide additional details such as **manner** (how? *with great care*), **cause** (why? *because of the rain*), and **accompaniment** (*alongside her friend*). • **Types of connections:** Some are **receptive**, where a recipient undergoes an action (*She was given an award*), while others are **operative**, where an action does not directly affect another (*He dreamed of traveling*).

(Continued)

Table 3.2 (Continued)

Metafunction	Definition and grammatical resources	Examples
Interpersonal Meanings (influenced by the tenor of discourse)	• Meaning-making resources are shaped by **mood** and **modality**, which reflect speaker attitudes and social roles.	• **Mood choices:** Sentences can be **declarative** (e.g., *They are studying*), **interrogative** (*Did you see the announcement?*), or **imperative** (*Turn off the lights!*). • **Modality:** Expresses levels of certainty or obligation, ranging from **low** (e.g., *might, could, possibly*), **median** (e.g., *should, probably, will*), to **high** (*must, certainly, has to*).

Textual Meanings (influenced by the mode of discourse)	• Meaning-making resources are framed by **theme** and **cohesion**, which help structure information flow in a text.	• **Theme and rheme:** The **theme** introduces the topic of a clause (e.g., "*This report*" in *This report outlines the findings*), while the **rheme** follows and contains new information (*outlines the findings*).
		• **Cohesion:** Uses **connective devices** to maintain coherence and link ideas, including the following:
		  • **Reference:** (e.g., "he" referring to *the manager* mentioned earlier in the text).
		  • **Conjunctions:** (e.g., *however, therefore, afterwards*), which establish logical relationships between ideas.

SOURCE: Adapted from Halliday (2002).

Comparing Halliday's Grammar with Other Approaches

While traditional and transformational grammars concentrate almost exclusively on the sentence or clause, SFG examines multiple layers (or strata) of language—from its expressive forms in phonology and graphology, through lexico-grammar, to the structures of whole texts and their social purposes. For example, consider a newspaper report on a new medical discovery, a narrative about an illness and its cure, or a doctor–patient conversation. Each of these is viewed as a different genre or type of whole text. Here, *genre* refers not to style (as in literary studies), but to a text type structured to fulfill an overall meaning purpose. In other words, a genre carries a social purpose; it is "staged" in that it typically has a characteristic beginning, middle, and end, and it is composed of clauses that adopt specific experiential, interpersonal, and textual forms (Martin, 1992).

For instance, consider the scenario of a local restaurant linked to a sudden food poisoning outbreak:

- **In the written genre of a *news report*, the structure might be as follows**: An announcement of the outbreak → background on the restaurant's recent safety record and inspection history → detailed accounts from affected patrons and health officials, with an emphasis on the unfolding events and contributing factors.
- **A *narrative story* on the same incident, on the other hand, might follow a structure such as**: Orientation, where a diner enjoys a meal at the restaurant → complication, as the diner begins to experience alarming symptoms → resolution, culminating in recovery and personal reflection, focusing on internal reactions and the progression of time.
- **And an oral genre like a *doctor–patient conversation* about the incident might progress in this sequence**: Greeting and invitation for the patient to describe their symptoms → the patient's detailed account of gastrointestinal distress → diagnosis of food poisoning → prescription for treatment and care instructions → departing greetings.

In every case, a purposeful social exchange of meanings results in a distinct structure and specific word choices—a point illustrated by the varying approaches to reporting on the restaurant's food poisoning outbreak. Written text involves a process of making deliberate choices that best convey meaning (see pages 34–36 in Chapter 2). For example, a news report on the outbreak uses a structured progression—from the initial announcement, through contextual background, to detailed accounts to effectively inform the public, much like a written procedure (such as a recipe) clearly outlines steps to achieve a result. In contrast, a narrative retelling of the incident, with its orientation, complication, and resolution, emphasizes personal experience and internal reactions; however, this format might be less effective when precise information is required. Similarly, an oral exchange (an example of speech; see pages 52–54 in Chapter 2)—like a doctor–patient conversation that follows a systematic sequence from symptom description to diagnosis and treatment—demonstrates how the genre (and meaning form) shapes communication strategies. In each instance, the overall genre unfolding in the communicative act is key to effective meaning-making, a concept that will be further explored in Chapter 4 in relation to literacy pedagogy.

As shown in the previous sections, like other grammatical frameworks, the systemic-functional approach offers far more detail than is usually required for everyday reading, writing, and literacy development. Language is so complex that it is impossible for users to consciously disentangle every element. Linguists are the professionals who undertake this detailed work as part of their scholarship, with applications ranging from machine translation and semantically informed search engines on the web to generative artificial intelligence (GenAI) models capable of synthesizing text and conduct linguistic analysis of, for example, students' written work, as well as computer vision systems that might extract and interpret text from images (Hristova et al., 2023; Tzirides et al., 2024; Voss, 2024).

Nonetheless, many aspects of language that captivate linguists are not necessarily interesting and/or useful for everyday users, who often rely on an intuitive grasp of meaning without needing technical explanations. In fact, the practical benefits of such detailed grammatical knowledge for everyday communication have been questioned. In the past, some critics have argued that teaching grammar in schools is irrelevant and disconnected from students' real-life language use—especially among advocates of what is known as authentic literacy pedagogy (more on this in Chapter 4).

Against this backdrop, it is important for teachers to understand these varied emphases and approaches, particularly in a constantly shifting landscape of educational practices and policies that rest on different assumptions about language and learning. To summarize our discussions so far, in Table 3.3, we compare Halliday's approach to traditional grammar and Chomsky's model.

Table 3.3 Different approaches to grammar

Aspect	Traditional grammar	Generative-transformational grammar	Systemic-functional grammar
View of language	Language is a set of rules.	Language is rule-governed creativity.	Language is a social process.
View of grammar	Focuses on rules of formation and usage.	Seen as an innate device in the human mind.	Considered a resource for making meaning in social contexts.
Derivation	Rooted in Ancient Greek and Latin.	Theorizing about universal principles of language.	Analysis of what people do through language.
Related disciplines	Philosophy	Philosophy; cognitive psychology	Sociology; anthropology
Form vs. function	Mainly concerned with form.	Emphasis on syntactic form, with some interest in semantics.	Maintains a principled relationship between form and function.
Meaning—form emphasis	Text (writing).	Not specifically concerned with meaning forms.	Incorporates both text and speech.
Unit of analysis	Parts of speech and their combinations.	Ranges from phonemes to complex syntactic forms.	Encompasses text, clause, group, word, and phoneme.
Key figures	Dionysius Thrax and Bishop Lowth	Chomsky	Halliday
Classroom implications	Overt teaching of rules, often as ends in themselves.	Teachers' knowledge of acquisition sequences guides input selection.	Discussion of relevant grammar points in context to enhance language awareness and proper use.

The three approaches so far discussed focused on the intricacies of linguistic systems. However, as we saw in Chapters 1 and 2, language is only one component of a broader suite of communication systems within a culture, which also involves other meaning forms, such as image, space, body, object, and sound. Considering the multimodal nature of meaning-making, in the following section, we introduce our proposal for a grammar where multimodality is considered. We have called our model *transpositional grammar*.

Transpositional Grammar

Overview

Transpositional grammar emerges from a longstanding tradition of meaning studies, particularly the SFG approach we presented in the previous section. Gunther Kress and Theo van Leeuwen later expanded Halliday's grammar to encompass multimodal communication, integrating text, image, gesture, and sound (Kress & Van Leeuwen, 2021).

Building on these foundations, in previous works (e.g., Cope & Kalantzis, 2020; Kalantzis & Cope, 2020), we proposed *transpositional grammar* as a comprehensive framework for understanding multimodal meaning-making in the digital age. We chose the term *transposition* to reflect the movement of meaning across different meaning forms (see pages 32–54 in Chapter 2] and to analyze how these forms interact. In other words, an idea can be expressed through various modalities, such as picturing it, articulating it in words, using gestures, engaging with an object and its symbolic significance, experiencing a feeling, or writing about it. Although these different forms may convey similar meanings, they can never be entirely identical. As a result, meaning often takes on multiple forms, layering one over another, expressing something in one way, then another. As discussed in Chapters 1 and 2, communication frequently involves multiple meaning forms simultaneously to elaborate, deepen, or extend meaning, a phenomenon that has become particularly relevant in the digital age.

Given this dynamic nature of meaning making, transposition underscores movement, emphasizing that meaning is never static but constantly shifting, expanding, and deepening itself. For example, consider a social media post: While the image and accompanying text convey the same message, they do so differently, allowing for redundancy and reinforcement. Similarly, in scientific communication, meaning can be expressed through text, photography, video demonstrations with gestures, audio recordings or podcasts, or numerical representation in tables or infographics. In the digital era, these diverse tools for constructing scientific meaning are readily accessible, making multimodal literacy crucial. Therefore, mastering science today requires the ability to "read" and "write" across multiple meaning forms, ensuring that learners can engage with and produce knowledge effectively.

At the core of this conceptualization of meaning making and transpositional grammar lies the concept of *design*, which in our framework carries a dual significance: (1) *Design as a noun*, conveying the inherent patterning or structure that underpins meaning, and (2) *Design as a verb*, reflecting the active, intentional process of creating meaning. We live and learn in a world shaped by existing designs, using them as resources to create our own meanings. The way we appropriate and apply these existing, *found designs* is inherently a social practice, influenced by historical conditions.

Because the designs and contexts in which we engage in meaning-making are so diverse, no two design processes or artifacts are ever identical. While they may follow recognizable social and historical patterns—such as genres—they are never exact replicas. The subtle differences between them are just as significant as the overarching continuities in form. Consequently, we do not simply reproduce pre-existing forms of meaning. Instead, the variations in our *design processes* and the artifacts they create reflect unique aspects of experience, voice, identity, and personal interest. Meaning is thus never purely an act of replication; it is also a means of transforming the world, as *newly designed meanings* reenter the world as found designs (Figure 3.2).

The dynamics of participation in meaning introduce an additional dimension of agency, incorporating difference and

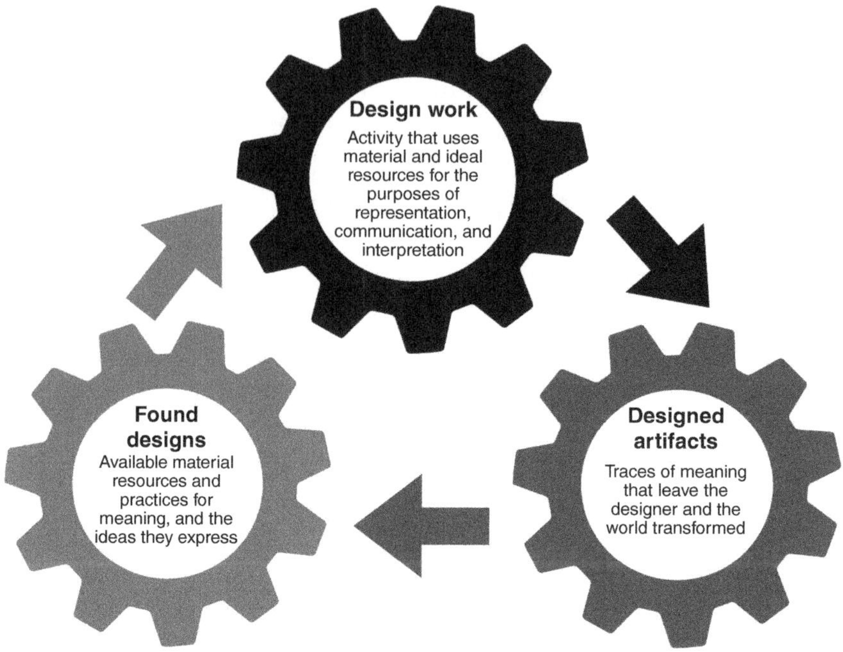

Figure 3.2 Meaning-making as design.

transformation into the meaning-making process. *Representation* serves as meaning for oneself, encompassing not only the "inner speech" described by Vygotsky (1986) but also mental imagery and the internal rehearsal of actions or wayfinding strategies (Cope and Kalantzis, 2020; Kalantzis & Cope, 2020). While representations may facilitate communication, they often function primarily as tools for personal sense-making. In other words, representation differs significantly from communication, as it allows for assumed contexts rather than explicitly stated ones, relying on only the most essential features to come to mind. *Communication*, in contrast, is never a direct translation of representation; it demands greater explicitness, requiring the reframing of contexts—for instance, incorporating subjects into spoken sentences or providing contextual cues through image framing—before establishing the focus of new meaning, such as predicates in sentences or focal points in images. Furthermore, when another person encounters a meaning,

Figure 3.3 Participation in meaning.

a subsequent transformation takes place: *interpretation*, shaped by their own experiences and interests (Figure 3.3).

The ongoing process of meaning-making as dynamic, participatory design unfolds across two simultaneous primary dimensions:

1. **Between and across different forms:** Meaning shifts as it moves from one medium to another—whether through text, image, space, object, body, sound, or speech.
2. **Between and across different functions:** Meaning acquires new nuances and implications as it transitions among its five core functions—*reference*, *agency*, *structure*, *context*, and *interest*.

In the following two sections, we explore these two dimensions.

Transposition 1: Between and Across Meaning Forms

Transposition of forms refers to the process of making sense of lived experience by employing historically developed and socially acquired forms of meaning. It involves the mental and physical work of navigating across and between the various meaning forms we discussed in Chapter 2, i.e., text, image, space, object, body, sound, and speech.

Transpositional grammar takes inspiration from Bogdanov's (1923/2016) concept of substitution but introduces a crucial shift. Like Bogdanov, we view the substitution of meaning as a process that entails transitions in meaning activity between the social mind and the material world (Cope & Kalantzis, 2020). However, rather than using the term *substitution*, we prefer *transposition* to emphasize that this relationship is not about mere replacement. Instead, it is a multimodal overlay, wherein a sense-maker constructs composite meaning by employing one form and then another—either sequentially or simultaneously.

At its core, *transposition* is a meaning-act performed by an individual as a distinct cognitive and bodily entity. Meaning is created through movement between embodied mind and sensory experience. However, the systems of transposition we engage with are not solely personal; they are also socially acquired products of human history. In our framework, text, image, space, object, body, sound, and speech constitute the fundamental forms of meaning that facilitate our navigation between embodied mind and sensuous experience. These forms function as practical actions, shaped by the materiality of their respective mediums (see Chapter 2). Each form and its multimodal expression extend immediate experience into social meaning. These extensions are both cognitive and material, serving as tools of thought and tangible artifacts that enable us to make sense of our experiences.

For instance, text connects with prior encounters with digital documents and historical manuscripts as visible objects and mediums. Similarly, speech links to previous experiences of recorded podcasts and whispered secrets in dimly lit rooms as audible objects and mediums. These are artifacts of socially embedded meaning and social cognition, leaving behind material traces of mental and physical labor—such as the cognitive process of structuring ideas in writing and the physical act of inscribing symbols onto a scroll or composing a social media post.

On the level of meaning forms (i.e., between and across forms), transposition entails that one form can transpose for another—being swapped, juxtaposed, or layered—because they serve a shared function. Through both mental and physical labor, thoughts become materialized in text, image, space, object, body, sound, and speech. This process, whether simultaneous or sequential, shapes our thinking. Meaning forms are conceived in our minds, take shape as tangible representations, and, in turn, influence our cognition through the work we invest in their creation. Cowan and Kress (2019) describe this as *transcription* or *transduction*—the rematerialization or reconstitution of meaning.

Consider this example, in which the same meaning is expressed across multiple forms:

- **Text**: The name "Ava" encoded in binary on a computer screen
- **Image and space**: An AI-generated representation of Ava standing at the entrance of a museum in London (Figure 3.4).
- **Object**: A sculpture of Ava.
- **Body**: Ava's synchronized dance movements in an immersive performance.

Figure 3.4 Example of meaning-making relying on image and space. (SOURCE: Generated with AI using DALL·E 3.0.—OpenAI).

- **Sound**: The echo of Ava's voice in an underground cavern.
- **Speech**: Ava delivering a passionate presentation on climate change in one of her university classes.

Each of these meaning forms represents a bridge between cognition and the material mediums through which thinking occurs, functioning as cognitive prostheses. While socially constructed, these forms are also tangible, materially embedded in the world, and ultimately linked to nature through human labor.

Our capacity to engage with meaning is therefore shaped by our interactions with these material mediums. The acquisition of social and personal meaning-making abilities is a result of lifelong engagement with these forms. As we participate in meaning-action throughout our lives, we inherit a socio-historical and personal legacy that influences each new moment of meaning-making. Each time we engage with these forms, we employ them for representation, communication, or interpretation.

Transposition 2: Between and Across Meaning Functions

The concept of *function* in meaning-making has its origins in the systemic-functional linguistic approach pioneered by M.A.K. Halliday, Ruqaiya Hasan, and their colleagues, which we discussed in Section "Systemic-Functional Grammar" of this chapter. Inspired by these scholars' foundational theories, we sought to extend their applicability beyond linguistic analysis into broader, multimodal realms of meaning-making.

As we saw in Section "Systemic-Functional Grammar", Halliday and Hasan (1985) proposed three primary metafunctions for analyzing text and speech: *ideational*, *interpersonal*, and *textual*. Ideational meanings involve the thematic and content-related aspects of meaning. Interpersonal meanings define the relationships between participants in a communicative act, while textual meanings pertain to the organization and coherence of a text. While these categories offer a robust framework for linguistic analysis, our work expands on them by renaming and revising their contents and adding two additional functions: *context* and *interest*.

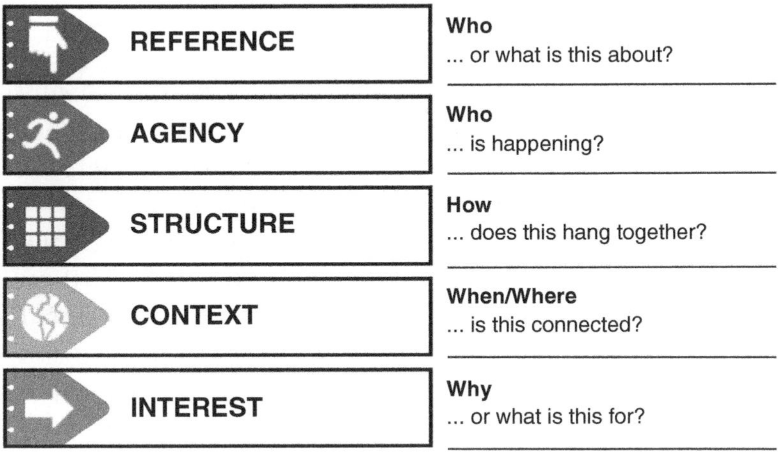

Figure 3.5 Functions of meaning.

Our approach, therefore, identifies five meaning functions—-*reference*, *agency*, *structure*, *context*, and *interest* (Figure 3.5). Reference aligns closely with SFG‘s ideational function but with distinctions regarding time, place, cause, and effect, which we place under *context*. *Agency*, corresponding to SFG's interpersonal metafunction, extends beyond human interactions to include impersonal and broader social dynamics. *Structure*, similar to textual meaning, acknowledges meaning systems beyond traditional text and speech. *Context,* which aligns with traditional pragmatics, highlights the framing conditions that influence meaning. Finally, *interest* addresses the motivations, purposes, and social dynamics underlying meaning, drawing from critical discourse analysis and social theory.

In the next five sections of the chapter, we describe each function in detail. We then discuss their transpositions with meaning forms.

Reference

Reference pertains to the identification of entities and their properties, whether as particular instances or general concepts. It operates at both specific and general levels, distinguishing between individual entities and collective categories. This conceptual shift between singularity and plurality—between unique instances and overarching classifications—represents a fundamental cognitive and practical process. Reference also establishes attributes, whether through linguistic elements like adjectives, visual characteristics in images, or tactile properties in physical representation.

In a multimodal grammar, reference answers the question: *Who or what is this about?* Traditionally, it has been expressed through nouns and adjectives. However, a broader framework includes instances (specific, identifiable entities), concepts (categories or general types), and properties that describe quality or quantity.

For example, in language, nouns represent entities such as mountains, rivers, or planets, while adjectives describe their attributes. In images, shape, perspective, and shading delineate individual instances, while spatial arrangements, textures, and gestures indicate general categories or properties.

Agency

Agency defines meaning through patterns of human and natural activity, shaping interpretations of causation and interaction. It answers the question: *Who or what is happening?* Agency encompasses both structured roles and interpretative potentials, influencing how meaning is conveyed and understood. Conditionality plays a key role, as meaning varies depending on assertion, requirement, or possibility. Beyond interpersonal communication, agency extends to systemic and cultural structures that shape meaning-making processes.

Agency manifests through linguistic elements such as tone, emphasis, and syntactic structures, as well as spatial and visual factors that determine interaction and constraint. It directs events through interpersonal structures, including declarative and imperative forms in language, placement and directional cues in images, and gestures that signal or emphasize intent.

In various contexts, meaning-making establishes roles such as chef/diner, architect/client, musician/audience, and teacher/student. Agency determines how these roles interact, influencing both communication and action. For example, in images, vectors and spatial arrangements suggest movement or direction, while in embodied action, gestures can be directive or open-ended, shaping interpretation and response.

Structure

Structure establishes networks of interconnection that provide coherence across the different meaning forms we introduced in Chapter 2, i.e., text, image, space, object, body, sound, and speech. It answers the question: *What makes this meaning hang together?* Structure, as a meaning function, therefore involves classification schemes and logic systems that organize both digital and analog meaning environments. These systems are defined by their ontological connections, internal relationships, design principles, and patterns of organization.

Meaning structures are both reflections of reality (*meanings-in-the-world*) and human-constructed frameworks (*meanings-for-the-world*). They function through multimodal cohesion mechanisms such as linguistic conjunctions and discourse markers, visual symmetry and contrast, spatial orientation, rhythmic sound patterns, and logical sequencing in functional objects. The concepts of *multimodality*—where meanings are layered across different meaning forms—and *synesthesia*—where one form of meaning transposes into another—highlight the dynamic nature of structure.

In practical terms, structure operates at multiple scales. In written text, it ranges from clauses to entire novels; in images, from individual frames to full galleries; and in bodily communication, from micro gestures to extended performances. Across all forms, structure provides coherence, ensuring that meaning is both comprehensible and adaptable to different contexts.

Context

Context situates meaning within its broader environment, determining its relevance through resemblance, directedness, and abstraction. It answers the question: *Where or when is this?* Meanings are shaped by the time and place in which they occur, as they are inseparable from their surroundings and deeply influenced by their temporal and spatial positioning. The interplay of context with structure, reference, and agency determines how meanings emerge and evolve within communicative acts.

Framing is a critical aspect of context, as meanings are positioned in relation to others through motifs, styles, genres, and historical associations. Contextual markers in meaning-making include linguistic prepositions, demonstratives, visual associations, and spatial configurations.

The evolution of digital media has intensified the role of context, where time is precisely measured in Coordinated Universal Time (UTC) and location is pinpointed with Global Positioning System (GPS) coordinates. These factors shape meaning in ways that were previously less explicitly defined, reinforcing the deep connection between meaning and its environment.

Interest

Interest addresses the motivations behind meaning-making, including emotional, social, and cognitive impulses. It answers the question: *Why?—What is the meaning? What are its purposes? Whose interests does it serve?* This raises broader concerns of ideology and change, as meaning is often shaped by competing interests, whether through persuasion, advocacy, or strategic omission.

An analysis of interest moves beyond congruent and harmonious meanings to examine ideological differences, power structures, and instances of (mis)representation. Critical analysis tools help uncover the unstated dimensions of interest, revealing deeper social, political, and cultural motivations that drive meaning-making.

In practical contexts, interest plays a role in persuasion within advertisements, the emotional resonance of art, and the influence of ideology in journalism. These examples illustrate how meaning is actively shaped by underlying motivations, reinforcing the dynamic nature of meaning-making.

Transpositions of Functions (and Forms)

Having explored the key functions of meaning—*reference*, *agency*, *structure*, *context*, and *interest*—it becomes evident that these are not static categories but dynamic processes. Meaning is constantly in motion, shifting across different forms and reconfiguring itself within and between these functions. This movement is at the heart of transpositional grammar, which recognizes how meaning is expressed fluidly across *text*, *image*, *space*, *object*, *body*, *sound*, and *speech*.

We bring these axes of form and function together into a map of multimodal meaning (Figure 3.6). Transposition happens along both axes. On one axis, we continuously move between and combine different forms of meaning—whether linguistic, visual, spatial, gestural, or auditory. On the functional axis, meaning is understood by shifting attention between different aspects of what it does: the things to which it refers (*reference*); the patterns of action it represents (*agency*); its organization as a meaning (*structure*); its surroundings that add meaning (*context*); and its purposes (*interest*) (Cope & Kalantzis, 2020; Kalantzis & Cope, 2020). This framework provides the foundation for a metalanguage that can enable learners to analyze found designs across all forms of meaning while also reflecting on their own design activities (more on this in Chapter 4).

One significant aspect of this movement is the continuous transformation within each function. Take *reference*, for example. In traditional textual literacy, reference was categorized through grammatical labels such as "noun." However, in a broader transpositional framework, this is more accurately described as "entity," allowing for identification across different meaning forms. In images, we encounter entity-like elements in depicted objects, while spatial arrangements, textures, and perspectives contribute to their interpretation. Yet, even this distinction is not fixed. Pictured objects are rarely static—they have arrived at their positions and can shift again. Likewise, linguistic reference is fluid: A common noun such as "storm" may become a specific event like "Storm Éowyn," which took place in the United Kingdom in January 2025; an abstract term such as "justice" can take on different meanings

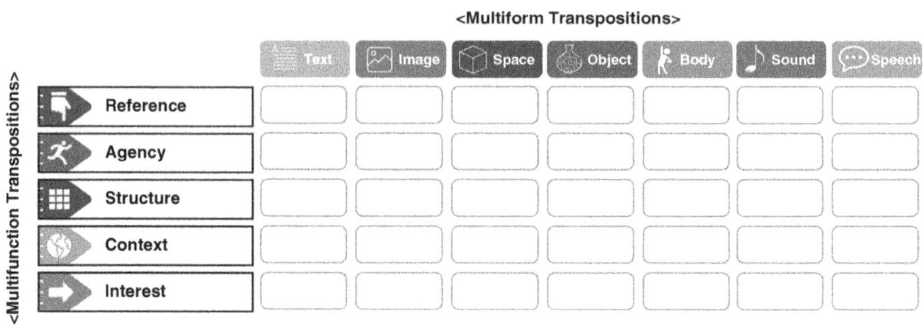

Figure 3.6 Form meets function in the matrix of transpositional grammar.

depending on context. Similarly, categories of reference can change as objects are recontextualized—an "artifact" in a museum may once have been an ordinary "tool" in daily life.

Bringing together our analyses of *form* and *function*, we see that every meaning function can be expressed through any form or combination of forms. This perspective transcends the traditional, text-bound framework of literacy, allowing for a more comprehensive mapping of meaning across different modes. However, while a matrix of transpositional grammar such as the one shown in Figure 3.6 may suggest neat categorization, meaning itself is far more fluid. It is always overlapping, evolving, and shifting, which is precisely why we describe this as a *transpositional* approach to grammar.

The Differences Between Human Meaning and Generative AI

The examination and conceptualization of literacy in the digital age raises critical questions about the nature of meaning-making, particularly in the contrast between human meaning-making and AI-generated meaning. This distinction becomes evident when examined through the lens of the meaning forms and functions we introduced in the previous section. In the following two sections, we describe the differences between humans and GenAI as meaning makers.

Human Meaning: Theoretical, Embodied, and Contextualized

Human meaning-making is not merely an arrangement of linguistic signs but rather an integrated, multimodal process in which the meaning forms we introduced in Chapter 2—i.e., text, image, space, object, body, sound, and speech—are used to construct and convey meaning across multiple social contexts. Embedded in the transpositions between and across meaning forms are the five meaning functions we described in the previous sections—i.e., reference, agency, structure, context, and interest—which ensure that meaning is dynamic, interactive, and socially situated. When examined through this lens, we can synthesize human meaning as follows:

1. **Reference and conceptual structuring**:
   - Humans do not rely solely on empirical word relations; instead, they actively classify, categorize, and create semantic hierarchies. Meaning is not latent but explicitly structured through grammar, social conventions, and cognitive schemas.
   - The functional classification of morphemes plays a key role in organizing reference, enabling precise distinctions between objects, actions, and abstract concepts.
2. **Agency and interaction**:
   - Human meaning-making extends beyond individual cognition—it is socially co-constructed through interpersonal interactions.
   - Through metalinguistic semantic primitives, such as parts of speech, phrase structures, and sentence constructions, humans actively shape discourse in intentional ways.
   - Meaning is not just received or predicted (as in AI) but actively produced by agents with social, cultural, and historical perspectives.
3. **Structure and coherence**:
   - Humans construct meaning through structured relationships between ideas, ensuring coherence both within and beyond the sentence level.

- Human meaning-making is grammatically, semantically, and pragmatically ordered to establish logical, thematic, and narrative *connections*.

4. **Context and material embodiment**:
   - Meaning is deeply tied to embodied experience—it is felt, lived, and situated in the material world.
   - Unlike AI, which lacks a physical presence, humans use gestures, spatial positioning, and sensory experience (e.g., images, sounds, tactile objects) as key contributors to meaning.
   - The context in which meaning is expressed influences interpretation—the same word, phrase, or non-linguistic meaning form can shift in meaning depending on time, place, and cultural context.
5. **Interest and intentionality**:
   - Meaning is never neutral: It is shaped by personal, social, and ideological interests.
   - Even in written texts which might be considered "objective" (e.g., a research paper), meaning reflects the author's purpose, emotions, and communicative goals. Human meaning is always pragmatically directed toward particular communicative and social functions.

This perspective underscores how human meaning operates beyond the word and sentence level, extending into multimodal, contextualized, and socially meaningful engagements.

GenAI Meaning: Empirical and Statistical

In contrast to human meaning, GenAI operates purely on statistical and empirical principles, lacking the deep structures of cognition, embodiment, and individual intentionality that characterize human meaning-making. For instance, AI does not classify or construct meaning with intention; instead, it identifies statistical relationships between words based on large text corpora and their fine-tuning by humans. Additionally, it functions within a "flat" world of one-to-one token relationships, where differentiation occurs only through weighted probabilities across vectors. Furthermore, while AI can reproduce grammatical structures, it lacks an underlying conceptual framework for meaning—it does not "understand" language but rather predicts word sequences based on training data. This fundamental difference limits AI's ability to generate new knowledge or adapt meaning to context in the same way humans do. GenAI's reliance on pre-existing texts and fine-tuning regimes means its limits are the limits of the corpus it was trained on and the ways in which responses to prompts are framed by the human designers of these systems.

Implications for Meaning and Literacy

The differences between human meaning and AI-generated meaning are particularly significant in the context of literacy education. As discussed in this chapter, meaning is not just a static arrangement of words but a socially and multimodally constructed process—*a process of design*. While AI can synthesize textual patterns, it cannot participate in the full range of human meaning-making, which integrates multimodal experience, contextual awareness, and intentional discourse.

As we advance into an era where GenAI-generated text will become increasingly prevalent, educators and learners must develop critical literacy skills to recognize the differences between statistical generation and intentional human meaning-making. In Chapters 4 and 5, we will explore these implications in greater detail, considering how literacy pedagogy can critically engage with AI while preserving human agency, multimodal fluency, and transformative meaning-making.

Conclusion

In this chapter, we have examined the evolving nature of grammar and meaning-making, moving from traditional grammar to transformational-generative grammar, SFG, and, finally, transpositional grammar. Each of these frameworks contributes to our understanding of how meaning is structured, communicated, and interpreted. While traditional and generative grammars focus on rule-based structures and cognitive mechanisms, SFG shifts the emphasis to the social contexts in which meaning is created. Building on these insights, transpositional grammar broadens the scope of literacy by integrating multimodal meaning-making across text, image, space, object, body, sound, and speech.

A key insight emerging from this discussion is the recognition that meaning is not static but dynamic—constantly evolving through representation, communication, and interpretation. This dynamism is particularly relevant in the digital age, where meaning moves fluidly across multiple modalities and is shaped by social, cultural, and technological factors. The distinction between human meaning-making and GenAI further underscores this point: While human meaning is deeply embodied, contextually situated, and driven by intentionality and social interaction, AI-generated texts operate through probabilistic patterns. Behind this, of course, is an army of humans curating the corpora, developing the algorithms, and fine-tuning the responses to user prompts.

As we move forward, the implications of these theoretical perspectives for literacy education become increasingly significant. In an era of rapidly evolving digital tools, educators must cultivate both digital and critical literacy skills that enable learners to engage with both human and AI-generated meaning. The ability to discern, critique, and adapt meaning across different forms and functions will be essential for navigating contemporary communication landscapes.

In the following chapter, we will explore how these theoretical insights translate into literacy pedagogy. We will examine different instructional approaches and consider how educators can create learning environments that empower students as critical thinkers, creative meaning-makers, and active participants in a complex, multimodal world.

Consolidate, Explore, Reflect, Do

We end this chapter with activities that will allow you to apply the concepts discussed in novel ways. Our goal is that these tasks will facilitate further exploration and reflection and will inspire your present and/or future teaching practice.

Task 1: Deconstructing Grammar Through Meaning-Making

To complete this task, you will work in groups of 3–4 to analyze and manipulate grammar structures to explore how they shape meaning.

Step 1. With your group mates, choose a short passage from a book, article, or digital text. Identify the parts of speech, sentence structures, and grammatical rules present.

Step 2. Rewrite the passage in multiple ways by modifying sentence structures, verb tenses, and word order. For example,

- Try converting active sentences to passive voice.
- Change the tense of key verbs.
- Experiment with different word orders.

Step 3. Compare your revised versions. How do these changes affect meaning and readability? How does traditional grammar shape understanding?

Step 4. Compare your findings with another groups'. How different/similar are your outcomes and reflections on traditional grammar? Together, consider the following:

- Do you believe there is still a place for traditional grammar in education? Why?/Why not? In what context(s) might it be appropriate?
- Create a short, multimodal reflection to present your views to the rest of the class.

Task 2: Exploring Transformational Grammar and Its Impact on Second Language Teaching and Learning

This activity will help you explore the basic principles of transformational-generative grammar in more depth, as well as its influence on second language (L2) teaching and learning.

Step 1. Conduct more in-depth research on Chomsky's transformational grammar. Use your course readings and additional resources.
Step 2. In small groups of 3–4 students, analyze how transformational grammar has influenced L2 teaching and learning. Focus on:

- How it has shaped modern L2 acquisition theories (e.g., focus on the work of scholars such as Lydia White, Harald Clahsen, Kevin R. Gregg, and Silvina Montrul).
- Its role (if any) in L2 pedagogy.
- Whether it is still relevant in L2 acquisition research.

Step 3. Based on your collaborative work, discuss the implications of transformational grammar for L2 learning and teaching. Consider whether this theory can help learners understand and use language more effectively, and how it compares to traditional and functional grammar approaches.
Step 4. Summarize the results of your work in a multimodal presentation highlighting the strengths and weaknesses of this theory in connection with L2 learning and teaching. Support your work with evidence from the literature you examined.

Task 3: Investigating SFG in Context

This task will help you understand how SFG explains language use in different contexts and how it contributes to meaning-making. By analyzing real-world texts, you will explore how language choices shape communication and reflect social interactions. You will work in pairs.

Step 1. Review the information on SFG we presented in this chapter, including its three metafunctions (i.e., ideational, interpersonal, and textual).
Step 2. With a classmate, choose a real-world text (e.g., a news article, a political speech, or a social media post) and analyze it using the three metafunctions:

- **Ideational**: What information is being communicated? What processes and participants are present?
- **Interpersonal**: How does the language used establish relationships between participants?

- **Textual**: How is the text structured for coherence and emphasis? How is the structure connected to the medium of which the example is part?

Step 3. Compare your analysis with that of another pair. Focus on how SFG helps explain meaning in different contexts, and what advantages it offers over both traditional grammar and Chomsky's model for understanding language in use.
Step 4. Combine both pairs' views and present them to the rest of the class. Explain how SFG can contribute to students' critical understanding of real-world communication and their growth as effective communicators.

Task 4: Analyzing Different Meaning Forms

This activity allows you to explore how different meaning forms (text, image, space, etc.) affect communication.

Step 1. Choose a multimodal artifact (e.g., an advertisement, a meme, an infographic, an Instagram or TikTok post, or a webpage).
Step 2. Identify the meaning forms present in the artifact. For example, focus on:
Text: Language variety, typography.
Image: Photographs, illustrations, colors.
Space: Layout, composition.
Step 3. Determine how each meaning form contributes to the message. Would the artifact mean the same thing without one of the forms?
Step 4. Create a multimodal message of your own using at least two meaning forms. Share it with another classmate, explaining why you chose specific meaning forms to convey meaning. Compare ways in which you communicated your messages as well as your preferred meaning forms. How are your choices connected to your identities, lifeworlds, and academic backgrounds/goals?

Task 5: The Five Functions of Meaning in Everyday Communication

In this task, you will be analyzing how the five functions of meaning shape communication. You will work in groups of 3–4.

Step 1. With your group mates, choose a news headline or a public statement.
Step 2. Working collaboratively, rewrite the chosen text in at least three different ways, changing one of the following functions each time:

- Reference (New Policy Affects University Students → University Students Affected by Policy Change);
- Agency (Government Introduces New Law → New Law Restricts Freedom);
- Structure (rearrange sentences/the presentation of information to emphasize different elements)
- Context (change details to frame the event differently);
- Interest (adjust wording to influence the audience's emotional reaction).

Step 3. Analyze and discuss the effects of your changes. How might each of the changes affect the intended audience's interpretation? Would any of the changes modify the intended audience per se (i.e., would different people be drawn to the text as a result of some of your changes)?
Step 4. Working with another group, analyze posts from different social media (e.g., Instagram, Facebook, TikTok, X) dealing with the same issue or event. Identify how each of them uses the five functions of meaning. How does each post differ from the others? How is this connected with the intended audience?
Step 5. Present the results of your work to the rest of the class. What have you learned from working on the two activities in this task? To what extent has this worked changed your understanding of *interest*? What else have you learned about meaning functions and their role and importance in meaning making?

Task 6: Multimodal Transposition Challenge

This task allows you to explore how meaning is expressed through different meaning forms.

Step 1. With a classmate, choose a short, written text (e.g., a poem, a news article, or a book passage).
Step 2. Working together, transform the text into a different artifact, involving other meaning forms, such as:
- a comic strip or infographic
- a spoken podcast segment
- a dance performance

Step 3. Compare the original artifact and the one you and your classmate have created. Discuss:
- What meanings were lost, gained, or changed?
- How would transpositional grammar explain these shifts (e.g., think of the five meaning functions and the affordances and limitations of different meaning forms)?

Step 4. Share your work and insights with another pair. How similar or different are your artifacts? Where do similarities/differences originate? Consider representation, communication, and interpretation. What do the different ways in which you have used meaning forms and convey meaning say about these three conceptualizations?

Task 7: Ethics and Power in Meaning-Making

In this activity, you will work with 3–4 classmates. Your group will analyze bias and power in communication.

Step 1. Choose a controversial multimodal text (e.g., a news article, a recorded political speech, or a social media post).
Step 2. Focusing on the five meaning functions, analyze the chosen artifact to answer these questions:
- Who created the text?
- What interests does it serve?
- What role do the chosen meaning forms play in the expression of the message?

Step 3. Change the artifact to convey a different ideological perspective. What meaning forms do you need to change? How?
Step 4. Discuss how different meaning forms influence public perception. Which would you say are the most effective meaning forms?
Step 5. Go back to the personal definition of literacy you developed in Chapter 1 and modified in Chapter 2. What changes would you make to it based on the contents of this chapter and your experience in this activity? What has changed? What remains the same? Why?

References

Aristotle. (350 BCE). *Poetics*. The Internet Classics Archive. MIT. https://classics.mit.edu/Aristotle/poetics.1.1.html

Bogdanov, A. (2016). *The philosophy of living experience: Popular outlines.* (D. G. Rowley, Trans.) Brill. (Original work published 1923.)

Carter, R. & McCarthy, M. (2006). *Cambridge grammar of English.* Cambridge University Press.

Cazden, C. B. (2001). *Classroom discourse: The language of teaching and learning*. Heinemann.

Chomsky, N. (2002). *Syntactic structures.* de Gruyter Mouton. (Original work published in 1957.)

Chomsky, N. (2024). Review of the book verbal behavior, by B F. Skinner. *Language, 100*(3), 579–603. https://dx.doi.org/10.1353/lan.2024.a937190. (Original work published in 1959.)

Cope, B. & Kalantzis, M. (2017). Conceptualizing e-Learning. In B. Cope & M. Kalantzis (Eds.), *ELearning ecologies* (pp. 1–45). Routledge.

Cope, B. & Kalantzis, M. (2020). *Making sense: Reference, agency and structure in a grammar of multimodal meaning*. Cambridge University Press.

Cowan, K. & Kress, G. (2019). Documenting and transferring meaning in the multimodal world: Reconsidering 'transcription. In F. Serafini & E. Gee (Eds.), *Remixing multiliteracies: Theory and practice from New London to new times* (pp. 66–77). Teachers College Press.

Halliday, M. A. K. (1975). *Learning how to mean: Explorations in the development of language*. Edward Arnold.

Halliday, M. A. K. (2002). In J. J. Webster (Ed.), *On grammar* (Vol. 1). Continuum.

Halliday, M. A. K. (2009). Context of culture and of situation. In J. J. Webster (Ed.), *The essential Halliday* (pp. 55–84). Continuum.

Halliday, M. A. K. & Hasan, R. (1985). *Language, context, and text: Aspects of language in a social-semiotic perspective*. Deakin University Press.
Herndon, J. H. (1970). *A survey of modern grammars*. Holt, Rinehart & Winston.
Hristova, T., Magee, L., & Soldatic, K. (2023). The problem of alignment. *ArXiv*. https://doi.org/10.48550/arXiv.2401.00210.
Kalantzis, M. & Cope, B. (2020). *Adding sense: Context and interest in a grammar of multimodal meaning*. Cambridge University Press.
Kress, G. & van Leeuwen, T. (2021). *Reading images: The grammar of visual design* (3rd ed.). Routledge.
Martin, J. R. (1992). *English text: System and structure*. John Benjamins.
Searle, J. R. (2002). End of the revolution. *The New York Review of Books*, *49*(3). https://www.nybooks.com/articles/2002/02/28/end-of-the-revolution/
Tzirides, A. O., Zapata, G. C., Bolger, P., Cope, B., Kalantzis, M., & Searsmith, D. (2024). Exploring instructors' views on fine-tuned Generative AI feedback in higher education. *International Journal on E-Learning*, *23*(3), 319–334. https://www.learntechlib.org/primary/p/225173/
Voss, E. (2024). Artificial intelligence and linguistic landscape research: Affordances, challenges & considerations. *Linguistic Landscape*, *10*(4), 400–424. https://doi.org/10.1075/ll.24011.vos
Vygotsky, L. S. (1986). *Thought and language*. MIT Press.

Chapter 4
Literacy Pedagogies

Introduction

The ways in which we understand and teach literacy have always been shaped by historical, technological, and social changes. In Chapter 1, we explored the evolution of literacy across time, from the first languages and early writing systems to the emergence of digital and multimodal literacies. Chapter 2 expanded on this by examining how meaning is made through multiple meaning forms—text, image, space, object, body, sound, and speech—revealing that literacy is not just about written language but a complex and multimodal process. Chapter 3 built on these ideas by exploring how literacy operates within social, institutional, and cultural spaces, emphasizing that meaning-making is shaped by power, ideologies, identities, personal experiences, cultural contexts, and social structures. It also introduced the concept of grammars—not just linguistic, but multimodal grammars that can help us understand how meanings are constructed, interpreted, and negotiated.

Building on these discussions, this chapter turns to literacy pedagogies—how literacy has been conceptualized, taught, and

Literacies in the Age of AI: Teaching and Learning in the Digital Era,
First Edition. Gabriela C. Zapata, Bill Cope, and Mary Kalantzis.

learned throughout history. We first define the concept of *pedagogy* and offer a framework for exploring major pedagogical traditions. We then examine diverse frameworks, starting with didactic approaches that emphasize structured instruction, and moving to more immersive and functional models that connect literacy to real-world practices and critical perspectives that interrogate the ideological dimensions of texts and their grammars. Finally, we introduce the pedagogy of multiliteracies. This is followed by the related framework *Learning by Design*, which integrates these approaches while recognizing literacy as an evolving, context-dependent practice shaped by digital technologies and multimodal communication. We examine its principles, tenets, and proposal for a reflexive pedagogy. By tracing these traditions, we aim to provide a foundation for understanding how literacy education can be designed to equip learners with the skills to navigate, contribute to, and critically engage with the complex meaning-making systems of contemporary society.

Understanding Pedagogical Approaches

At its core, *pedagogy* refers to a deliberately structured sequence of learning activities designed to support and guide students toward specific educational goals and expected outcomes, preparing them as citizens, workers, and lifelong learners. It is not just about transmitting knowledge; rather, it involves understanding how knowledge is constructed, shared, and applied within particular social, historical, cultural, and work contexts (Kalantzis et al., 2016). Pedagogy is thus shaped by a set of beliefs about what counts as valuable knowledge, how students learn best, and which forms of engagement foster deeper understanding and creative application. These beliefs influence every aspect of the teaching and learning process—from selecting content and resources to designing tasks and cultivating relationships in the classroom.

To explore the diverse ways literacy has been conceptualized and taught over time, it is useful to adopt a framework that captures

Table 4.1 A framework for analyzing classroom learning ecologies and literacy pedagogy

Dimension	Description
The contents of literacy knowledge	What literacy skills, understandings, or texts are deemed important to learn?
The organization of the literacy curriculum	How is the subject matter arranged and sequenced, and what is the rationale for that arrangement?
Learners doing literacy	Which activities or practices enable learners to construct and communicate meaning?
The social relationships of literacy learning	How do power dynamics, identities, and interactions among teachers, learners, and the broader community influence the teaching and learning process?

the complexity of these pedagogical choices. Table 4.1 provides one such framework for analyzing classroom learning ecologies and literacy pedagogy. It encompasses four dimensions that together illuminate how literacy knowledge, curriculum design, and social interactions shape the learning environment.

Each dimension highlights a different aspect of pedagogical design:

1. The *Contents of Literacy Knowledge* focuses on the subject matter—what students are expected to learn and why it is considered important.
2. The *Organization of the Literacy Curriculum* is about how this subject matter is selected, arranged, and connected.
3. *Learners Doing Literacy* examines the specific tasks, strategies, and experiential activities that enable students to engage with and make purposeful meaning of the content.
4. The *Social Relationships of Literacy Learning* underscores the significance of context, exploring the roles and interactions between teachers, learners, and the social environment in which literacy practices occur.

By considering these four dimensions in tandem, we can see the underlying principles of different pedagogical approaches more clearly. This analytical lens will guide the exploration of literacy pedagogies throughout this chapter, laying the groundwork for understanding how they have emerged, evolved, and adapted in response to new societal needs and technological innovations.

Didactic Literacy Pedagogy

Didactic literacy pedagogy has been the foundational approach to reading and writing since the 19th century, when mass, compulsory, institutionalized schooling first emerged (Graff, 1979, 1987). It has roots stretching back even further, to the invention of the printing press in the 15th century, and persists in many classrooms today despite ongoing calls to prepare learners for 21st-century complexities (Cuban, 1993; Kalantzis & Cope, 2012). As discussed in Chapter 3, the contents of literacy knowledge in didactic pedagogy emphasize formal correctness, memorization of spelling and grammar rules, comprehension of a singular authorial meaning, and reverence for canonical texts (Bennett, 1984; Hirsch, 1988). This approach organizes the literacy curriculum around fixed syllabi and textbooks, which teachers and students are expected to follow methodically. It positions learners to engage in literacy activities by copying and repeating prescribed content, focusing on memorization and drill techniques ("skill and drill," or, to critics, "drill and kill"), and absorbing knowledge in a manner consistent with "direct instruction" or "transmission pedagogy" (Schoenfeld & Pearson, 2009; Snyder, 2008). In its social relationships, didactic teaching locates authority firmly with the teacher and the textbook, leaving students as largely passive recipients of content (Aristotle, 350 BCE; Cazden, 2001).

Historically, this pedagogy served societal aims by promoting punctuality, discipline, and compliance, shaping a workforce willing to follow orders (Graff, 1979). The classroom itself was organized accordingly, with students facing the teacher in rows, learning literacy in preordained timeslots, and progressing in strictly sequenced steps (Figure 4.1). Textbooks played a pivotal role in enforcing these arrangements: they broke down knowledge into digestible chunks and placed it in a linear order that culminated

Figure 4.1 Example of a classroom reflective of didactic pedagogy.
(SOURCE: Lee, Russell/GetArchive/Public Domain).

in standardized testing (Ong, 1958). Direct instruction programs typify this approach, scripting teacher–student exchanges down to the anticipated student responses (Engelmann, 1992; Goeke, 2009).

While critics label didactic pedagogy inflexible and take issue with its tendency to cast students as silent recipients of expert knowledge, didactic approaches persist in various forms, including technology-mediated versions like recorded lectures or "flipped classrooms" that retain the classic initiate–respond–evaluate cycle (Cope & Kalantzis, 2015a). The digital era has not necessarily diminished teacher-centered or textbook-driven instruction: e-textbooks and computerized quizzes can replicate the same one-way patterns of knowledge transmission (Cope & Kalantzis, 2019). Even so, some educators and researchers see value in preserving aspects of didactic pedagogy, particularly its strengths in explicit conceptual instruction and its emphasis on the systematic organization of disciplinary

Table 4.2 Classroom learning ecologies grounded in didactic literacy pedagogy

Dimension	Description
The contents of literacy knowledge	Emphasis on formal rules (grammar, spelling), canonical texts, and singular authorial meanings.
The organization of the literacy curriculum	Rigidly follows standardized syllabi and textbooks; teachers and students are expected to adhere to a set sequence.
Learners doing literacy	Focus on memorization, drill practices, correct application of rules, and comprehension of one "correct" interpretation.
The social relationships of literacy learning	The teacher assumes authority; learners are viewed as passive recipients of expert knowledge, with limited peer interaction.

knowledge (Cope & Kalantzis, 2017; Kirschner et al., 2006). In these ways, a didactic approach remains influential, especially where high-stakes testing or calls for "cultural literacy" and "back to basics" resonate.

In Table 4.2, we apply the framework introduced in Section "Understanding Pedagogical Approaches" to summarize the classroom learning ecologies grounded in didactic literacy pedagogy outlined in this section.

Authentic Literacy Pedagogy

Almost from the moment it was applied to mass, institutionalized schooling, didactic education attracted its share of critics, from popular culture's enduring image of the stern schoolteacher to the ranks of the education profession itself. These critics questioned the moral and intellectual implications of requiring passive acceptance of "one right answer," wondered whether formal academic disciplines truly prepared young people for life, and asked how meaningful knowledge could be if it did not engage a learner's identity, interests, and motivations. Out of these questions emerged an alternative view of education—often labeled "progressivism" or, more precisely, *authentic pedagogy*—that places the learner at the center of the educational process. This shift reflected broader economic and cultural changes in the 20th century, as well as a sense that didactic education might even betray what some perceived to be "human nature" (Kalantzis & Cope, 2012).

One of the ironies of the didactic approach was that it reduced teachers to mere conduits between the textbook or syllabus and their students, with modest expectations for teacher training or professional autonomy. By contrast, the new focus on learning redefined the teacher's role, enhancing their professional standing and increasing the required training. Key early figures in this change were Maria Montessori and John Dewey. Montessori (1912/1964) created experimental "Children's Houses" in Rome, organized around practical, hands-on activities; children worked on projects that interested them or honed fundamental skills through tangible, sensory materials (Montessori 1917/1973; see Figure 4.2). Meanwhile, Dewey founded the University of Chicago's Laboratory School, advocating "direct experience" through making, doing, and solving real-world problems (Dewey, 1938/1963; Dewey & Dewey, 1915)

Figure 4.2 Example of an early Montessori classroom.
(SOURCE: Dolph Kohnstamm/Wikimedia Commons/Public Domain).

These thinkers critiqued the "bookish" learning and rigid discipline of didactic pedagogy (Dewey, 1915/1956). Instead, they proposed classrooms where students could move at their own pace, selecting tasks that engaged their motivations and life experiences. In Dewey's vision, teachers were to act as facilitators or "watchers and helpers," rather than authorities who deliver knowledge from on high. By focusing on authentic, purposeful activities, children would therefore see the practical value of spelling, punctuation, and grammar; for instance, learning punctuation rules because they needed clear communication to print a pamphlet, rather than memorizing rules for a test (Dewey & Dewey, 1915). Montessori (1917/1973) similarly advocated learner autonomy in language, allowing children to form sentences and discover linguistic patterns rather than subjecting them to the "assassin" of grammar-as-dissection.

Over time, others carried these ideas into more specialized domains of literacy learning. For example, Kenneth Goodman (2005) advanced the "whole language" approach, suggesting that children learn written language most effectively in ways analogous to how they learn oral language—through immersion in personally meaningful reading and writing. Donald Graves (2003) and Donald Murray (1982) promoted "process writing," contending that students should choose their own writing topics, work through drafting and revising, and focus on voice rather than merely reproducing "correct" forms. These notions challenged the central premises of didactic literacy teaching: They shifted attention away from memorizing isolated language facts to cultivating real communication, student interest, and purposeful practice.

Like didactic pedagogy, authentic pedagogy was also a cultural product of its time, tied to a sense of modern progress and technological mastery. Dewey's (1915/1956) "pragmatism" held that problem-solving and practical experiences prepared learners for a rapidly changing world. Yet even as they critiqued didactic orthodoxy, authentic educators did not wholly relinquish the aim of producing standardized, educated language use; standard English was still treated as a key requirement for future success. This tension underscores the moral economy of authentic pedagogy, in which teachers are to create inclusive, learner-focused environments while often still expecting learners to conform to particular norms of literacy (Kalantzis et al., 2016).

Despite its limitations—such as sometimes overlooking cultural and linguistic diversity or ultimately reinforcing a single standard form of literacy—authentic pedagogy reoriented classrooms toward the learner's experience, interests, and motivations. In this sense, it represented a striking break from the passivity and rote discipline of didactic pedagogy, giving learners a more active role and asking teachers to develop richer, more flexible learning environments (Cook-Gumperz, 2006; Kalantzis & Cope, 2012). By establishing a friendlier space for student collaboration, personal expression, and practical engagement, authentic pedagogy opened the door to subsequent innovations in functional literacy, critical literacy, and other pedagogical models.

Below, in Table 4.3, we offer a summary of how the four dimensions of classroom learning ecologies apply to authentic literacy pedagogy.

Table 4.3 Classroom learning ecologies grounded in authentic literacy pedagogy

Dimension	Description
The contents of literacy knowledge	Focus on meaningful, relevant texts that connect to learners' experiences; emphasis on real-world language use rather than abstract rules.
The organization of the literacy curriculum	Flexible, learner-centered design; process-oriented tasks; reduced reliance on fixed textbooks; integration of practical, hands-on activities aligned with learners' interests.
Learners doing literacy	Active engagement in purposeful reading and writing; immersion in collaborative projects; writing as a multi-stage process (drafting, revising, publishing); emphasis on personal voice and discovery.
The social relationships of literacy learning	The teacher as facilitator or guide, rather than authority; learner-centered discourse; peer collaboration; recognition of individual needs and experiences to foster motivation and ownership of learning.

Functional Literacy Pedagogy

Functional literacy pedagogy emphasizes that reading and composing texts should serve real-world purposes and enable learners to participate fully in both school and society. Instead of starting with discrete rules for phonics, spelling, or grammar, functional literacy begins by asking, "What is the purpose of this whole text?" and then moves on to, "How is the text organized to meet that purpose?" This approach is grounded in the tenets of the systemic functional grammar developed by Halliday and colleagues (Halliday, 1975, 2002, 2009; Halliday & Hasan, 1985), which we introduced in Chapter 3. In this pedagogy, reading and writing are seen as closely linked processes, and learners are encouraged to examine how different text types, or *genres*, function in the world to achieve distinct communicative goals.

In other words, genres are defined as more than individual utterances spontaneously created in the moment; they are textual interventions in society, representing familiar patterns of meaning that have developed over time for particular social purposes (Martin, 1997). Different genres grant users access to particular social spaces of influence and power—for instance, the specialized language of lawyers, chess players, or academics. Those who have grown up immersed in these social realms may "pick up the language" naturally, while those who have not may find it more difficult to gain entry. Because schooling purports to equalize opportunities, functional pedagogy aims to make explicit how these genres work, thereby expanding each learner's linguistic repertoire without displacing the genres and dialects of their home communities.

School is a unique social site where language is both reflected and transformed for teaching and learning. It must represent a broad sweep of knowledge and yet deliver that knowledge through systematic generalizations rather than mere immersion. School subjects—such as science, history, and English—often privilege different types of texts, which vary in their generic structures and purposes. These "genres at school" are mapped to specific goals; for example, a scientific report describes phenomena in a way that can be replicated or tested, while a historical argument might analyze evidence to interpret events from multiple perspectives. To discuss these structural and organizational features of texts, functional literacy pedagogy deploys a *metalanguage*—a vocabulary for talking about language.

While speakers do not need to be consciously aware of every linguistic choice they make, explicit instruction in text organization and language features can be crucial for learners who come from historically disadvantaged groups and may not have had early immersion in the "genres of power" (Cope & Kalantzis, 1993). A primary goal of functional pedagogy, then, is to use this metalanguage to connect the "hows" of language structure to the "whys" of social purpose. In contrast to "authentic" approaches that rely on student interest and natural growth, functional pedagogy underscores the need for systematic scaffolding, showing how each genre's structure (macrostructures) and language choices (microstructures) serve a text's overarching aims (Halliday & Hasan, 1985; see Figure 4.3).

A common tool in functional pedagogy is the teaching–learning cycle (Figure 4.4), which systematically guides learners from teacher-led modeling of a target genre to joint construction of a text, and finally to independent writing (Callaghan & Rothery, 1988; Martin, 1986). In the *modeling and deconstruction* phase, the teacher and students read or analyze exemplary texts, identifying typical structures, key vocabulary, and patterns of organization. The second phase, *joint construction*, allows the teacher to act as a "language expert," co-writing a text with the class by focusing on the genre's social purpose and linguistic features. Finally, in *independent construction*, students compose their own texts—preparing by researching and note-taking, writing drafts, conferring with teachers and peers, and revising for publication. This deliberate scaffolding makes visible the steps required for success in school-based literacies and beyond, addressing critiques of learner-centered approaches that can fail to provide explicit instruction on how language works (Cope & Kalantzis, 1993).

Through these phases, functional pedagogy aims to offer "genres of school success and social power" to all students (Martin, 1997).

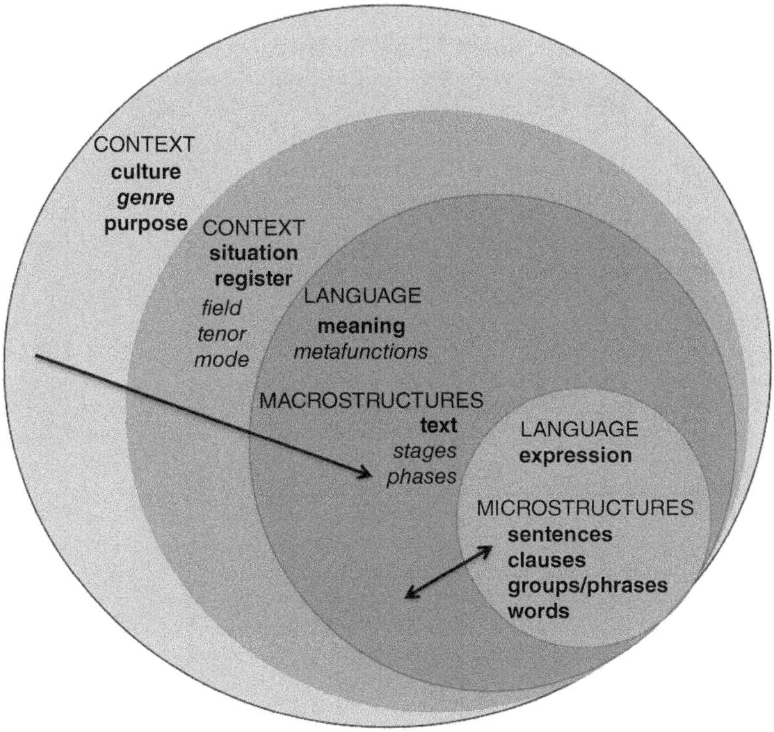

Figure 4.3 A model of text in context—meaning and form.

That is, the approach recognizes that specialized genres—such as scientific reports, analytical essays, and technical procedures—are increasingly important in workplaces and civic discourse. By teaching students to see how social purpose drives language choices, functional literacy stands apart from didactic pedagogies that stress rule-based accuracy for its own sake, and from purely authentic pedagogies that may lack the structural rigor some learners need.

In sum, ultimately, functional literacy pedagogy links language form to its social function. Writers select grammatical constructions and vocabulary not arbitrarily but to serve specific communicative goals. By making these relationships explicit, functional educators seek to ensure that all learners—not just those born into particular language communities—can access and reshape the social

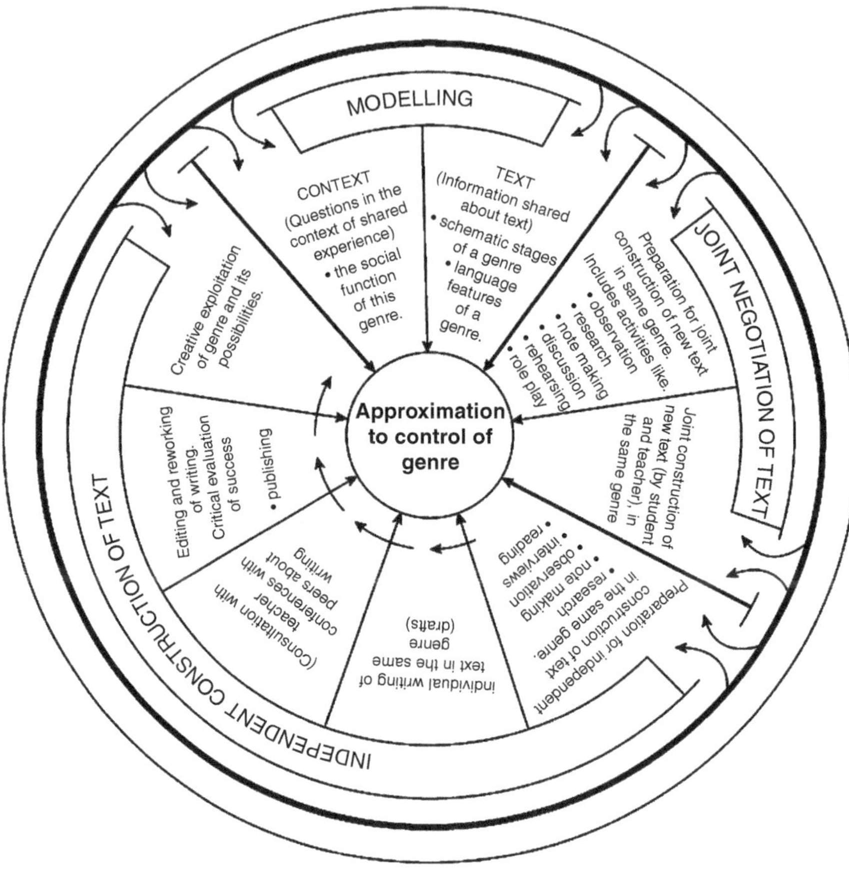

Figure 4.4 An example of the teaching and learning cycle: Phases of reading and writing in a genre approach.

realms where language is a source of power and status. In Table 4.4, we show the four dimensions of classroom learning ecologies in functional literacy pedagogy.

Critical Literacy Pedagogy

Critical pedagogies fundamentally embrace the notion that literacies are multiple, acknowledging the diverse voices, cultural backgrounds, and knowledge systems that learners bring into the

Table 4.4 Classroom learning ecologies grounded in functional literacy pedagogy

Dimension	Description
The contents of literacy knowledge	Emphasis on learning genres that serve social, academic, and professional functions; understanding how text structures and language features relate to real-world purposes and contexts.
The organization of the literacy curriculum	A systematic teaching-learning cycle: Modeling texts, joint construction, and independent writing; explicit connections between macrostructures (overall text organization) and microstructures (sentence-level grammar, vocabulary).
Learners doing literacy	Supported apprenticeship model where learners analyze, co-create, and eventually compose texts independently; focus on explicit knowledge of how language works to achieve communicative goals; use of metalanguage for deeper understanding.
The social relationships of literacy learning	The teacher as an expert guide showing how language confers access to realms of power; scaffolding designed to broaden learners' linguistic repertoires; commitment to equitable social outcomes by expanding students' genre capacities.

classroom (Kalantzis & Cope, 2012; Kalantzis et al., 2016). This perspective extends beyond traditional literacy practices to include various sites of popular culture, new media, and the evolving landscape of real-world texts. Recognizing that literacy is not merely about decoding written words but also about navigating, interpreting, and creating meaning across contexts, critical literacy approaches position students as active meaning-makers, agents of change, and engaged citizens (Apple & Beane, 2007; Freire & Macedo, 1987). Rather than being passive consumers of knowledge, students are encouraged to critically engage with texts and contexts that shape their realities, resisting alienation and fostering empowerment (Ayers, 2010).

Recent scholarship has expanded critical literacy into the domain of creating and interrogating media texts that tackle pressing societal issues such as discrimination, marginalization, and social inequities. Through an emphasis on participatory learning and co-construction of knowledge, critical literacy invites students to challenge dominant narratives, question ideologies embedded in texts, and use their literacy skills as tools for social transformation (Kalantzis & Cope, 2012). This orientation also aligns with the related *syncretic approaches*, which value "horizontal learning"—the blending of everyday knowledge with academic knowledge to create new ways of understanding (Gregory et al., 2013; Gutiérrez, 2008, 2014).

When learning is grounded in real-world problems connected to students' lifeworlds and/or communities, they can be encouraged to compose authentic texts that reflect their lived experiences. This is what Apple and Beane (2007) refer to as a "democratic curriculum," not merely in the sense of civic participation but as a fundamental commitment to collective problem-solving. Similarly, Ayers (2010) argues that genuine education is transformative, enabling students to "tear down walls" and reimagine new possibilities. Freire and Macedo (1987) extend this view, advocating for literacy as a means of transformation—teaching individuals not just how to read and write, but how to "read the world." This concept resonates with syncretic literacy studies, which emphasize the blending of cultural, linguistic, and epistemic resources to create new, contextually relevant ways of knowing (Gregory et al., 2013).

Also, from a critical pedagogy and syncretic perspective, popular culture and digital media are not peripheral to literacy learning but are central sites where young people construct meaning, form identities, and engage with the world. Older didactic models of pedagogy often dismissed media and popular texts as distractions from "serious" academic work. In contrast, critical and syncretic pedagogies recognize these texts as rich cultural artifacts that influence social norms, ideologies, and individual self-perception. Engaging with these texts through the lens of "critical reflexivity" and "syncretic literacies" allows students not only to interrogate their assumptions, biases, and the exclusions embedded within mainstream discourse but also to remix and repurpose textual resources from different domains to create new, hybrid forms of meaning (Gutiérrez, 2014).

Thus, a core tenet of both critical literacy and syncretic learning is that knowledge is socially constructed and deeply intertwined with identity. Students from diverse linguistic, cultural, and socioeconomic backgrounds bring distinct discourses into the learning space. By validating and amplifying these multiple voices—while also equipping learners with the tools to critique dominant literacy norms—educators can disrupt power imbalances and foster a more inclusive and equitable learning environment. And both critical pedagogy and syncretic literacy studies can also offer an analytical framework for understanding how students blend home, community, and school literacies in ways that both challenge and expand conventional literacy practices.

In sum, taking action is ultimately central to both critical and syncretic literacy approaches. This can manifest in the classroom through a range of activities, from rewriting stories to make them more inclusive to designing community-based projects that address social injustices. In these contexts, teachers act as facilitators rather than authoritative figures, guiding students toward critical inquiry and transformative engagement. These types of pedagogical interventions can therefore provide a way to reorganize traditional relationships between everyday and school-based practices, fostering more just and equitable learning environments.

As in previous sections, in Table 4.5, we summarize the classroom learning ecologies reflective of both critical and syncretic literacy approaches.

We believe that, by integrating critical and syncretic pedagogical approaches, literacy education can become a powerful space for fostering transformative knowledge-making. These approaches do not simply include more voices in existing structures but actively reconfigure learning to be more inclusive, dynamic, performance-driven, and reflective of the complex realities in which students live and learn. As syncretic frameworks suggest, learning is an ever-evolving process of repurposing, blending, and reimagining knowledge across boundaries, opening up new pathways for understanding and action (Gutiérrez, 2014).

Table 4.5 Classroom learning ecologies grounded in critical and syncretic literacy approaches

Dimension	Description
The contents of literacy knowledge	Emphasis on multiple perspectives and real-world social issues; engaging students' home languages, interests, and life experiences as starting points; highlighting power relations, cultural differences, and questions of identity.
The organization of the literacy curriculum	Curriculum structured around learners' concerns, addressing local or global problems; texts drawn from popular culture, new media, or authentic community contexts; teacher facilitates inquiry and scaffolds reflection, discussion, and critique.
Learners doing literacy	Collaborative investigation of complex questions; interrogation of texts for ideology and bias; active creation of alternative or redesigned texts; focus on voice, agency, and taking socially meaningful action; explicit support for minoritized discourses.
The social relationships of literacy learning	Horizontal, democratic engagement; teacher as co-learner and guide rather than authority; acknowledgment of different cultures, dialects, and identity positions; fostering participation, debate, and mutual respect; pursuit of equity and social transformation.

While the pedagogical traditions discussed so far offer distinct approaches to literacy instruction, they also intersect, evolve, and respond to critique. The ongoing transformation of literacy education reflects a growing recognition that learning is not a one-size-fits-all process but rather a dynamic, context-dependent practice shaped by technological advances, cultural shifts, and diverse learner experiences.

This chapter now turns to the pedagogy of multiliteracies and *Learning by Design*—frameworks that integrate key elements of the pedagogical approaches examined earlier. These frameworks allow for purposeful choices among these traditions in order to facilitate high-performance outcomes as well as inclusive and adaptable literacy education models that can foster deeper engagement, analytical capacities, critical thinking, and creative problem-solving. Ultimately, these approaches aim at equipping learners with the skills to effectively navigate and communicate within the complex world of meaning-making in contemporary society.

The Pedagogy of Multiliteracies

In 1994, a group of 10 international scholars, of which two of us (Bill and Mary) were part, gathered in New London, New Hampshire, to reflect on why scholarship had hitherto not had a significant impact on stubborn student inequalities and uneven performance outcomes. The group discussed how globalization, cultural and linguistic diversity, and emerging digital technologies were reshaping literacy education. New London had been recommended as a quiet and out-of-the-way location for the meeting by Courtney Cazden, who was a professor at Harvard at the time. Additionally, we felt it would serve as a central meeting point, given our widely dispersed locations across the United States, Australia, and the United Kingdom. We also found some interesting ironies in the name—after all, old London had once been the center of a local dialect in what was originally a small language but would later expand into a global-imperial one. This led us to wonder: What could be next for a "new" London? And so, as group members, we chose to transcend our personal profiles and use this name for the collective thinking of the group (see Kalantzis & Cope, 2025).

Our discussions led to the seminal article we published under our collective name in 1996 (New London Group [NLG], 1996). In it, we explored how monolingual, print-centric conceptions of literacy instruction had put a drag on literacy outcomes. Consequently, we argued that learner differences (cultural, socioeconomic, and linguistic) and global connectedness (international interactions, digital links) rendered a single "standard" form of literacy inadequate. That is, at the time, trends in globalization and technology made it clear that the traditional concept of literacy—tied primarily to the printed medium and to "a single, official, or standard form of language" (Cope & Kalantzis, 2015b, p. 1)—was inadequate for a generation whose learning already extended far beyond the printed, "official word." We therefore posited that literacy education needed to move beyond a sole focus on written language and incorporate the multiple modalities of communication that were increasingly shaping the everyday experiences of learners (these are the meaning forms we discussed in Chapters 2 and 3).

Moreover, the new approach needed had to explicitly address learner performance and harness learners' diverse identities and life experiences (Kalantzis et al., 2005). It was evident that we were living in a more challenging, international world where multilingualism not only continued to prevail, but, more importantly, multimodal meaning-making was flourishing. The traditional notion of literacy (the one we introduced in Chapter 1) was thus no longer sufficient. Instead, we needed a pedagogy that would

> facilitate [learners'] active engagement with new and unfamiliar kinds of [multimodal] texts, without arousing a sense of alienation and exclusion, [and would focus on the] increasing complexity and inter-relationship of different modes of meaning (Cope & Kalantzis, 2006, pp. 37–38).

To describe this educational shift and a new, more appropriate view of literacy and its instruction, we coined the concept of *multiliteracies* (NLG, 1996).

Broadly speaking, *multiliteracies* refers to the multiple ways in which we create and communicate meaning, encompassing the two fundamental dimensions of meaning as design (also connected to the forms and functions we saw in Chapter 3)—the *situational* (or *social*) *dimension* (context and function) and the *modal dimension* (form) (Cope & Kalantzis, 2023; Kalantzis et al., 2016).

The first dimension, *situational*, refers to symbolic, embodied, and material differences (for an in-depth discussion of these concepts, see Chapter 7, pp. 261–264). It highlights the variability of meaning conventions across different social, cultural, material, and domain-specific contexts, shaped by personal experiences, cultural and community settings, socioeconomic backgrounds, interpersonal relationships, identities, subject matter, and disciplinary domains, among other factors (more on this in Chapter 7). These diverse contexts significantly influence how we engage in meaning-making in everyday life (and are reflected in the five meaning functions we discussed in Chapter 3; i.e., reference, agency, structure, context, and interest). Therefore, literacy education today cannot remain focused solely on the rigid rules of a single, standardized national language, as it did in the past. Instead, it must recognize and harness the diversity of learners (in all its forms and complexities) that shape communication and meaning in our classrooms (Cope & Kalantzis, 2023; Kalantzis et al., 2016).

The second dimension, *modal*, refers to the various meaning forms we use to create meaning (i.e., text, image, space, object, body, sound, and speech). The increasing complexity of these meaning forms is directly connected to new media and the digital tools and practices that influence contemporary communication. As technology advances, meaning-making is no longer confined to traditional, text-based literacy but extends across multiple platforms and formats, requiring an expanded and more inclusive approach to literacy education (Cope & Kalantzis, 2023). We present both dimensions in Figure 4.5.

To help educators enact the pedagogy of multiliteracies in the classroom, the NLG (1996) proposed four key, epistemically based, pedagogical options—*Situated Practice*, *Overt Instruction*, *Critical Framing*, and *Transformed Practice*. Rather than prescribing a linear sequence, these pedagogical practices were seen as a set of options through which teachers could design learning experiences. Pedagogical choices depend on the needs of individual students, classrooms, or subject matter, so not every practice needs to be included in the instructional sequence, nor is there a specific order in which they must be implemented. Nevertheless, pedagogical choices play a crucial role in fostering students' multiliteracies and expanding teachers' instructional repertoires (Cope & Kalantzis, 2006).

Regardless of the chosen approach, instruction must always begin with an understanding of the learner and their needs. We and

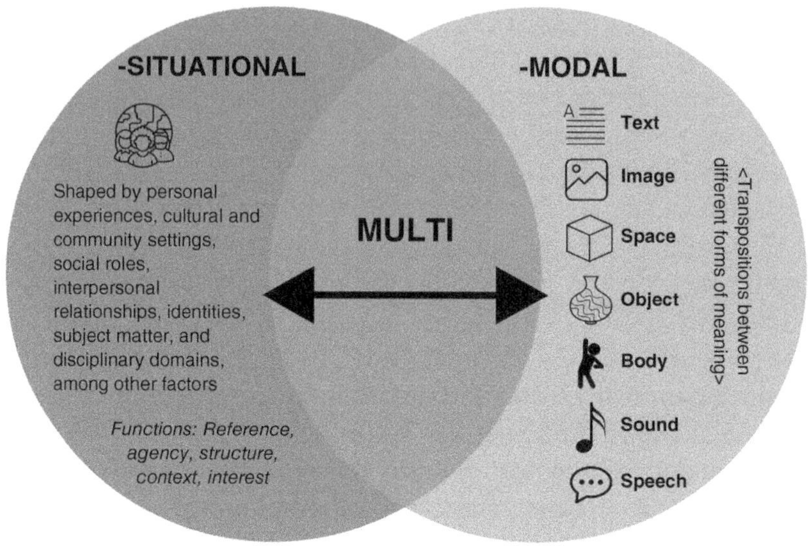

Figure 4.5 The two multi of multiliteracies.

our NLG colleagues argued that, for instruction to be meaningful, it needs to harness the diverse life experiences students bring to the classroom, and connect with their "different subjectivities and with their attendant languages, discourses, and registers, and use these as a resource for learning" (NLG, 1996, p. 72).

Consequently, students' personal language use and experiences become part of what we have termed *found designs* (see page 52 in Chapter 2). That is, what they were born into, use in community life, and bring with them into the classroom needs to be recognized in the curriculum.

Through active engagement with any combination of the four multiliteracies pedagogical practices, both instructors and students collaborate in *designing* new, creative, and goal-specific meanings as they analyze, utilize, and modify their found designs.

This process ultimately leads to the *redesigned*, which consists of newly constructed meanings and representations—essentially, new knowledge—not only in relation to the found designs but also in how meaning-makers themselves evolve. In the process of designing, therefore, both educators and students "transform their relations with each other, [and] themselves, [and also] configurations of subjects, social relations, and knowledges are worked upon and transformed" (NLG, 1996, p. 76).

Educators can make pedagogical choices from the multiliteracies framework as appropriate for the learner, class, or subject focus. Each of the four practices is discussed as follows:

- **Situated Practice (Experiencing)** primarily draws upon the known knowledge students bring to the classroom, which is deeply connected to their communities, personal backgrounds, and prior academic experiences (NLG, 1996). Thus, links are established between curricular objectives and students' identities and academic and personal needs. New knowledge can also be introduced seamlessly and integrated into what students have already encountered or understand (Cope & Kalantzis, 2015b).
- **Overt Instruction (Conceptualizing)** entails instructors guiding students in analyzing meaning-making. This pedagogical move provides learners with explicit concepts and metalanguages that they can use to critically examine meaning forms and functions, understanding how these elements have been employed to convey meaning. The objective of this phase is for students to "have a way to describe the processes and patterns of [meaning] design in a meaningful way" (Cope & Kalantzis, 2006, p. 40).
- **Critical Framing (Analyzing)** involves students' understanding the power of meaning-making. At this stage, the focus shifts to what Kress (1993) describes as the motivated aspect of a sign (or design)—that is, the underlying reasons for its creation. Students critically analyze *found designs* by considering their creators' intentions, exploring context, and ideological and sociocultural connections in relation to the meaning forms employed and the messages being conveyed. The goal of critical framing is for learners to "gain the necessary personal and theoretical distance from what they have learned, constructively [analyze] it, account for its [purpose], cultural location, [and] creatively extend and apply it" (NLG, 1996, p. 87).

- **Transformed Practice (Applying)** provides students with opportunities to apply their learning appropriately and/or creatively. They can rework found designs into new creations (e.g., multimodal texts).

The NLG's (1996) multiliteracies pedagogy provided a foundation for a reimagined educational approach—one that not only addressed the evolving landscape of communication and meaning-making shaped by information technology and digital media but also integrated students' diverse lived experiences into curricula. We have since revisited the initial concepts from the NLG's proposal and reconceptualized them (Cope & Kalantzis, 2015b, 2023; Kalantzis & Cope, 2025; Kalantzis et al., 2005, 2016).

Our objective was to refine the NLG's (1996) pedagogy of multiliteracies, making it more accessible and comprehensible for both educators and students while also providing guidelines for designing clear instructional repertoires. Furthermore, we introduced new pedagogical conceptualizations, which, together with the revised NLG ideas, became the *Learning by Design* framework (henceforth, LbyD).

Learning by Design

Overview

The emphasis placed by the NLG's (1996) pedagogy of multiliteracies was on purposeful choices based on an epistemological framework; i.e., rigorous, intentional instructional designs along with the harnessing of learners' identities and their personal and community experiences as valuable learning resources. This is also a fundamental aspect of LbyD. One of the core premises of our framework is the need to integrate both *informal* and *formal learning*. The former pertains to what students acquire organically and implicitly in their daily lives—knowledge that stems from their personal experiences and lifeworlds. The latter, on the other hand, is academic, connected to schooling, and characterized as structured and systematically designed. We argue that the most effective formal learning experiences are those that incorporate informal learning into curricula by engaging with students' experiential world and applying what is learned in that world (Kalantzis et al., 2005). This is particularly relevant in today's digital and globalized society, where learners have access to diverse learning opportunities through their interactions with digital media and virtual communities—opportunities that often surpass those available in traditional school settings (Green & Beavis, 2013; Tzirides et al., 2023; Zammit, 2010). Additionally, students may find informal learning more engaging and personally relevant, further emphasizing the necessity of its integration into formal education.

The incorporation of informal learning into formal education is directly linked to two fundamental conditions that we have identified as essential for learning to occur. The first is *belonging,* which underscores the importance of creating instructional environments in which learners feel a deep personal connection—not only in terms of curricular content but also in relation to the broader learning community and context. Learners' identities and *funds of knowledge*, which Moll et al., (1992, p. 133) define as "the historically accumulated and culturally developed bodies of knowledge and skills essential for household and individual functioning and well-being," are central to this sense of belonging. In other words, belonging to learning is founded on the learning ways (i.e., the learner's identities and learning preferences), the learning content (i.e., curricula), and the learning community (i.e., the learning environment).

The second essential condition for learning is *transformation*, which refers to the lifelong changes that result from students' active participation in the learning process, as well as the instructional components necessary to facilitate such change. For learning to be transformative, instruction must take learners into new and unfamiliar terrains. However, the journey into the unfamiliar needs to stay within a zone of intelligibility and safety. At each step, it needs to travel just the right distance from the student's lifeworld starting point. In LbyD, failure to meet these two conditions—*belonging* and

Table 4.6 Comparison between the pedagogy of multiliteracies and learning by design

Pedagogy of Multiliteracies	Learning by Design
Situated Practice	Experiencing the Known Experiencing the New
Overt Instruction	Conceptualizing by Classifying Conceptualizing with Theory
Critical Framing	Analyzing Functionally Analyzing Critically
Transformed Practice	Applying Appropriately Applying Creatively

transformation—can hinder the realization of equitable education. These principles serve as the foundation for designing instructional interventions and curricula that foster the equitable development of learners' multiliteracies.

LbyD originates in the NLG's (1996) multiliteracies pedagogy. However, we have redefined, expanded, and renamed the practices embedded in the original multiliteracies proposal. For instance, in LbyD, instructional approaches are conceptualized as *knowledge processes* or *epistemic moves*. These processes can be defined as foundational types of thinking-in-action or things we can do to know. In Table 4.6, we offer a comparison between the instructional practices in the pedagogy of multiliteracies and the knowledge processes in LbyD.

The eight knowledge processes in LbyD align closely with those found in informal learning, and they also resonate with the distinct pedagogical traditions we presented in previous sections of this chapter. In formal academic contexts, these knowledge processes are embedded within instruction, and they frame instructional interventions. We describe each process as follows:

1. **Experiencing** (related to *authentic pedagogies*; immersive, real-world contexts)
   - **(a)** *Experiencing the Known*: Activates learners' existing cultural and social knowledge, anchoring new material in familiar lifeworlds.

   (b) *Experiencing the New:* Invites learners into unfamiliar or more challenging material, broadening perspectives and capacities within a supportive zone of proximal development (Vygotsky, 1978).
2. **Conceptualizing** (aligned with *didactic approaches* [i.e., explicit instruction] but goes beyond to incorporate learner-centered critical reflection and analysis)
   (a) **Conceptualizing by Classifying**: Offers explicit instruction, delineating key terms, genres, and multimodal features, mirroring didactic transmission but in a design-oriented way.
   (b) **Conceptualizing with Theory**: Takes learners beyond discrete terms or labels, prompting them to synthesize patterns, form generalizations, and critically reflect on how meaning works in context.
3. **Analyzing** (fuses *critical pedagogy*—revealing power/ideology—with *functional literacy*—understanding how texts achieve social purposes)
   (a) **Analyzing Functionally**: Investigates how textual or multimodal structures accomplish communicative aims—echoing functional approaches.
   (b) **Analyzing Critically**: Draws explicitly on critical pedagogy, interrogating bias, power relations, and the social interests that textual designs may serve.
4. **Applying** (connected to *functional pedagogy* and *transferable learning*, also reflecting *syncretic approaches*)
   (a) **Applying Appropriately**: Learners demonstrate new skills in conventional or widely accepted formats (e.g., academic essays, formal presentations). While reminiscent of traditional pedagogy, it remains flexible and integrative.
   (b) **Applying Creatively**: Encourages pushing boundaries and remixing knowledge in contextually inventive ways, embodying the spirit of syncretic and inquiry-based pedagogies that prioritize agency and creativity and foster applications and connections beyond the classroom (e.g., with learners' communities; focus on citizenship and civic participation).

Learning that integrates these knowledge processes involves "weaving" backward and forward across and between purposeful choices. However, it is important to note that LbyD does not impose rigid curricular designs, specific classroom activities, or predetermined instructional sequences. Instead, it provides flexible guidelines for instructional tasks and strategies, emphasizing that learning must be tailored to the unique needs of each educational context and group of students. Consequently, the selection and sequencing of epistemic moves depend on the learners and the specific educational setting.

Within this pedagogical approach, it is also important to emphasize that different knowledge processes have distinct orientations. *Experiencing* and *applying* are primarily socio-material, while *conceptualizing* and *analyzing* lean more toward cognitive processes. Here, we use the term "orientation" intentionally, as socio-material activity always involves cognition, just as cognition is never entirely disembodied or separate from social and material contexts.

This constant movement between socio-material and cognitive dimensions is central to the learning and teaching process. Cognitive engagement often needs to be reoriented toward socio-material contexts, just as socio-material activities require cognitive reflection. This interplay exemplifies the process of transposition we discussed in Chapter 3, where pedagogy involves an ongoing negotiation between these different focal points to foster meaningful learning.

Regardless of the chosen epistemic moves or how they are implemented in the classroom, the crucial aspect of our approach is the development and enactment of a *transformative curriculum*. Such a curriculum integrates students' diverse lifeworld experiences into instruction, aiming to establish comparable learning outcomes without prejudice to difference so that the effects are pluralism—a community of productive diversity, high performance, and equity. This type of curriculum is materialized in the classroom through what we have defined as *reflexive literacy pedagogy*.

Reflexive Literacy Pedagogy

A transformative curriculum with a focus on literacy instruction grounded in LbyD is only feasible through the adoption of a *reflexive pedagogical approach*. This approach is characterized by its dynamic and iterative nature, involving a continuous exchange between various knowledge processes. Additionally, it fosters a dialogic interaction among learners, educators, peers, family members, experts, and the community, thus facilitating a rich and evolving learning experience. Also, in a classroom where literacy pedagogy is informed by LbyD's reflexive pedagogy, it is crucial to design learning activities that align with the principles of belonging and transformation. These goals can be achieved through educational practices that

- Connect learning to real-life experiences and incorporate students' identities and lifeworlds as well as mutual understanding into all instructional aspects.
- Create inclusive tasks—reflective of learners' diversity and personal and academic needs—that allow for their critical exposure to and use of varied meaning forms, digital media, and technologies (including generative AI—more on this in Chapter 5), as well as position them as legitimate knowledge creators. This involves instruction that fosters critical citizenship and civic participation.
- Integrate varied, purposeful knowledge processes, facilitating learners' dynamic engagement with different epistemic moves.
- Foster collaborative knowledge construction and students' joint meaning-making within their zone of proximal development (Vygotsky, 1978).
- Challenge learners to develop increasingly sophisticated conceptual frameworks, defining concepts, formulating theories, analyzing critically, and evaluating thoughtfully.
- Provide ongoing, recursive feedback and track performance.
- Encourage learners to articulate their cognitive processes, offering guidance and opportunities for metacognitive reflection.

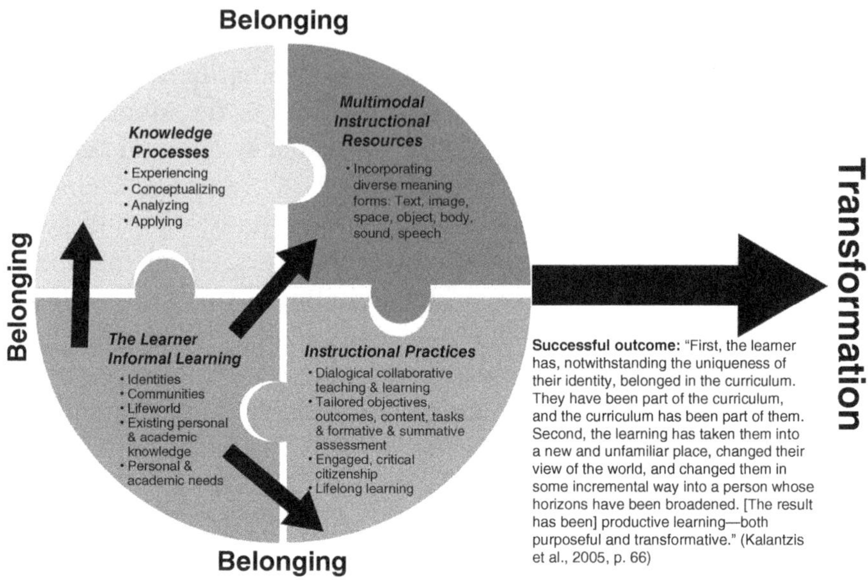

Figure 4.6 Elements of a reflexive literacy approach grounded in learning by design.

By integrating these practices into literacy pedagogy, educators can foster inclusive, learner-centered environments that enhance engagement, analytical thinking, collaborative meaning-making, and high performance. In Figure 4.6, we offer a visual representation of reflexive literacy pedagogy grounded in the principles and tenets of LbyD (see also Lim et al., 2022).

In the following chapters of the book, we will establish connections between our reflexive pedagogy and literacy development in today's digital world. But before we conclude our discussion, let's summarize, in Table 4.7, LbyD's classroom learning ecologies as we did with the other approaches we examined in previous sections.

Conclusion

This chapter has examined the evolution of literacy pedagogies, illustrating how different approaches have shaped the ways in which literacy is taught and learned. We began by exploring

Table 4.7 Classroom learning ecologies grounded in learning by design

Dimension	Description
The contents of literacy knowledge	Emphasizes integrating informal and formal learning. Recognizes learners' identities and lifeworld experiences as essential knowledge resources.
The organization of the literacy curriculum	A flexible and responsive curriculum that weaves between different epistemic moves (experiencing, conceptualizing, analyzing, applying), tailored to students' needs and contexts.
Learners doing literacy	Engages learners in diverse knowledge processes that involve authentic, experiential, conceptual, analytical, and applied learning activities. Collaborative construction of knowledge and high-performance goals.
The social relationships of literacy learning	Prioritizes belonging and transformation that leads to positive outcomes, fostering inclusive learning communities, dialogic interactions, and critical engagement with varied literacy practices. Fosters lifelong learning, productive work practices, citizenship, and civic engagement.

didactic pedagogy, which emphasizes structured instruction, and contrasted it with more learner-centered frameworks such as authentic, functional, and critical literacy pedagogies, also touching on syncretic approaches. Each of these frameworks offers distinct insights into literacy education, reflecting broader societal, technological, and ideological transformations.

In the last part of the chapter, we introduced two frameworks directly connected with our scholarship, the pedagogy of multiliteracies and LbyD. We posited that this latter one integrates the pedagogical traditions discussed in the first sections of the chapter and also recognizes the multimodal and digital dimensions of contemporary literacy. By combining explicit instruction with active engagement, collaborative learning, and critical inquiry, we believe our model offers a comprehensive way to prepare learners for the complexities of meaning-making in a rapidly changing world.

A significant challenge for literacy education today is the integration of digital tools and artificial intelligence (AI) into teaching and learning. These technologies have transformed the ways in which we engage with texts, shifting literacy practices beyond traditional reading and writing to encompass multimodal and algorithmically generated content. As these developments continue, educators must rethink how literacy is taught to ensure learners develop the critical skills needed to navigate, interpret, and produce digital texts responsibly.

In the next chapter, *Digital Literacy and Artificial Intelligence*, we will explore how AI is reshaping literacy practices. From generative text production to personalized learning environments, AI presents both opportunities and challenges for educators and learners. We will consider how these emerging technologies influence digital literacy, addressing ethical concerns such as bias, misinformation, and the implications of automated content creation. By engaging with these issues, we aim to provide a foundation for understanding the role of AI in shaping the future of literacy education.

Consolidate, Explore, Reflect, Do

We end this chapter with activities that will allow you to apply the concepts discussed in novel ways. Our goal is that these tasks will facilitate further exploration and reflection and will inspire your present and/or future teaching practice.

Task 1: Tracing Pedagogical Shifts in Literacy

To complete this task, you will work in groups of 5 to analyze and compare different literacy pedagogies and their evolution over time.

Step 1. Assign each member of your group one of the following pedagogical approaches: *didactic*, *authentic*, *functional*, *critical*, or *multiliteracies/LbyD*. Each member should conduct more in-depth research on their assigned approach and prepare a brief report on their findings. Possible information to include:

- key figures;
- main principles for literacy teaching and learning;
- theories that might ground the pedagogy or have given origin to it;
- sample classroom practices.

Also, group members might want to create a timeline that illustrates the historical evolution of the pedagogy assigned to them.

Step 2. Share your report and timeline with the members of your group. As a group, discuss and document the following:

- Which pedagogies do you recognize in your own education?
- What are the strengths and limitations of each approach?
- How do these approaches shape literacy learning in contemporary classrooms? Consider educational benefits and limitations.

Step 3. Compare insights with another group. Identify similarities and differences in your analyses and reflect on how different pedagogical approaches can intersect. Have you been exposed to the same pedagogies in your educational trajectories? Why?/Why not? Where might similarities and differences originate?

Task 2: Designing a Learning Task Using the LbyD Framework

To complete this task, you will work in groups of 3–4 to create a literacy-focused learning task that aligns with the LbyD framework.

Step 1. Examine the LbyD Pedagogical Intervention Planning Tool in Appendix 1. Discuss in your group:

- What are the key ideas in each section?
- What aspects of literacy learning and meaning-making can you connect each knowledge process to?

- Reflect on and share your collaborative understanding of the knowledge processes. Do you all have the same understanding? Can you think of examples of possible archetypal activities for each process? For inspiration, we recommend the tasks proposed by Lim et al., (2022, pp. 9–11) and Zapata (2018, 2022).

Step 2. Brainstorm a literacy-focused learning task using the framework. Your task should:

- engage students in experiencing (using personal knowledge or exploring something new);
- guide students in conceptualizing (connecting ideas or theories);
- encourage analyzing (examining meaning forms and/or functions—reference, agency, structure, context, and/or interest);
- support applying (demonstrating understanding in expected or creative ways).

Step 3. Using the planning tool in Appendix 1, outline a step-by-step lesson plan or pedagogical intervention incorporating these elements. Be specific about:

- the learning objectives and expected outcomes;
- the student population of focus;
- the types of texts, media, or activities involved;
- how students will interact in pairs or groups;
- how they will demonstrate their understanding.

Step 4. Exchange your results of your work with another group and provide feedback on:

- how well/effectively the task integrates the chosen knowledge processes;
- the clarity and engagement level of the task;
- possible improvements or extensions.

Step 5. Revise your task based on feedback and incorporate revisions in a new planning tool. Share it with the rest of the class to compile a class portfolio.

Task 3: Literacy in Everyday Life

To complete this task, you will work in small groups (3–4 students) to explore how literacy connects to real-world challenges and community engagement.

Step 1. Identify a real-world literacy challenge in your community/ies (e.g., barriers to accessing educational resources, misinformation, digital literacy gaps).
Step 2. Gather information to understand the issue's impact. For example, you could examine social media posts, news articles, local government reports, census data, etc.
Step 3. Identify one or two key issues, and with the members of your group, design a practical literacy intervention and create a multimodal blueprint of your idea. Possible ideas:

- a social media campaign raising awareness about misinformation;
- a community workshop to teach specific skills;
- a multimodal tool such as a brochure, infographic, or video.

Step 4. Share your blueprint with your classmates and reflect on the literacy pedagogies embedded in your work. What do you think might be the most appropriate approaches to inform real-world literacy practices?

Task 4: Analyzing Syncretic Approaches in Action

This activity involves the analysis of a research study carried out by Eve Gregory and her colleagues (Gregory et al., 2013) on syncretism, literacy, and pedagogy. You will work in groups of four.

Step 1. Read Gregory et al.'s work, which you can download using this link: `https://research.gold.ac.uk/id/eprint/8093/1/EDU_Gregory_et _al_2013.doc`.
Step 2. Each member of the group will focus on one case study from the article (e.g., Tanja, Isha, Adam, or Bema). Read your assigned section and highlight key ideas about:

- how children blend faith, culture, and literacy;
- the role of syncretic approaches in shaping their literacy learning;
- the impact of family, school, and community on their literacy practices.

Step 3. After you have finished your analysis of the case study assigned to you, get together with your group and discuss the following questions:

- How does the child in your case study integrate different linguistic and sociocultural influences?
- What pedagogical implications does this have for teaching literacy?
- How do syncretic approaches challenge traditional literacy education?

Step 4. As a group, create a mind map or infographic illustrating how syncretic approaches expand traditional views of literacy. Include examples from your case study and address broader implications for teaching.

Step 5. Present your mind map/infographic to the rest of your classmates. Together, reflect on the following:

- As pre- or in-service educators, how could you support syncretic literacy approaches in your classroom(s)?
- What role might syncretic approaches play in curriculum design and the enactment of inclusive classroom practices?

Task 5: Exploring Literacy Pedagogies in the Classroom

To complete this task, you will work in groups of 5. You will base your work on Figure 4.7.

Step 1. Look at Figure 4.7 and consider the classroom setup and the children's interactions. With the members of your group, analyze how literacy pedagogies influence learning in hands-on activities. Guiding questions:

- What kinds of materials are the children engaging with?

Figure 4.7 Primary school children completing a classroom task. (SOURCE: The Bakken Museum/Flickr/CC BY-SA 2.0).

- What skills are they using (e.g., problem-solving, collaboration, critical thinking)?
- What does this reveal about their learning process?

Now you will analyze the image, making connections with the pedagogies presented in this chapter.

Step 2. Each group member will analyze Figure 4.7 through one of the following literacy pedagogies:

- **Didactic Pedagogy**:
  - What structured elements, if any, do you observe?
  - What could the expected outcomes for this activity be if students' work were grounded in didactic literacy pedagogy?
- **Authentic Pedagogy**:
  - How might this activity connect to real-world tasks and the children's identity and lifeworld?
  - What could the expected outcomes for this activity be if students' work were grounded in authentic literacy pedagogy?

- **Functional Pedagogy**:
  - What is the social purpose of this learning experience?
  - How are students applying literacy or problem-solving strategies, and how could this be related to the expected outcomes for this activity?
- **Critical Pedagogy/Syncretic Approaches**:
  - What power dynamics are at play in this activity?
  - How might this task support identity, agency, and diverse perspectives (think of syncretic approaches)?
- **Multiliteracies/LbyD**:
  - What meaning forms are involved in the activity? What knowledge processes might this activity be structured around?
  - How does the activity engage multimodal literacy practices?

Each member should prepare a brief report summarizing their analyses and findings.

Step 3. Compare your findings. After each member presents their work, discuss and document the following:

- Are there any pedagogical approaches that might intersect in the observed activity? How?
- What is the main pedagogical approach reflected in the activity? Why? Explain your answer making reference to the tenets/principles/methods discussed in this chapter.
- Explain why the activity in Figure 4.7 can be considered an example of meaning-making as design.

Step 4. Compare your insights with another group's observations. Reflect on similarities and differences in interpretations. Where do you think they originate? Also consider how different pedagogical perspectives might change the way we understand classroom activities.

Step 5. Now, with the members of your group, considering the main pedagogical approach reflected in the activity (identified in **Step 3**), hypothesize on the educational context, background, and guidance involved in students' work. Address the following:

- educational context and type of classroom;
- a description of the activity: e.g., instructions offered to students to guide their work, time limits, objectives, expected outcomes;

- what meaning forms learners might employ to complete the task (consider their identities and lifeworlds);
- ways in which students' work could be assessed.

Once completed, share with and receive feedback from another group.

Task 6: Exploring Literacy in the Age of Generative AI

We end this section with a task that will help you prepare for the next chapter while establishing connections with this one. To complete your work, you will work in pairs. You will explore how generative artificial intelligence (GenAI) tools might shape literacy practices, comprehension, and meaning-making.

Step 1. Working with your partner, choose a type of text (e.g., news article, advertisements, or social media posts) and obtain both a human-written and an AI-generated version of it. To generate the AI text, you can choose one of the following tools:

- ChatGPT/OpenAI's GPT-5;
- Claude (Anthropic AI);
- Google Gemini.

Each of you should focus on one text type. Analyze the structure, vocabulary, clarity, and intended audience of both the human and AI-generated texts. Focus on the five functions of meaning we discussed in Chapter 3. You can use/adapt the questions in Figure 4.8. to carry out your analysis.

Step 2. Share your analyses and compare both texts. Focus on similarities and differences. Also, consider the following:

- Who has easy access to understanding AI-generated texts? Who might struggle with them?
- What background knowledge is required to interpret them accurately?
- How does AI reinforce or challenge power structures in literacy? (e.g., bias in AI-generated content, misinformation, accessibility, or influence on traditional literacy skills).

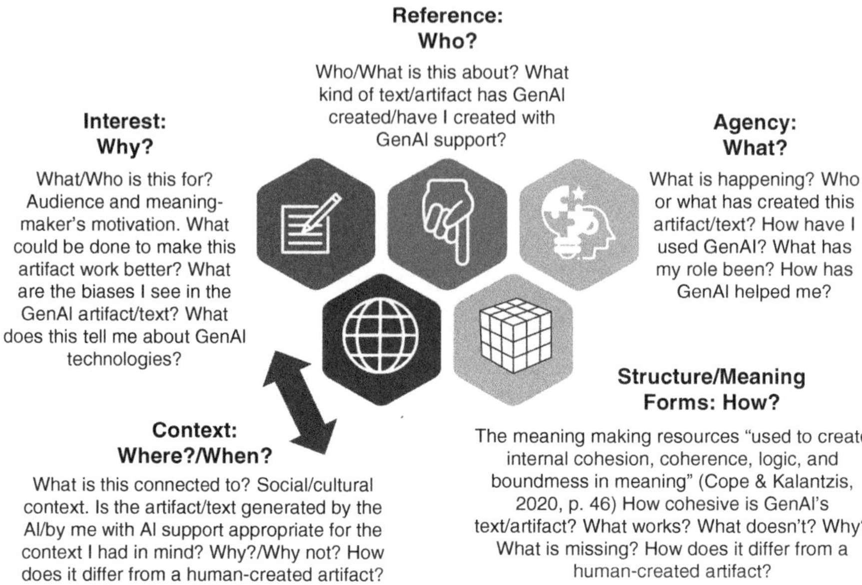

Figure 4.8 Functions of meaning: Questions to critically assess GenAI-supported meaning-making.

Step 3. Compare your findings with another pair and discuss how different literacy approaches (e.g., functional literacy, critical literacy, multiliteracies) might influence the way people understand and engage with GenAI-generated texts. For instance, consider the following:

- **Functional Literacy**: How does AI assist or hinder real-world literacy skills?
- **Critical Literacy**: How can AI-generated texts be analyzed for bias and ideology?
- **Multiliteracies/LbyD**: How does AI impact multimodal communication and global digital literacy?

Step 4. Go back to the personal definition of literacy you developed in Chapter 1 and modified in Chapters 2 and 3. What changes would you make to it based on the contents of this chapter and your experience in this activity? What has changed? What remains the same? Why? Think of literacy needs in connection with GenAI.

References

Apple, M. W. & Beane, J. A. (2007). *Democratic schools: Lessons in powerful education* ((2nd ed.). ed.). Heinemann.

Aristotle. (350 BCE). *Poetics*. The Internet Classics Archive, MIT. https://classics.mit.edu/Aristotle/poetics.1.1.html

Ayers, W. (2010). *To teach: The journey of a teacher* ((3rd ed.). Teachers College Press.

Bennett, W. (1984). *To reclaim a legacy: A report on the humanities in higher education*. National Endowment for the Humanities.

Callaghan, M. & Rothery, J. (1988). *Teaching factual writing: A Genre based approach (Report of the Disadvantaged Schools Program Literacy project)*. NSW Department of Education.

Cazden, C. B. (2001). *Classroom discourse: The language of teaching and learning*. Heinemann.

Cook-Gumperz, J. (2006). Literacy and schooling: An unchanging equation? In J. Cook-Gumperz (Ed.), *The social construction of literacy* (pp. 19–50). Cambridge University Press.

Cope, B. & Kalantzis, M. (1993). *The powers of literacy: Genre approaches to teaching writing*. Falmer Press.

Cope, B. & Kalantzis, M. (2006). From literacy to 'multiliteracies': Learning to mean in the new communications environment. *English Studies in Africa*, *49*(1), 23–45. https://doi.org/10.1080/00138390608691342

Cope, B. & Kalantzis, M. (2015a). Assessment and pedagogy in the era of machine-mediated learning. In T. Dragonas, K. J. Gergen, S. McNamee, & E. Tseliou (Eds.), *Education as social construction: Contributions to theory, research, and practice* (pp. 350–374). Worldshare Books.

Cope, B. & Kalantzis, M. (2015b). The things you do to know: An introduction to the pedagogy of multiliteracies. In B. Cope & M. Kalantzis (Eds.), *A pedagogy of multiliteracies: Learning by Design* (pp. 1–36). Palgrave Macmillan.

Cope, B. & Kalantzis, M. (2017). Conceptualizing e-Learning. In B. Cope & M. Kalantzis (Eds.), *ELearning ecologies* (pp. 1–45). Routledge.

Cope, B. & Kalantzis, M. (2019). Education 2.0: Artificial intelligence and the end of the test. *Beijing International Review of Education*, *1*(2-3), 528–543. https://brill.com/view/journals/bire/1/2-3/article-p528_528.xml?language=en

Cope, B. & Kalantzis, M. (2023). Towards education justice: Multiliteracies revisited. In G. C. Zapata, M. Kalantzis, & B. Cope (Eds.), *Multiliteracies in international educational contexts: Towards education justice* (pp. 1–33). Routledge.

Cuban, L. (1993). *How teachers taught: Constancy and change in American classrooms, 1890–1990*. Teachers College Press.

Dewey, J. (1915/1956). *The school and society*. University of Chicago Press.

Dewey, J. (1938/1963). *Experience and education.* Collier Books.
Dewey, J. & Dewey, E. (1915). *Schools of tomorrow.* Dutton.
Engelmann, S. (1992). *War against the schools' academic child abuse.* Halcyon House.
Freire, P. & Macedo, D. (1987). *Literacy: Reading the word and the world.* Bergin & Garvey.
Goeke, J. L. (2009). *Explicit instruction.* Merrill.
Goodman, K. S. (2005). *What's whole in whole language.* RDR Books.
Graff, H. J. (1979). *The literacy myth: Literacy and social structure in the nineteenth-century city.* Academic Press.
Graff, H. J. (1987). *The legacies of literacy: Continuities and contradictions in Western culture and society.* Indiana University Press.
Graves, D. H. (2003). *Writing: Teachers and children at work.* Heinemann.
Green, B. & Beavis, C. (2013). Literacy education in the age of new media. In K. Hall, T. Cremin, B. Comber, & L. C. Moll (Eds.), *International handbook of research on children's literacy, learning, and culture* (pp. 42–53). John Wiley & Sons.
Gregory, E., Volk, D., & Long, S. (2013). Guest editors' introduction: Syncretism and syncretic literacies. *Journal of Early Childhood Literacy, 13*(3), 309–321. https://doi.org/10.1177/1468798413478025
Gutiérrez, K. D. (2008). Developing a sociocritical literacy in the third space. *Reading Research Quarterly, 43*(2), 148–164. https://doi.org/10.1598/RRQ.43.2.3
Gutiérrez, K. D. (2014). Integrative research review: Syncretic approaches to literacy learning. Leveraging horizontal knowledge and expertise. In P. Dunston, L. Gambrell, K. Headley, S. Fullerton, & P. Stecker (Eds.), *63rd Literacy Research Association yearbook* (pp. 48–61). Literacy Research Association.
Halliday, M. A. K. (1975). *Learning how to mean: Explorations in the development of language.* Edward Arnold.
Halliday, M. A. K. (2002). In J. J. Webster (Ed.), *On grammar* (Vol. 1). Continuum.
Halliday, M. A. K. (2009). Context of culture and of situation. In J. J. Webster (Ed.), *The essential Halliday* (pp. 55–84). Continuum.
Halliday, M. A. K. & Hasan, R. (1985). *Language, context, and text: Aspects of language in a social-semiotic perspective.* Deakin University Press.
Hirsch, E. D. (1988). *Cultural literacy: What every American needs to know.* Vintage Books.
Kalantzis, M. & Cope, B. (2025). Multiliteracies since social media and artificial intelligence. *Harvard Educational Review, 95*(1), 135–151. https://doi.org/10.17763/1943-5045-95.1.135

Kalantzis, M. & Cope, B. (2012). *New learning: Elements of a science of education*. Cambridge University Press.
Kalantzis, M., Cope, B., & the Learning by Design Project Group. (2005). *Learning by Design*. Victorian Schools Innovation Commission and Common Ground Publishing.
Kalantzis, M., Cope, B., Chan, E., & Dalley-Trim, L. (2016). *Literacies* (2nd ed.). Cambridge University Press.
Kirschner, P. A., Sweller, J., & Clark, R. E. (2006). Why minimal guidance during instruction does not work: An analysis of the failure of constructivist, discovery, problem-based, experiential, and inquiry-based teaching. *Educational Psychologist*, *41*(2), 75–86. https://doi.org/10.1207/s15326985ep4102_1
Kress, G. (1993). Against arbitrariness: The social production of the sign as a foundational issue in critical discourse analysis. *Discourse and Society*, *4*(2), 169–191. http://www.jstor.org/stable/42888774
Lim, F. V., Cope, B., & Kalantzis, M. (2022). A metalanguage for learning: Rebalancing the cognitive with the socio-material. *Frontiers in Communication*, *7*, 830613. https://doi.org/10.3389/fcomm.2022.830613
Martin, J. R. (1986). *Writing to mean: Teaching genres across the curriculum*. Applied Linguistics Association of Australia.
Martin, J. R. (1997). Analyzing genre: Functional parameters. In F. Christie & J. R. Martin (Eds.), *Genres and institutions: Social processes in the workplace and school* (pp. 3–39). Cassell Academic.
Moll, L. C., Amanti, C., Neff, D., & Gonzalez, N. (1992). Funds of knowledge for teaching: Using a qualitative approach to connect homes and classrooms. *Theory Into Practice*, *31*(2), 132–141. https://www.jstor.org/stable/1476399
Montessori, M. (1912/1964). *The Montessori method*. Schocken Books.
Montessori, M. (1917/1973). *The Montessori elementary material*. Schocken Books.
Murray, D. M. (1982). *Learning by teaching: Selected articles on writing and teaching*. Boynton/Cook.
New London Group. (1996). A pedagogy of multiliteracies: Designing social futures. *Harvard Educational Review*, *66*, 60–92. https://doi.org/10.17763/haer.66.1.17370n67v22j160u
Ong, W. J. (1958). *Ramus, method and the decay of dialogue*. Harvard University Press.
Schoenfeld, A. H. & Pearson, D. P. (2009). The reading and math wars. In G. Sykes, B. Schneider, & D. N. Plank (Eds.), *Handbook of education policy research* (pp. 560–580). Routledge.
Snyder, I. (2008). *The literacy wars: Why teaching children to read and write is a battleground in Australia*. Allen & Unwin.

Tzirides, A. O., Cope, B., & Kalantzis, M. (2023). Contemporary contexts for learning: An overview. In R. J. Tierney, F. Rizvi, & K. Erkican (Eds.), *International Encyclopedia of Education* (4th ed.), (pp. 258–266). Elsevier. https://doi.org/10.1016/B978-0-12-818630-5.14034-5

Vygotsky, L. S. (1978). *Mind in society: The development of higher psychological processes.* Harvard University Press.

Zammit, K. (2010). The new learning environment framework: Scaffolding the development of multiliterate students. *Pedagogies: An International Journal, 5*(4), 325–337. https://doi.org/10.1080/1554480X.2010.509479

Zapata, G. C. (2018). A match made in Heaven: An introduction to Learning by Design and its role in heritage language education. In G. C. Zapata & M. Lacorte (Eds.), *Multiliteracies pedagogy and language learning: Teaching Spanish to heritage speakers* (pp. 1–26). Palgrave Macmillan. https://doi.org/10.1007/978-3-319-63103-5_1

Zapata, G. C. (2022). *Learning by Design and second language teaching: Theory, research, and practice.* Routledge.

Chapter 5
Digital Literacy and Artificial Intelligence

Introduction

In our discussion so far, we have traced the changing contours of literacy—from its historical roots to the expanding possibilities of multimodal meaning-making; from traditional pedagogies to reflexive, learner-centered approaches. This chapter builds on those foundations by situating literacy within the rapidly evolving contexts of digital media, the internet, and emerging generative artificial intelligence (GenAI) technologies. We begin by examining how the internet and digital tools and media have amplified multimodality and participatory culture, reshaping both social structures and educational practices. We then move to e-learning ecologies, exploring how ubiquitous computing and collaborative knowledge production can enrich literacy learning, while also considering the persistence of inequities and the power imbalances that shape these digital spaces.

Literacies in the Age of AI: Teaching and Learning in the Digital Era, First Edition. Gabriela C. Zapata, Bill Cope, and Mary Kalantzis.

Against this backdrop, we turn to GenAI—both, as discussed in Chapter 1, a textual and multimodal technology that complicates our understanding of meaning-making and the way in which we conceptualize literacy education. In this chapter, we argue that while GenAI tools promise new opportunities for active, inclusive, and personalized literacy learning, they also raise serious concerns, such as algorithmic bias and fake content, as well as questions of privacy, security, and corporate control. We also examine the evolving roles of teachers in guiding learners through these challenges and emphasize the need to develop both their and their students' AI literacy as an essential dimension of digital citizenship. Through this lens, we explore how education can remain responsive to shifting technological landscapes, ensuring that learners not only master emerging tools but also critically and effectively navigate the power structures and ethical dilemmas originating from their use.

Digital Media, Participation, and Multimodal Meaning-Making

As discussed in Chapters 1 and 2, the advent of digital technologies in the 20th century transformed the production, reproduction, and distribution of meaning, overcoming prior constraints deriving from our historical reliance on writing as the predominant mode of communication. As digitalization progressed, different forms of meaning converged into a unified system based on binary notation (see Chapter 1, pages 10–11). This has enabled computing machines to process text and images as two-dimensional pixel arrays, create three-dimensional (3D) virtual spaces, facilitate 3D object capture and printing, and integrate wearables and video for bodily representation. Sound and speech are similarly encoded through digital audio (Cope & Kalantzis, 2017, 2024a).

These changes have reshaped knowledge production, cultural participation, and meaning-making. New media and social platforms have cultivated a participatory culture that reconfigures cultural and epistemic agency (Haythornthwaite, 2009; Jenkins, 2006;

Lessig, 2008). The boundaries between consumers and creators have blurred, as social media posts and smartphone images now serve as primary news sources. Traditional news outlets no longer monopolize information dissemination; instead, individuals capture and share real-time events. The dominance of mass media has been disrupted by the participatory nature of the social web, where anyone can act as both a reporter and a creator.

Beyond major news events, participatory media also extend to personal experiences—documenting daily activities, sharing opinions, and engaging in interactive discourse. The once rigid hierarchies of cognitive and cultural labor have dissolved, as readers become writers and viewers become image-makers. This shift has given rise to new forms of social reciprocity—liking to be liked, following to be followed, and friending to be friended. This dynamic oscillates between mutual affirmation and self-exhibition, reinforcing the idea that everyone contributes to meaning, culture, and knowledge. The traditional distinctions between creation and consumption have collapsed, merging into an ongoing, dialogical process.

However, these changes have also been characterized by inherent contradictions. While new media encourage participation, they also subject users to extensive surveillance, whether for commercial profit or regulatory control. Tech corporations, including those who own social media platforms, extract significant financial value from user-generated content, capitalizing on participatory labor without compensating individuals. The economic power amassed by platforms such as Facebook and X underscores the extent to which user engagement translates into corporate profit. Individuals generate epistemic and cultural value, yet the vast majority receive no direct financial remuneration, raising critical concerns about agency and exploitation (Kalantzis-Cope, 2016). All these aspects of today's communication landscape have, of course, become an essential part of what we do in our classrooms, particularly when it comes to learning how to critically understand who is accessing the content we create and why (more on this later in the chapter).

Also important in the digital communication reality in which we live is multimodal meaning-making, deeply embedded in the materiality of industrial design. Digital devices—phones, tablets, and laptops—function as cognitive prostheses, supporting both individual thinking and remote communication. The convergence of meaning forms such as text, image, sound, body, and speech within a single platform or digital artifact has transformed how meaning is created, shared, and consumed.

Given these changes, as posited in previous chapters, education must evolve beyond its traditional focus on handwriting and word processing. Learners need to critically engage with 21st-century technologies, not only utilizing multimodal tools for meaning-making but also understanding the issues of power, agency, and economic exploitation embedded within these technologies—crucially important, as we will see, when it comes to GenAI. This shift, which will be addressed in more detail in later in the chapter, is both pedagogically and practically necessary to prepare students for an increasingly complex, interconnected digital world (Cope & Kalantzis, 2019; Kalantzis & Cope, 2025).

The Internet and Mass Connectivity

Embedded in the changes discussed in the previous section is, of course, the emergence of the internet as a ubiquitous, multimodal medium of communication, tracing its origins to ARPANET in 1969 (Figure 5.1) and maturing into a mass phenomenon by the early 1990s (Abbate, 1999; Paloque-Bergès & Schafer, 2019). The ubiquity of the internet has ensured that multimodal communication channels, integrating text, images, audio, and video, are accessible to virtually everyone, fostering mass connectivity and resulting in profound transformations at all societal levels, including education. That is, this vast networked availability has not only accelerated the dissemination of diverse content but also enriched the ways in which knowledge is constructed, shared, and contested. Mass connectivity now empowers individuals to engage in an ongoing process of creation, critique, and co-construction of meaning. In this new environment, expertise and authority are no longer confined to

Figure 5.1 ARPANET first router (SOURCE: Steve Jurvetson/Wikimedia Commons/CC BY 2.0).

a select few but are distributed across an expansive, interconnected digital public (Cope & Kalantzis, 2009).

In educational contexts, the confluence of ubiquity and multimodality has given rise to collaborative learning environments that transcend traditional classroom boundaries. Learners can now access a vast array of resources and perspectives, thereby having the opportunity to cultivate critical digital literacy skills and participate actively in knowledge-making processes. This fluid, interactive model of learning—enabled by the mass connectivity of the internet—blurs the lines between formal and informal education and supports more inclusive, dynamic, and learner-centered pedagogical practices (Cope & Kalantzis, 2017, 2019; Kalantzis et al., 2005).

Socioculturally, the effects of mass connectivity are equally transformative. Online communities—characterized by their decentralized and dynamic nature—have reshaped how identities are formed and cultural capital is negotiated. These platforms facilitate the co-creation of meaning through sustained dialog and interaction, acting as fertile grounds for social innovation and enabling individuals to challenge traditional norms and redefine social values (Cope & Kalantzis, 2017). Moreover, the integration of multimodal channels amplifies these effects by allowing for more nuanced and context-sensitive expressions of cultural identity and civic engagement.

The intersection of mass connectivity and the ubiquity of the internet thus reconfigures both social interactions and educational practices. By dismantling conventional hierarchies and fostering a participatory culture, these digital affordances open new avenues for collective knowledge construction and social inclusion. In the following section, our discussion will further explore how digital environments can be harnessed to create dynamic, inclusive, and flexible learning spaces that respond to the evolving demands of literacy in contemporary society.

Reflexive Pedagogy and E-Learning Ecologies: Digital Affordances for Literacy Learning

Building on our discussion of reflexive literacy pedagogy in Chapter 4, we now extend our focus into its core tenets and transformative potential. This approach recalibrates the balance of agency so that learners assume considerable responsibility for epistemic action while operating within an activity sequence carefully scaffolded by the instructor. Central to our ergative *Learning by Design* (LbyD) pedagogical framework (see pages 160–162), reflexive literacy pedagogy envisions knowledge as a dialogical process characterized by continuous, bidirectional exchanges among instructors, peers, and the broader community. Rather than relying solely on the singular, monological voice of a lecturer or textbook writer, this approach draws on diverse, authentic resources, from the vast repositories of the internet to the rich, lived experiences that learners bring to the classroom (Cope & Kalantzis, 2023; Lim et al., 2022; Zapata, 2018, 2022).

A redistribution of agency thus occurs between instructor and learner, granting the learner significant latitude and responsibility for epistemic action, albeit within an activity sequence that the instructor has carefully scaffolded. Knowledge activities unfold in a dialogical manner, featuring reciprocal movement between instructor and students as well as among the students themselves.

This implies that the instructional emphasis shifts to the artifacts and representations of knowledge that learners construct, and the processes involved in their construction. In an era where personal digital devices provide constant access to information, the role of long-term memory is diminished. Although long-term memory will naturally develop, it becomes merely an incidental by-product of deep disciplinary engagement. There is no longer a pressing need to stress long-term memory in pedagogy. When a fact is momentarily forgotten, it can be instantly retrieved; if a procedure is not recalled, an app can execute it—a calculation, a sequence of directions, a data mashup. Thus, the objectives of learning transform in an age of ubiquitous cognitive prostheses, with the focus moving away from pure cognition to the creation of epistemic artifacts (Cope & Kalantzis, 2015, 2019, 2023).

Also crucial, as discussed in Section "Digital Media, Participation, and Multimodal Meaning Making", are the social origins of knowledge. Knowledge is now not merely about what I know individually; it encompasses my ability to navigate the expansive epistemic world available at my fingertips, to critically determine what is significant, to acknowledge the social provenance of my knowledge through citations and links, and to collaborate with others in creating collective knowledge where the whole exceeds the sum of its parts. It also involves my capacity for synthesis and the creative extension of socially acquired knowledge.

We believe that reflexive pedagogy can address the shifting balance of agency between instructors and learners, the reduced emphasis on memorization in an age of instant access to information, and the understanding that knowledge is socially constructed and dialogical. That is, by empowering learners to create and share knowledge artifacts that draw on diverse resources, reflexive pedagogy can foster experiences that are more engaging—since they involve learners in genuine, agency-rich activities—while also promoting deeper understanding, using resources more efficiently through on-demand access to knowledge, and responding equitably to a broad range of learner profiles. In the sections that follow, we illustrate how these outcomes can be realized through seven affordances introduced by digital media—*ubiquitous learning, active knowledge production, multimodal knowledge representations, recursive feedback, collaborative intelligence, metacognitive reflection*, and *differentiated learning*. We have summarized these principles in Figure 5.2, and we will discuss each of them separately as follows, before turning to the additional transformative potential of GenAI.

Ubiquitous Learning

Ubiquitous learning refers to the ability to learn anytime and anywhere (Cope & Kalantzis, 2009). Earlier iterations of formal out-of-school learning—such as homework, self-paced textbooks, and distance education—hinted at this concept. Today, ubiquitous learning builds on the notion of "ubiquitous computing" (Twidale, 2009). Once relegated to the realm of science fiction, ubiquitous computing has become a pervasive reality with the advent of laptops, tablets, and smartphones; it now appears in virtually every store, workplace, and even in every handbag or pocket. However, its integration into schools remains a more recent development, and when it does occur, it is often implemented in ways that fail to fully exploit the dynamic knowledge potentials offered by new media.

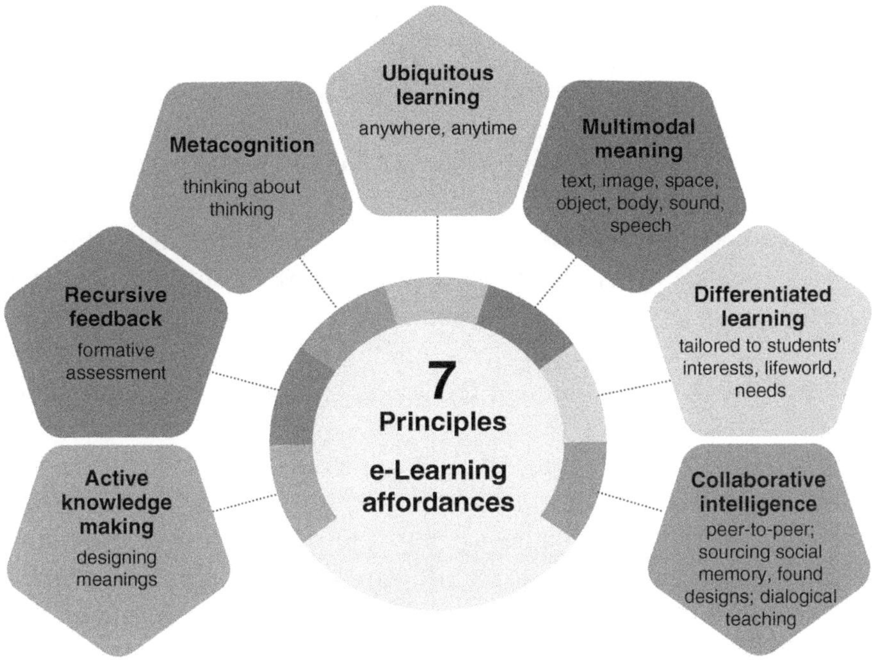

Figure 5.2 Principles of e-learning affordances.

The advent of internet-mediated computing—and particularly innovations such as "Web 2.0" (O'Reilly, 2005), "cloud computing" (Reese, 2009), and "semantic publishing" (Cope et al., 2011a)—opened up possibilities that would be truly transformative for education. Ubiquitous learning environments can now offer a range of novel opportunities, from enabling students to discover multimodal content sourced from a diverse array of authentic materials to supporting intensive, simultaneous interactions where every member of the learning community is actively involved. They also allow for more responsive feedback and assessment systems, particularly in the era of GenAI (more on this later).

Perhaps the most significant change is that the traditional constraints of time and space in education become irrelevant. In the past, learning was confined to the physical boundaries of the classroom and the rigid schedules imposed by timetables. With ubiquitous learning, all the activities typical of a conventional classroom—and more—can be carried out anywhere, at any time (as was evident during the COVID-19 mandatory lockdowns). Learners equipped with ubiquitous computing technology can engage in the same acts of knowledge creation and interaction, whether they are inside or outside the classroom.

Moreover, the factor of scale is effectively neutralized. Whether a class consists of three students or 3,000, the configuration can remain consistent—be it the video lecture, textbook, and test routine typical of didactic pedagogy, or the more dynamic, reflexive interactions that include peer feedback, collaborative writing, and threaded discussions.

Does this herald the end of the traditional school? Not necessarily. Schools remain a valuable setting for technology-mediated learning, primarily because society continues to entrust them with the duty of caring for children during designated times, thereby enabling parents to work. However, the concept of the classroom as a broader learning ecology may evolve to accommodate either larger or smaller groups of students than historically observed.

Multimodal Meaning

As discussed since the beginning of this book, today's communication is inherently multimodal, as we routinely combine meaning forms such as text, still images, moving images, sound, and speech in meaning-making. Devices like phones, tablets, and laptops serve as our cognitive prostheses for multimodal communication, supporting both representation—by bolstering our individual thinking—and communication—by connecting us through telepresent messaging. With the capability for fully multimodal knowledge representation at our fingertips, we can offer these tools to our learners. Our times demand that we move beyond the traditional handwritten book or word processor. Instead, students need to engage with 21st-century tools and media. This shift is a pedagogical imperative as much as it is a practical one.

Effective multimodal communication entails multimodal literacy, defined by van Leeuwen (2017) as

> the ability to use and combine different [meaning forms] in ways that are appropriate to the given [social] context, both in the sense of the context-bound rules and conventions that may apply and in the sense of the unique demands made by each specific situation. (p. 18)

In educational contexts, developing multimodal literacy involves explicit pedagogical strategies that equip students with a shared vocabulary for critically deconstructing multimodal artifacts, understanding not only the affordances and limitations of different meaning forms (see Chapter 2) but also meaning functions that these forms realize (see Chapter 3). And, of course, being multimodally literate also means students need to be able to design coherent, communicatively effective multimodal artifacts.

Moreover, the integration of multimodal literacy into curriculum, pedagogy, and assessment practices can foster more inclusive and equitable learning environments. A focus on multimodal communication can not only bridge the gap between students' diverse lifeworld experiences and formal educational practices but can also equip all learners with the essential skills to navigate and contribute to the digital age. We believe instruction grounded in LbyD's reflexive pedagogy (see Chapter 4, pages 139–140) can facilitate the achievement of these goals (see also Lim et al. 2022; Zapata, 2022, and the example we offer in Task 1, on pages 142–145).

Active Knowledge-Making

Since the advent of mass-institutionalized education in the 19th century, the typical mode of acquiring knowledge has followed a fixed configuration: A bureaucratic system prescribes specific content areas in the syllabus; textbooks lay out that content; teachers recite the material; and teacher–student question-and-answer routines take place. Also, students fill in answers in workbooks, read texts and respond to comprehension questions, and write brief pieces to demonstrate what they have learned. These practices were predictable and straightforward. Essentially, this traditional classroom represents an epistemic architecture built on a particular communications technology—one defined by the classroom's physical walls, where approximately 30 children gather and where only one person, be it the teacher or a student, speaks at any given time.

In this setting, teachers and textbooks deliver concise representations of the world—whether in history, language arts, mathematics, or another subject—in the form of monologs, a singular and synoptic voice emanating from either the teacher or the textbook author. Students read silently, write quietly, and avoid lateral "copying" glances as they work through worksheets or answer quizzes. These processes are almost solitary, even when learners are physically close to one another. The aim is for facts to be memorized and for theorems to be learned so that unequivocal answers can be deduced. These memories, along with the application of the learned theorems, are then measured in tests that yield right or wrong answers at the end of a lesson, week, chapter, or course.

Within this knowledge architecture, reflective of didactic pedagogy (see Chapter 4), students are configured primarily as passive consumers. The knowledge transmitted to them is presented as a univocal narrative—declarative knowledge—characterized by unquestioning compliance in the face of epistemic authority, a lack of critical autonomy, and an absence of both epistemic and social responsibility. This approach may have suited an era of industrial discipline and mass conformity, aligning with the cultural logic of broadcast or mass media. In that older cognitive-epistemic regime, the capacity of a speaker addressing a large audience to receive feedback was extremely limited—a carefully vetted letter to the editor or an occasional call-in to a talk-show host, one interaction at a time. Discursively, this relationship was modeled on the image of a single student answering the teacher's question on behalf of the entire class, with moments of participation serving merely as tokens for rhetorical effect. Participation in media and discourse was, at best, vicarious.

In today's digital world, however, the sensibilities, habits of mind, and skills fostered by heavily didactic pedagogy are ill-suited. New media afford the opportunity to create learning environments in schools where students function as knowledge producers just as much as they are consumers. In fact, new media imply that this is the direction education should take, ensuring that it remains relevant and aligned with the media sensibilities of contemporary learners.

In order to bring their informal, digitally flooded world into formal instruction, it is imperative for learners to

- critically examine multiple, multimodal sources, dissecting the various perspectives embedded in these sources and even conducting their own observations to act as researchers;
- collaborate with peers in producing knowledge, working together as co-authors, peer reviewers, and readers and discussants of shared works; and
- generate original knowledge, not only by applying what has been learned but also being able to incorporate their unique life experiences and viewpoints as appropriate.

Learning that fosters this type of active learner engagement is supported by new media, which can supplement the predominantly hierarchical knowledge flows of our recent past—from expert to novice, from authority to the authorized, from teacher to student—with structures that promote lateral co-creation of knowledge. This shift aligns well with broader contemporary changes in the "balance of agency" (Kalantzis & Cope, 2012), where consumers are becoming "prosumers" through customizable products and interfaces, where reading (as a form of consumption) intermingles with writing (as a form of production) in the new media, where amateurs and professionals are scarcely distinguishable in web-based knowledge spaces like Wikipedia, and, more recently, GenAI platforms, and where the narrative pleasure in gaming is not merely vicarious as it is in television or cinema, because now the learner is positioned as a character sharing responsibility for the story's outcome.

Recursive Feedback

Old media operated in a linear fashion—information and culture flowed in one direction from the television studio to the viewer, from the newspaper office to the reader, from the radio studio to the listener, and from the movie lot to the audience. In contrast, new media are inherently recursive. At the outset of the computer age, Norbert Weiner (1965 [1948]) sought to encapsulate the logic of self-regulating systems, both mechanical and biological, under the term *cybernetics*. Much like the Greek *kybernetes*, or oarsman, who continually adjusts the rudder to keep a vessel on course, new media function in a dialogical and recursive manner, blurring the lines between creator and consumer. Feedback permeates these systems. For instance, web reputation and moderation systems introduce social filters to the feedback process (Farmer & Glass, 2010), while ubiquitous devices enable the "quantified self," providing continuous feedback on everything from navigation and exercise routines to the social reach of a posted message.

In traditional schools, feedback processes were as linear as old media, beginning with the curriculum and culminating in a test. In this model, the summative test (i.e., an assessment conducted at the end of an instructional period to evaluate cumulative student learning) is an afterthought, a managerial judgment that occurs at the end of a lesson, week, chapter, or course, offering little immediate support for learning. It also conceptualizes knowledge in a peculiar way, employing devices that are markedly different from the everyday processes of engaging with knowledge. Assessment in this regime often resembles a game where students are tasked with distinguishing isolated correct responses from trick "distractors" that are designed to seem plausible yet are deliberately incorrect. In recent decades, an obsession with testing for institutional accountability has amplified the shortcomings of these linear methods (Cope & Kalantzis, 2017, 2019).

New media technologies, however, provide an alternative approach to assessment (Cope et al., 2011b). They allow for a renewed emphasis on formative assessment—ongoing, immediate evaluations that contribute directly and constructively to student learning (Black & Wiliam, 1998; Wiliam, 2011). In today's era of social knowledge technologies and GenAI, no learning environment should be without ever-present feedback mechanisms, both machine-generated and machine-mediated social feedback. When it comes time for summative assessment, we can simply offer a retrospective overview of student progress, drawing on all the data gathered from formative assessments. In fact, it may not be long before we are able to do away with traditional summative assessment altogether, eliminating its peculiar artifacts and negative institutional impacts, because so much assessment is now occurring continuously—recursive feedback from numerous perspectives on every digitally mediated learning activity.

Moreover, new media have broadened the range of assessment modalities. Machines can now provide computable feedback using natural language processing algorithms, and there is also the possibility for constant, machine-mediated human feedback, "crowdsourced" from teachers, peers, and the students themselves (Surowiecki, 2004). And, of course, these possibilities have been exponentially expanded in the realm of GenAI (Figure 5.3; Cope & Kalantzis, 2024b; Dai et al., 2023; Steiss et al., 2024; Tzirides et al., 2023, 2024a, 2024b; Zapata et al., 2024, 2025a).

In technology-supported environments, teachers and learners alike are engaged in assessing learning, and each perspective contributes unique value. With varied perspectives, the feedback can be more extensive, thought-provoking, and timely than what even the most diligent solitary teacher marker might offer. By moderating and calibrating different ratings through inter-rater reliability processes, the overall assessment can become even more reliable. Distributing assessment responsibilities in this way not only makes the process more explicit and transparent but also democratizes it, ensuring that both teachers and students evaluate learning using the same criteria and methods.

Even survey-based assessments retain value when used formatively, especially with recent advances in survey psychometrics, such as computer-adaptive and diagnostic testing (Chang, 2012, 2015).

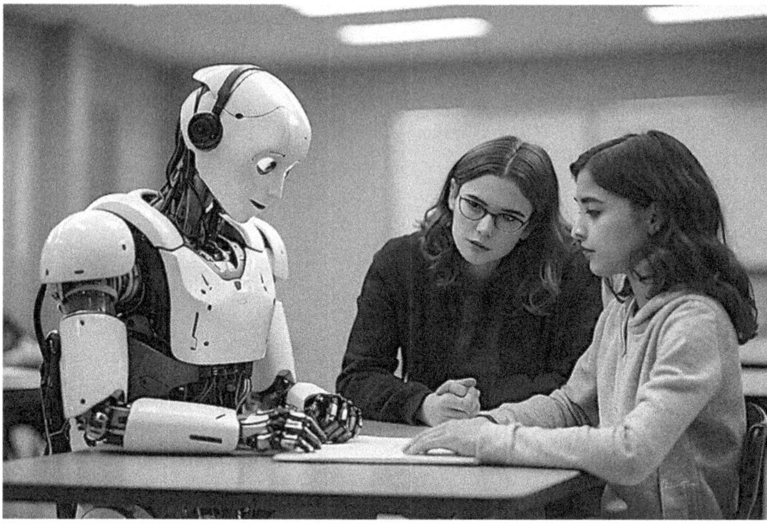

Figure 5.3 AI-generated representation of a student receiving formative feedback from a peer and a GenAI pedagogical agent. (SOURCE: Zapata et al., (2024)/University of Nottingham/CC BY 4.0). SOURCE: Zapata et al., (2024)/University of Nottingham/CC BY 4.0.

The convergence of these innovations has given rise to what is known as "big data" in education, along with the emerging field of "learning analytics." Leaders in this area argue that educational data mining and learning analytics have the potential to uncover data that has previously gone unseen, unnoticed, and thus unexploited (Bienkowski et al., 2012). West (2012), for instance, draws our attention to the "real-time" assessment potential for improved research, evaluation, and accountability through data mining, analytics and web dashboards. Behrens and DiCerbo (2013) contend that technology expands our conception of evidence: digital systems capture streams or traces of data from students' interactions, providing insights into the processes that lead to the final product—the only portion traditionally graded. As our activities become increasingly digital, the necessity for separate assessment tasks should be increasingly questioned.

Learning analytics can also better capture evidence of deep learning than standardized assessments, which have traditionally measured knowing in terms of long-term memory or the ability to select the correct answer (Knight et al., 2013). As Behrens and DiCerbo (2013), DiCerbo and Behrens, (2014) suggest, the shift to big data in education moves us from an item-based paradigm, where questions have fixed answers, to an activity-based paradigm, where learning actions provide multidimensional evidence of behavioral attributes. By raising evidentiary standards, therefore, educational data sciences can begin to draw conclusions about complex dimensions of learning, such as mastery of disciplinary practices, intricate epistemic performances, collaborative knowledge work, and multimodal knowledge representations. This may be achieved through a richer data environment and more sophisticated analytical tools, many of which can be preemptively integrated into the learning environment itself via "evidence-centered design" (Mislevy et al., 2012; Rupp et al., 2012). And, of course, as previously posited and later discussed in more depth, GenAI expands these possibilities into yet unknown but possibly instructionally richer realms.

So, what might we accomplish with these comprehensive assessment modes that extensively employ new media? One possibility is to reframe our assessment question from "How did we do?" to "How are we doing?"—with "we" encompassing the learner, the class, and the teacher (and possibly a GenAI pedagogical agent). In this model, assessment is not a retrospective, managerial process focused solely on results but a formative evaluation centered on ongoing progress and improvement, framed in the present continuous tense. Furthermore, in addition to measuring individual work, we can also assess social interactions and peer contributions through the feedback they provide. In other words, we can evaluate both learning interactions *and* learning artifacts. We can build recursive feedback systems—feedback that is itself subject to further feedback—and calibrate ratings through inter-rater reliability calculations. This approach enables crowdsourced assessments to become increasingly reliable, perhaps even more so than isolated expert evaluations.

We might even take a bold step toward a "no failure" educational paradigm, wherein students can continuously receive feedback until they achieve a standard of excellence. This contrasts sharply with the traditional bell-curve distribution, where only a few succeed while most are relegated to mediocrity or failure. A culture of mutually supportive, constructive feedback not only reflects the ideals of a knowledge economy—where teamwork and networked collaborations are highly valued—but also supports both the stronger and the weaker learners. It establishes community standards, where those who struggle can learn from exemplary works showcased in a shared web portfolio. In this feedback-on-feedback model, where constructive interactions are measured and valued, peers receive "help credits" rather than the competitive, zero-sum rewards typical of conventional grading systems (Cope & Kalantzis, 2019; Tzirides et al., 2023).

Collaborative Intelligence

Traditionally, schooling has been premised on the idea of individual intelligence, narrowly defined as personal memory and the mechanical ability to deduce. Yet the human mind is inherently social (Gee, 2014). Our cognitive capacities are embedded in the language we inherit and the perceptual frameworks we learn. In essence, intelligence is our ability to draw upon an ever-available social memory and utilize shared logics and computational tools. It is the collective capability that emerges when individuals work together within communities of practice.

Today, ubiquitous computing and the social web have made externalized memory and powerful computational tools accessible on an unprecedented scale. Meanwhile, work, public life, and community activities are increasingly driven by collaboration. In the realm of new media, peer-to-peer collaborations—ranging from platforms like Wikipedia to the vast video repository of YouTube—are prime examples of massive social cooperation. This renders the old model of closed-book exams and isolated, individual student work increasingly outdated.

As students engage with their schoolwork in digital environments, the emphasis shifts from mere memorization to focusing on the knowledge artifacts they create using new media. These artifacts might include a science experiment report, an information piece on a social phenomenon, a history essay, an artwork accompanied by exegesis, a video narrative, a business case study, a worked example in mathematics or statistics, an executable computer code with user stories, or a GenAI-generated image resulting from trial and error reflected in several prompt iterations. These are the signature knowledge artifacts of our era.

In the digital age, learners construct their knowledge representations using rich, multimodal resources—text, images, diagrams, tables, audio, video, hyperlinks, infographics, and interactive data visualizations. These outputs are clearly the products of distributed cognition, where not only the final artifacts but also the processes behind their creation—such as source selection, peer feedback, and collaborative production, including perhaps GenAI assistance—carry significant evidentiary weight. They provide tangible evidence of high-quality disciplinary practice, collaborative effort, the ability to locate secondary sources, and the capacity to generate original knowledge from observations and interactions, as well as the use of GenAI technologies.

These artifacts are identifiable, assessable, and measurable, with verifiable provenance. Every step in their construction can be tracked, and the tools for measuring them have expanded to include natural language processing, time-on-task analysis, peer, GenAI, and self-reviews, annotations, and navigation paths through sources. In this way, the volume and variety of data related to knowledge work have increased dramatically.

Our evidentiary focus may thus shift. We no longer need to chase after elusive constructs like the "theta" of latent cognitive traits in item response theory or the "g" factor of intelligence measured by IQ tests. In the digital era, there is no need to speculate about latent variables when we can capture abundant, readily analyzable evidence regarding the tangible products of knowledge work, along with records of every step taken in their creation.

Moreover, we must extend our understanding beyond individualized, "mentalist" constructs (Gergen & Dixon-Román, 2013) to include the social origins of knowledge—evidenced by quotations, paraphrases, remixes, links, citations, and similar references. In a world where information is always accessible, these elements do not need to be memorized; they only need to be used effectively (Cope & Kalantzis, 2019).

Furthermore, collaborative intelligence recognizes that the collective knowledge of a working group often surpasses the sum of its individual contributions. We now have analyzable records of social knowledge work that can highlight and credit, for instance, the peer or GenAI feedback that significantly enhanced a knowledge construct, or trace the varied contributions of participants in a jointly created work (Tzirides et al., 2023; Zapata et al., 2024). In this way, the artifacts and their production processes provide ample evidence of knowledge actions, demonstrating both the thinking involved and the practical outcomes of that thinking as represented in tangible knowledge artifacts.

Metacognition

Metacognition enables deeper, more abstract forms of thinking and enhances the efficiency of both thought and learning. By conceptualizing at higher levels of abstraction, individuals can broaden the range of applications and the transferability of their ideas and understandings. An existing body of literature (e.g., Bereiter, 2002; National Research Council, 2000) underscores the importance of metacognition in learning, positing that the incorporation of metacognitive strategies into instruction not only benefits students when completing a specific task but also results in lifelong learning that can be applied to other novel academic or personal situations. Indeed,

> "in research with experts who were asked to verbalize their thinking as they worked, it was revealed that they monitored their own understanding carefully, making note of when additional

> information was required for understanding, whether new information was consistent with what they already knew, and what analogies could be drawn that would advance their understanding. These meta-cognitive monitoring activities are an important component of [the learning process]." (National Research Council, 2000, p. 18)

Metacognitive processes naturally align with the logic inherent in new media. For instance, Gee (2007) suggests that computer games require meta-level thinking about their semiotic domain, i.e., playing a game well demands an understanding of its underlying design principles and architecture, not merely playing it. This implies that, unlike traditional texts that can be read sequentially, new media require familiarity with navigational schemes and information architectures.

In contrast, traditional didactic pedagogy operates within a flat epistemic framework, where cognition is confined to memorization, routine procedures for deducing correct answers, and the accurate application of established concepts. Metacognition, however, introduces a second layer of thought—analogous to the navigational structures found in new media—which involves developing a meta-understanding of the nature of disciplinary practice. This higher-order layer is generative; it supports the transfer of understanding to new, even unforeseen, contexts and aids mnemonic work through tools such as tags, annotations, and bookmarks that highlight overarching meanings (National Research Council, 2000).

Consider, for example, the use of student peer reviews in evaluating written science arguments. When students revise their work in light of peer feedback, they are prompted to analyze whether a claim is sufficiently supported by evidence. This exercise fosters a dialectical interplay between first-level cognition—such as thinking about topics like climate change or hydraulic fracturing—and a second level of reflective thought about how scientific claims should be substantiated (Cope et al., 2013). Through this formative assessment process, students externalize and critically examine their scientific writing against specific criteria, thereby deepening their analytical skills in science (Driver et al., 2000).

Munford and Zembal-Saul (2002) summarize the metacognitive benefits for students as including opportunities to learn not only content but also the underlying disciplinary theories and processes. This involves gaining insights into the role of documentary knowledge representations and social interactions in knowledge construction, engaging in discourse that makes learners' understanding and thought processes visible for reflection and assessment, and developing diverse ways of thinking to enhance comprehension of disciplinary concepts.

Differentiated Learning

Mass media once built mass audiences and transmitted a uniform mass culture. Culture was homogenized—assumed to be identical and, as far as possible, made so through the mass production and distribution of newspapers, television, radio, and best-selling books. The logic of mass production brought with it cultures of mass consumption, an intrinsic feature of the economies of scale that dominated cultural production and distribution during the era of mass communications. Today, such economies of scale no longer exist in media. Every Facebook feed and X stream is uniquely tailored for and by the user, reflecting individual interests, identities, and local contexts. Major contributors—celebrities, corporations, large movements—receive the same visibility as friends, colleagues, and even the smallest niche interests. Learner differences are paramount; divergence of identity, taste, affiliation, stance, and interest is now the norm.

In the era of new media, our individual identities and their differences are increasingly pronounced. Traditional classroom communication architectures resemble the old mass media—they are designed for one-size-fits-all transmission of identical content. The teacher addresses the middle of the class, meaning that the lesson may be incomprehensible for some and tediously obvious for others. As students work through a textbook, everyone is forced to be on the same page at the same time. And when it comes to testing, there is only one set of correct answers—standardization is treated as a virtue. This arrangement relies on a homogenizing focus on knowledge and a uniform learning pace. Yet homogenization is an approach that fails as often as it succeeds. Few would dispute today that differentiated learning is superior, although it requires considerably more effort than uniform teaching. It poses a logistical challenge for the teacher, who must possess a broader repertoire of strategies and exceptional classroom management skills (though things might change in educators' favor with the advent of GenAI—more on this later in the chapter).

New media make differentiated instruction far more feasible. Learners can work at their own pace or engage in different tasks based on their needs or interests. This is the goal of adaptive, personalized, or differentiated instruction, which calibrates learning to the individual (Conati & Kardan, 2013; Cope & Kalantzis, 2019; Shute & Zapata-Rivers, 2012; Walkington, 2013; Wolf, 2010; Zapata, 2022). The process becomes even more manageable when a teacher can immediately monitor a student's progress on a project status screen, even clicking into their work to view their most recent keystroke. Moreover, positioning the learner as a knowledge producer creates more space for their voice, interests, experiences, and local relevance. While the overarching intellectual project may remain consistent, the topics explored can vary. In collaborative knowledge creation, each student might work on a unique piece of a jigsaw puzzle of class knowledge, which is later assembled and shared with the community. Rather than enforcing uniformity, such a classroom operationalizes the principle of *productive diversity*, valuing the complementarity of different knowledge and experiences. Students might even cite one another's work as sources of distributed expertise. This type of learning ecology harnesses learner identities, deepens engagement, and increases motivation to invest time in tasks and interact with their knowledge community.

In this type of educational context, assessment focuses on comparing higher-order equivalences between knowledge artifacts that may differ in substance, rather than measuring the capacity to remember identical facts or deduce the same answers. In this approach, sameness is not required for equality, and managing learner differences may become easier than imposing a one-size-fits-all approach. Computer-mediated learning environments now available are designed to embrace divergence—often referred to as adaptive or personalized learning (Conati & Kardan, 2013; Cope & Kalantzis, 2019; Wolf, 2010). In these environments, recursive, dynamic, and recalibrating systems are the norm. They are unstandardized by design, generating dynamic data through their self-adjusting mechanisms. In the following section, we revisit this affordance, as well as the previous ones, in connection with GenAI, focusing on how these new technologies further support e-learning ecologies.

E-Learning Ecologies, GenAI, and Cyber-Social Learning

Recent developments in GenAI have accelerated a broader transition toward what we define as *cyber-social learning*—the complementary, dynamic relationship between a human meaning maker and a machine in the production (i.e., design) of meaning (see also Cope & Kalantzis, 2022). Although the seven e-learning affordances we introduced in the previous sections offer a set of choices and opportunities for harnessing new media (Cope & Kalantzis, 2017, 2019), they need to be conceptualized in light of recent GenAI affordances and the theoretical underpinnings of cyber-social learning. This section synthesizes these perspectives, outlining a comprehensive framework for technology-mediated education.

Cyber-Social Learning: Opportunities

At its core, cyber-social learning arises in the nexus between physical environments (classrooms, workplaces, homes) and the computational, networked systems that increasingly permeate these spaces. It leverages new "sociabilities" made possible by mobile and ubiquitous computing, thus enabling teaching and learning arrangements that transcend traditional boundaries of time and space (Cope & Kalantzis, 2017, 2022). GenAI intensifies these possibilities by offering on-demand, multimodal content generation, instant knowledge retrieval, and adaptive tutorials.

This dynamic context reconfigures learning in ways that are:

- **Agentive:** Emphasizing learners' and educators' capacity to self-regulate and creatively employ digital tools, in contrast to "transmission pedagogies" that treat learners as passive recipients.
- **Transpositional:** Bridging sensorimotor experiences with conceptual constructs, integrating human intelligence with GenAI-driven computation, and real-world contexts with digital representations.
- **Multilinear:** Exploiting the networked, non-linear knowledge flows that allow diverse entry points and iterative feedback loops.
- **Reflexive:** Offering rapid, actionable cycles of feedback—human–machine and human–human—thereby replacing the long, summative cycles of traditional assessment.
- **Modulated:** Alternating between stabilization (practice at a given level) and self-transformation (learning leaps, conceptual "upshifts"), rather than delivering knowledge as a lock-step, continuous stream.
- **Collaborative and Heterarchical:** Tapping into distributed meanings across multiple participants, resisting hierarchical one-size-fits-all transmission, and focusing on dynamic interactions that embrace academic identity and widely differing learner backgrounds.
- **Non-scalar:** Designed to function flexibly across small groups or large cohorts, scaling up digitally mediated collaboration and resource sharing without losing local relevance.

Within this cyber-social framework, the seven e-learning affordances previously discussed can serve to underpin and facilitate the agentive, transpositional, and heterarchical qualities of cyber-social learning to produce a nuanced model for contemporary education.

Mapping E-Learning Affordances onto Cyber-Social Learning

Building on the foundational principles of cyber-social learning, this section explores how the seven e-learning affordances—*ubiquitous learning*, *active knowledge-making*, *multimodal meaning*, *recursive feedback*, *collaborative intelligence*, *metacognition*, and *differentiated learning*—can converge with the agentive, transpositional, and heterarchical dynamics of digital education.

GenAI amplifies these digital affordances by enabling real-time, adaptive, and multimodal learning experiences, allowing learners to engage in non-linear, self-regulated, and collaborative knowledge-making. From AI-assisted tutoring that fosters ubiquitous learning to algorithm-driven personalization that supports differentiated instruction, these digital affordances reshape how knowledge is created, shared, and assessed. However, these GenAI innovations also introduce new ethical and pedagogical considerations, such as algorithmic bias and the potential oversimplification of multimodal outputs.

By examining how GenAI can be used, this section highlights both the affordances and challenges of integrating cyber-social learning into contemporary education. Let's revisit the seven e-learning affordances and their interface with GenAI:

1. **Ubiquitous Learning:** In cyber-social environments, ubiquitous learning is enhanced by GenAI's capacity to deliver real-time explanations and resources. For instance, a student might consult a GenAI-assisted tutoring system on a smartphone en route to school, receiving highly specific feedback or multimodal clarifications (text, diagrams, short videos). This 24/7 accessibility expands both informal and formal learning, reflecting the agentive principle of cyber-social learning. At the same time, educators must remain aware of new vectors of algorithmic bias, ensuring that the content served by these systems aligns with equitable pedagogical goals.
2. **Active Knowledge-Making:** GenAI empowers learners to move beyond passive absorption of facts, aligning with transpositional learning. In a science class, for example, students might

use GenAI to generate preliminary data analyses or textual explanations of experimental results. They then interpret these AI outputs within a collaborative workflow—editing text, integrating new data, and articulating novel hypotheses. By granting learners the autonomy to iterate between digital prompts and physical experiments, educators reinforce the multilinear knowledge pathways characteristic of cyber-social learning.

3. **Multimodal Meaning:** Cyber-social learning foregrounds transposition among meaning forms, and GenAI plays a critical role here by fluidly converting text to images (text-to-image generation) or data to infographics. In a social studies project, for instance, students may prompt an AI to visualize population growth data geographically while simultaneously annotating historical texts. This bridging of the sensorimotor (visual, spatial) with the conceptual fosters deeper meaning-making. Teachers can also encourage/guide students' critical reflection on how these multimodal outputs might broaden interpretive possibilities or risk oversimplification.
4. **Recursive Feedback:** In contrast to the protracted feedback cycles of standardized testing, cyber-social learning emphasizes short, reflexive loops. GenAI facilitates this kind of feedback with on-the-fly text critiques or problem-set hints. For example, a learner drafting an argumentative essay can receive immediate suggestions regarding structure, coherence, and evidence use. By aligning such feedback with teacher guidance and peer reviews, instruction remains modulated: Stable periods of practice interspersed with moments of conceptual breakthrough.
5. **Collaborative Intelligence:** Heterarchical collaboration—where ideas flow laterally rather than top-down—becomes more feasible with GenAI-facilitated group work. In a mathematics setting, for instance, small teams might tackle complex problems using a shared digital workspace that integrates multiple AI-driven solvers or data analytics tools. Each student contributes insights from unique perspectives, collectively refining solution paths. Meanwhile, GenAI can highlight conceptual overlaps or divergences, prompting reflective group discussions. This

approach not only fosters shared accountability but also leverages learner differences for richer problem-solving.

6. **Metacognition:** Generative AI systems can track student interactions, time-on-task, and learning trajectories to generate personal analytics dashboards. These dashboards invite learners to examine their own thinking strategies—how they approached tasks, where they hesitated, or which revisions improved clarity. Such metacognitive engagements align with the agentive and reflexive thrust of cyber-social learning, as students become more cognizant of their cognitive states and more adept at self-regulation.
7. **Differentiated Learning:** AI-driven personalization tools dynamically tailor content and pacing. For example, a physics class can offer multiple "pathways" through the subject matter, adjusting complexity in real time based on performance metrics. In a large online course, GenAI chatbots can provide varying degrees of scaffolding to novice, intermediate, and advanced learners, thereby fulfilling the non-scalar principle—equally adaptive in small peer-led groups or massive course enrollments. However, educators should remain vigilant regarding how personalization may mask underlying inequities, such as uneven broadband access or commercial platform biases.

Taken together, when these seven digital affordances are enacted through a cyber-social lens, they offer a comprehensive roadmap for integrating GenAI into educational contexts. Ubiquitous access, multimodal meaning-making, adaptive personalization, and iterative feedback loops transform classrooms into socially distributed, technologically enriched learning ecologies. At the same time, the principles of cyber-social learning remind us of potential pitfalls: the algorithmic manipulations of private platforms, the risk of overrelying on automated solutions, and the perpetuation of existing hierarchies through seemingly neutral technologies.

Ultimately, success in the convergence of digital affordances and cyber-social learning hinges on the ways educators and learners strategically adopt AI technologies. Rather than viewing GenAI as a replacement for human cognition, the model posits a transpositional relationship: AI handles the computational "what," while learners focus on reflexive "how," harnessing agentive, collaborative, and heterarchical pedagogies. By foregrounding awareness of social dynamics, identity, and the ethical implications of technology use, educators can shape an era in which cyber-social learning complements rather than displaces the transformative potential of human creativity and criticality.

Challenges of GenAI in Education: Bias, Fakes, and Policy Concerns

Building on the preceding discussion, in which we underscored the transformative potential of GenAI for cyber-social learning, it is equally important to consider the serious challenges that this technology poses. Recent work highlights how the very mechanisms that make generative systems so effective in producing seemingly coherent outputs also render them vulnerable to new forms of manipulation, bias, and deception (Cope & Kalantzis, 2024a; Pagano et al., 2023; Tzirides et al., 2023). In educational environments, these vulnerabilities extend beyond simple issues such as "AI cheating," touching instead on deep-seated concerns around bias in machine learning models, widespread creation of fake content and sources, and broader policy and security implications. The following sections examine each of these challenges through the lens of the scholarship on GenAI, drawing attention to how educators and policymakers must grapple with the complex ethical, social, and practical ramifications of these technologies.

AI Bias

A central challenge for educational applications of GenAI is algorithmic bias, an inherent by-product of using massive textual corpora to train large language models (LLMs) (Baker & Hawn, 2022; Kordzadeh & Ghasemaghaei, 2022; Tzirides et al., 2023). These corpora invariably mirror the cultural, social, and political prejudices embedded in public discourse—manifesting as racism, sexism, homophobia, ableism, or other ideologies that are at odds with educational equity. Computer scientist and poet Dr. Joy Adowaa Buolamwini has documented AI biases in both her scholarly work (e.g., Raji & Buolamwini, 2019) and creative pieces. For instance, the wonderful multimodal poem *AI, Ain't I a Woman?* (available at `https://tinyurl.com/AIAintIW`) offers evidence for AI's gender misidentification of well-known Black/African American women such as Shirley Chisholm, Serena Williams, and Michelle Obama. This piece celebrates these women's contributions while also critically highlighting AI's failure in recognizing their features and hairstyles as female.

Unfortunately, conscientious attempts to filter objectionable material and reduce bias often introduce new distortions; the machine's underlying statistical architecture remains captive to linguistic patterns with deeply rooted biases (Cope & Kalantzis, 2024a; Raji & Buolamwini, 2019). Consequently, schools and universities face the prospect of inadvertently endorsing texts or recommendations generated from tainted corpora.

In practical classroom terms, a GenAI-driven writing tool might propose word choices or topics steeped in cultural stereotypes, while tutors that generate feedback on student essays could offer subtly differential comments based on historically minoritized dialects. This poses ethical and pedagogical dilemmas: How to offer students equal learning opportunities and encourage their authentic voices if the system's "default" orientation risks othering their sociolects or lived experiences? Ongoing efforts in responsible AI development—such as the design of better filtering mechanisms and the refinement of reinforcement learning from human feedback (RLHF)—are noteworthy, but these remain partial solutions (Cope & Kalantzis, 2024b). In many respects, teachers themselves become mediators and interpreters of AI's outputs, deploying critical literacy strategies to highlight and disrupt moments where algorithmic bias might harm students' self-perception or narrow their intellectual horizons.

AI Fakes

GenAI systems frequently generate "facts" that are entirely fabricated or references that do not actually exist, a phenomenon often called "AI hallucination" or "machine confabulation" (Cope & Kalantzis, 2024a; Kalantzis & Cope, 2025; Zhou et al., 2023). While these model outputs may appear superficially consistent, they can mislead both instructors and students alike, particularly when integrated into high-stakes academic tasks such as research projects or evidence-based writing. The situation, also discussed in Chapter 1, is compounded by the fact that LLMs rarely disclose the authentic sources or logic behind their responses—indeed, part of their rhetorical success comes from presenting aggregated textual data as though it were spontaneously generated knowledge.

These "fakes" undermine fundamental academic principles that uphold accurate citation and transparent peer review (Cope & Kalantzis, 2024b). A system may propose citation data that seems plausible—correctly formatted, relevant to the topic—but upon further checking reveals nonexistent or misattributed sources. Faced with such outputs, learners risk absorbing unvetted information or building arguments around spurious evidence. Such a dynamic places additional strain on educators, who must rigorously teach students how to validate references through external databases or to check factual claims using well-established quality filters. Rather than passively receiving GenAI-generated information, both teachers and students must now adopt a critical stance, interrogating each detail to discern which fragments might be genuinely supported by validated sources and which are mere statistical "inventions" (Kalantzis & Cope, 2025; Tzirides et al., 2023).

Policy and Security

The integration of GenAI into education also raises vital policy and security questions (Akgun & Greenhow, 2022; Mollick & Mollick, 2023). In many jurisdictions, current frameworks for student data protection and digital literacy standards were formulated before the advent of AI-driven teaching aids. These regulations must be revisited to address the extraction and storage of student data used to train and refine AI models, as well as the ownership of GenAI-generated content. Additionally, the covert appropriation of copyrighted texts and images to build LLMs—what some have termed the "privatization of collective human intellect"—exposes educational institutions to complex intellectual property risks (Cope & Kalantzis, 2024b; Kalantzis & Cope, 2025).

Moreover, the infiltration of AI-generated content into broader social channels creates security gaps that can be exploited for "social engineering" or disinformation campaigns (Coeckelbergh, 2023). Educational settings are particularly vulnerable if teachers and students lack robust strategies to recognize deepfakes and manipulated text or media. Malicious actors could, for instance, fabricate exam solutions or disseminate harmful misinformation disguised as official communications. To counter such threats, education policymakers need to develop stricter guidelines on platform usage, mandate transparency measures (e.g., watermarks or disclaimers on GenAI-created text), and invest in ongoing professional development to ensure that all stakeholders—teachers, students, parents, and IT professionals—can spot and neutralize suspicious content (Kalantzis & Cope, 2025; Tzirides et al., 2023, 2024b).

Finally, these concerns dovetail with the broader ethical questions of whether public institutions should rely on proprietary GenAI platforms that may encode opaque, profit-driven motives into their recommendation algorithms or restrict data portability between vendor ecosystems. Public-school systems and universities may need to negotiate new contractual obligations that guarantee data sovereignty, open algorithms, and local hosting solutions, thereby balancing the benefits of adaptive, GenAI-augmented learning with the imperatives of communal trust and oversight.

GenAI in Education: New Roles for Teachers

The challenges posed by GenAI in education—manifested, as discussed in the previous section, through lingering algorithmic biases, the widespread proliferation of AI-crafted fakes, and policy and security vulnerabilities—point to a critical imperative for educators, administrators, and policymakers. While GenAI can accelerate pedagogical innovation and foster new forms of learner engagement, stakeholders must adopt proactive measures that integrate transparent data usage policies, robust teacher professional development, and critical AI literacy (Kalantzis & Cope, 2025; Tzirides et al., 2024b).

Far from rendering human expertise obsolete, these innovations open up new avenues for teachers to shape and support the evolving landscapes of writing, reading, and multimodal meaning-making (Kalantzis & Cope, 2025). Although recent scholarship documents the powerful affordances of AI for content creation and individualized student feedback, it also underscores the persistent need for educators who can steer these processes with a critical pedagogical lens (Cope & Kalantzis, 2024b; Tzirides et al., 2023, 2024a, 2024b; UNESCO, 2023). This section outlines how teacher roles are changing in curricula design, assessment, and the cultivation of higher-order cyber-social literacy practices in a world where the machine increasingly handles many aspects of the "what" of knowledge, freeing educators to focus on the "how" of meaningful learning.

Orchestrating Content Creation and Differentiation

GenAI excels at drafting lesson plans, generating structured activities, and customizing materials for diverse learner needs (UNESCO, 2023). This automation of content assembly repositions teachers from sole architects of instructional content to orchestrators who strategically select, refine, and contextualize GenAI-generated outputs. In practice, educators might take an AI-produced lesson outline in a subject such as biology and adapt it to emphasize local, context-specific data sources that tie directly to community issues—an approach that fosters both relevance and equity.

Furthermore, because GenAI-based resources can be tailored to varied skill levels, instructors can offer differentiated pathways that meet the needs of advanced, intermediate, and emergent learners. What remains vital, however, is the teacher's role in ensuring that all materials are pedagogically coherent, responsive to and reflective of student identities, and aligned with national and institutional standards (Cope & Kalantzis, 2024b; Kalantzis & Cope, 2025). Rather than merely employing GenAI's content as offered, educators must critically evaluate outputs for bias and/or misinformation, recalibrate learning objectives to reflect their students' personal and academic needs, and embed opportunities for self-reflection and peer collaboration.

Curating Assessments and Providing Formative Feedback

GenAI tools are already influencing the assessment lifecycle by generating quizzes, rubrics, and model answers, as well as providing formative feedback on student writing—all of which can streamline grading and deliver immediate, data-rich feedback (Tzirides et al., 2023, 2024a, 2024b; Zapata et al., 2024, 2025a, 2025b). In many instances, learners also enlist GenAI to brainstorm essay ideas or refine drafts, thus blurring the line between human and machine contributions. Teachers must respond by calibrating assessment tasks to promote skills that GenAI cannot fully replicate—such as context-specific problem-solving, advanced conceptual synthesis, and ethical decision-making (Kalantzis & Cope, 2025). Rather than primarily policing "cheating," educators can use AI-based analytics to flag potential issues early and direct students toward constructive revision, thus ensuring academic integrity while focusing on deeper learning.

Additionally, teachers who adopt cyber-social learning practices can leverage GenAI to democratize feedback loops, letting each student receive near-instant textual or even multimodal comments on their work (Kalantzis & Cope, 2025; Tzirides et al., 2024b; Zapata et al., 2025b). This mechanism can reinforce formative assessment, wherein small cycles of feedback enhance ongoing mastery (Cope & Kalantzis, 2019). Even so, however, constant GenAI oversight demands that teachers maintain the authority to override or adapt machine-generated judgments, especially in emotionally charged or academically complex situations. By integrating their disciplinary expertise with GenAI-driven insights, educators can ensure that assessment remains more than a series of mechanized correctness checks.

Sustaining Higher-Order Literacies in an Automated World

Beyond serving as instructors, orchestrators, and assessors, teachers are increasingly tasked with cultivating what might be called meta-literacy skills—helping learners negotiate the moral, esthetic, and societal implications of living in an environment saturated with AI-curated texts, images, and data (Cope & Kalantzis, 2024b). As a result, educators become ethical navigators, guiding students through GenAI hallucinations and highlighting the hidden labor behind machine outputs, from data cleaning to enforcement of content moderation filters (Tzirides et al., 2023). By teaching students to probe the intentions behind generative prompts, re-check claims using recognized disciplinary frameworks, and adopt a reflexive stance toward algorithmic recommendations, teachers deepen the very notion of literacy—steering it away from rote memorization and toward discerning, critical engagement (Kalantzis & Cope, 2025).

A corollary of this expanded literacy is the development of multimodal and transpositional skill sets (Kalantzis & Cope, 2020; see also Chapter 4). Given that many GenAI systems output not only text but also associated images, diagrams, and even short videos, educators can teach students how to interpret and remake such artifacts in ways that privilege local knowledge, cultural values, and domain-specific rigor. In effect, a teacher's role here resembles that of a knowledgeable guide and dialectical co-designer: clarifying the interplay of student agency and machine affordances, weaving in advanced conceptual structures that AI alone cannot authentically teach, and modeling the reflective iteration that characterizes genuine inquiry (Cope & Kalantzis, 2024b; Kalantzis & Cope, 2025).

Facilitating Collaborative Knowledge Work and Community Connections

Finally, where GenAI automates many of the procedures traditionally performed by individual learners, teachers can redirect the instructional focus to collaborative knowledge production. Teachers might, for instance, design group projects where students use GenAI to gather diverse resources, but the crux of the learning lies in the interpretive dialog among classmates—discussing the credibility of sources, synthesizing multiple viewpoints, and co-constructing a final product. Such endeavors can not only strengthen academic and metacognitive competencies but also build community within the classroom. By situating shared inquiries in meaningful sociopolitical and/or disciplinary contexts, teachers connect the micro-level of daily learning tasks to broader macro-level discussions about knowledge, power, and ethical responsibility (Cope & Kalantzis, 2024b).

Moreover, educators remain the pivotal link between school and home/community contexts, where parents, caregivers, and local stakeholders have their own questions and apprehensions regarding GenAI-supported instruction. In these broader ecologies, teachers can serve as trusted guides—helping families understand what it means for a bot to co-create a piece of writing with their child, explaining data privacy protocols, and outlining how new digital tools might equitably support diverse learners.

In sum, in an era where GenAI increasingly automates central dimensions of literacy—drafting lesson plans, revising student texts, generating feedback—teachers' roles are neither diminished nor rendered obsolete. Instead, they evolve toward orchestration, curation, ethical navigation, and community building. By thoughtfully applying cyber-social learning principles, educators can move beyond transmitting knowledge to nurturing deeper interpretive skills, collaborative dispositions, and shared moral accountability.

Although GenAI can offload many routine tasks and accelerate personalized learning pathways, it is the teacher's reflective leadership that ensures equitable, contextually rich, and ethically grounded education in the automated landscapes of 21st-century literacy. In Figure 5.4, we summarize the ways in which GenAI can support teachers' practices.

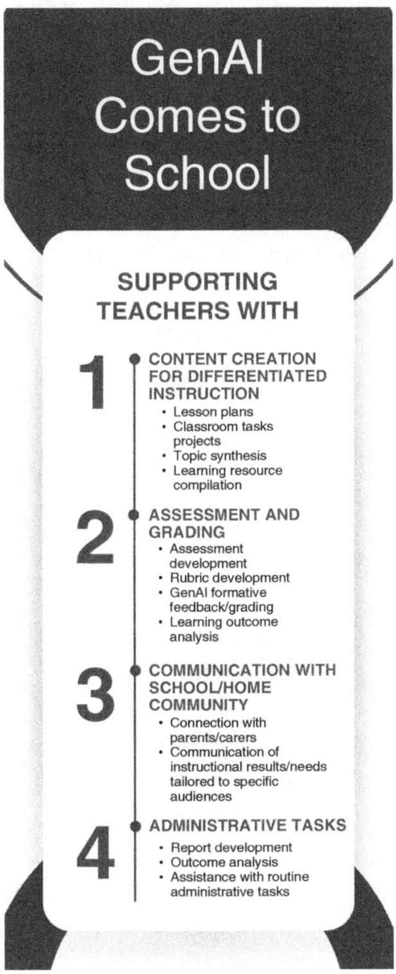

Figure 5.4 Summary of ways in which GenAI can support teachers' daily practices.

Developing AI Literacy

Transitioning from the discussion of teachers' evolving roles in an era of automated literacy, we turn now to the concept of *AI literacy*. The widespread integration of GenAI into classrooms and everyday life requires both teachers and students to develop competencies that extend beyond conventional digital skills. AI literacy is not simply about knowing how to use AI tools; rather, it encompasses a rich tapestry of technical, ethical, and critical dimensions that aim to empower individuals to harness, question, and shape AI in responsible and equitable ways (Cope & Kalantzis, 2024b; Laupichler et al., 2022; Long & Magerko, 2020; Ng et al., 2021). This section explores what AI literacy entails and how it can be cultivated within contemporary educational ecologies.

AI literacy can be understood as the capacity to understand, use, and critically evaluate AI systems in a manner that is informed, responsible, and context-aware (Laupichler et al., 2022; Ng et al., 2021). This type of literacy goes beyond mastering basic functionalities—such as prompting a chatbot or running a data analysis tool—to include awareness of GenAI's foundational mechanisms, recognition and, more importantly, identification of potential limitations such as the ones previously discussed, and engagement with broader ethical and social implications (Cope & Kalantzis, 2024b; Kalantzis & Cope, 2025). From a pedagogical standpoint, AI literacy is simultaneously an individual and collective endeavor, entailing the following:

1. **Technical Understanding:** Individuals develop a working knowledge of AI fundamentals—machine learning, algorithms, data processing—along with insights into how GenAI-generated outputs differ from human cognition and creativity.
2. **Critical Engagement:** AI-literate individuals routinely verify machine-generated content against reliable sources, question the validity of references, and remain vigilant to "hallucinations" or ideological/algorithmic bias. This analytical practice parallels established principles of critical digital literacy and is

intrinsically connected with the meaning functions discussed in Chapter 4, highlighting the need for ongoing skepticism and reflective practice.

3. **Ethical and Responsible Use:** Recognizing that AI systems can inadvertently encode unfair biases or produce harmful misinformation, AI literacy involves grappling with core values such as privacy, transparency, and accountability. Users learn to identify when human judgment is indispensable and how to integrate algorithmic insights without compromising social or moral imperatives.

We believe that the development of AI literacy for both teachers and students can be achieved through specific instructional pathways that involve:

1. **Curriculum Integration:** Rather than treating GenAI as a novelty or an extracurricular interest, schools and universities can embed AI literacy components into existing subjects. For instance, language arts classes might analyze the rhetorical strategies of chatbot-generated texts, while social studies courses might explore GenAI's impact on public discourse and policy. Of course, as with any other pedagogical intervention, the curricular implementation of GenAI tools must be grounded in established, research-guided pedagogical frameworks, such as LbyD.
2. **Collaborative Projects and Inquiry-Based Learning:** Group/pair work that integrates GenAI allows students to practice prompt engineering, data analysis, and critical reflection in shared contexts. By framing GenAI tasks within broader inquiry projects—e.g., researching local environmental challenges—learners see AI as a tool that can amplify but never replace, collaborative, real-world problem-solving.
3. **Ongoing Professional Development:** Teachers can benefit from structured workshops, peer mentoring, and iterative feedback loops on GenAI integration. Training must involve hands-on engagement and work with GenAI to develop educators' knowledge of "the nature of GenAI technologies (where and by

whom they have been developed, how, and for what purpose), their affordances and limitations, and the ethical implications (e.g., personal, social, cultural, and political) arising from GenAI use for education" (Zapata, 2025, p. 138). Additionally, professional learning communities can share best practices for prompt-engineering strategies, discuss emerging ethical concerns, and design robust student activities around AI literacy.

4. **Reflective, Critical Assessment:** Both teachers and students require opportunities to reflect on how effectively they are applying AI skills and employing GenAI tools, as well as whether they are doing so ethically. Structured self-assessments, peer reviews, or teacher-guided reflections can highlight the gaps and strengths in learners' approaches.

In an educational landscape increasingly shaped by automated text generation and adaptive computing, AI literacy emerges as an indispensable suite of competences—technical, critical, and ethical—that prepares both educators and learners to thrive in a rapidly shifting digital environment. Far from being a narrow skill set, AI literacy underpins practices of cyber-social learning in which human intelligence and machine algorithms become co-creative partners. By developing solid understandings of how GenAI works, interrogating its outputs with a skeptical and reflective eye, and ensuring ethical imperatives remain paramount, teachers and students alike can evolve into active participants in shaping the trajectory of GenAI in education.

Toward Digital Citizenship

In light of our explorations of GenAI's affordances and limitations, teachers' evolving roles, and the critical importance of AI literacy, we end this chapter by considering the notion of *digital citizenship*, which we view as an emerging unifying framework. Digital citizenship encompasses the capacities, dispositions, and ethical commitments needed for individuals to participate responsibly in complex, technology-mediated societies (Cope & Kalantzis, 2024b). It situates AI literacy within a broader ethos of democratic engagement, social justice, and civic agency, recognizing that a robust educational program must prepare learners not only to master computational and critical skills but also to shape the sociotechnical worlds they inhabit. This final section integrates the key themes of this chapter into a vision of learning that fosters active, principled digital citizenship.

Digital citizenship, in essence, transcends technical know-how or rule compliance. It centers on an ethos of responsible participation, interweaving the goals of personal growth, collective good, and future-ready competences. Building on the concept of cyber-social learning, we may conceive of digital citizenship in at least four interconnected dimensions:

1. **Critical-Reflective Dimension:** Learners and educators alike engage in continuous evaluation of GenAI-based tools and content—assessing potential biases, verifying sources, and questioning the social implications of machine outputs. This dimension aligns with the critical stance essential to AI literacy, ensuring that digital participants avoid unwittingly perpetuating misinformation, discrimination, or intellectual complacency.
2. **Ethical-Communal and Policy Dimension:** Acting as a principled digital citizen involves upholding norms around privacy, consent, and data responsibility. In educational contexts, teachers can guide students to recognize how personal data fuels AI analytics and to articulate a sense of collective responsibility for equitable technology use. The communal aspect also implies that social media spaces, classroom projects, and broader civic arenas remain inclusive and accountable, with participants attuned to preventing digital harm—ranging from cyberbullying to the encroachment of surveillance capitalism.
3. **Collaborative-Innovative Dimension:** As GenAI automates many aspects of literacy, digital citizens focus on creative, human–machine collaborations that magnify the best of both domains. Teachers may stage collaborative inquiry-based

projects, where AI handles data processing while students supply context awareness and interpretive nuance. In this environment, digital citizenship entails the capacity to orchestrate synergy across diverse inputs—human expertise, machine suggestions, community voices—to solve problems that matter to real-world communities.

4. **Sociopolitical Dimension:** Finally, digital citizenship implies stepping into public debates surrounding GenAI governance, educational policy, and social equity. Whether discussing algorithmic regulation in civics lessons or analyzing data ethics in science, technology, engineering, and mathematics (STEM) projects, learners practice the negotiation of public goods and legal frameworks that shape how GenAI is deployed at institutional, regional, and global levels. In such a stance, students build a foundation for lifelong civic engagement, informed by a comprehensive, critical understanding of how sociotechnical systems enact or subvert democratic values.

We believe teachers occupy a pivotal position in fostering the development of students as digital citizens who can productively navigate cyber-social realities. Through both curriculum design and everyday interactions, they model how GenAI might be used ethically for research, creative meaning design, or community engagement. Concretely, a teacher might lead a project-based unit on climate change in which students leverage GenAI-driven data visualization tools while also hosting peer discussions on how misinformation circulates through social networks. In doing so, they bridge the "ethical-communal" and "collaborative-innovative" dimensions, sustaining a learning culture in which learners see themselves as co-responsible for the direction and impact of GenAI-mediated inquiries.

Moreover, educators can help learners navigate tensions between individual freedoms and collective well-being in digital spaces. Students learn to question whether certain AI-driven services compromise broader social or environmental goals, and they glean strategies to mitigate potential harm, from using privacy-friendly tools to supporting open-source data resources. By weaving these ethical sensibilities into content instruction, teachers can reinforce the normative frameworks—both formal and informal—that keep digital participation constructive and compassionate.

The aspirations of digital citizenship do not end at the boundaries of formal education; ideally, they connect learners' classroom experiences to broader public forums and collaborative networks. School-based initiatives might partner with local civic organizations, libraries, or nonprofits, enabling students to apply GenAI skills to real-world challenges such as mapping neighborhood resources or analyzing community health data. Through these experiences, learners can refine problem-solving capacities while exercising ethical judgment, moving beyond rote academic tasks toward meaningful social impact.

In advanced educational contexts—secondary/high school or higher education—digital citizenship initiatives can explore policy-making roles, such as student advisory boards that interface with school district technology committees or local government GenAI task forces. Engaging students in these ventures underscores the premise that active digital citizenship is not merely about personal competence but about shaping—and being shaped by—public discourse. Blending teacher mentorship, interdisciplinary curricula, and authentic participatory venues, schools and universities can thus become incubators of sociotechnical leadership for future generations.

In sum, our digital citizenship call seeks to harness GenAI, AI literacy, and re-envisioned teacher roles for the larger purpose of ethical, engaged participation in digital culture that leads to enhanced performance. Encompassing critical reflection, ethical communal life, collaborative innovation, and sociopolitical awareness, digital citizenship weaves together the transformative potential of AI technologies with the abiding mission of education as a civic institution. By scaling AI literacy from individual skills to societal practices, it reaffirms that technology should serve human needs—and not vice versa—through inclusive, democratic systems of knowledge creation and use. The final outcome is neither utopian nor fatalistic but a grounded vision that underscores the shared responsibilities of educators, learners, and policy actors in stewarding AI-infused societies. As classrooms evolve into collaborative laboratories for future-making, digital citizenship emerges as the guiding compass—a concept both forward-thinking and morally anchored in its articulation of how we might collectively design the futures of human–machine symbiosis.

Conclusion

This chapter has explored the intersection of digital literacy and AI for enhancing learning experiences and outcomes, emphasizing how emerging technologies are reshaping meaning-making, education, and participatory culture. We examined how digital tools and GenAI-driven platforms have expanded multimodal communication, transforming literacy from a predominantly text-based practice into a dynamic, interactive, and algorithmically mediated process. While these advancements offer unprecedented opportunities for personalization, collaboration, and accessibility, they also raise critical concerns regarding ethical considerations, algorithmic bias, misinformation, and digital agency. As such, AI literacy has become an essential component of digital citizenship, requiring educators and learners to develop critical awareness and ethical engagement with these technologies.

As literacy practices continue to evolve in response to technological shifts, particularly those brought about by GenAI, it is essential to consider how literacy develops across different stages of learning. In the following chapter, we turn our attention to literacy development with a focus on GenAI across levels of education—from early childhood to higher education and beyond. We explore how literacy learning is shaped at each stage, from foundational literacy skills to advanced academic and lifelong literacies. By tracing this continuum, we seek to understand how literacy education can be designed to equip learners with the skills necessary to navigate an increasingly complex and interconnected human–AI world.

Consolidate, Explore, Reflect, Do

We end this chapter with activities that will allow you to apply the concepts discussed in novel ways. Our goal is that these tasks will facilitate further exploration and reflection and will inspire your present and/or future teaching practice.

Task 1: Picture Books and Multimodal Literacy

In his discussion on multimodal literacy, Serafini (2015) suggests that working with picture books might constitute a first step in our growth as effective multimodal communicators. Specifically, he posits:

> The use of contemporary, complex, and post-modern picture books with adolescent readers has been recommended by various reading educators and researchers for many years... [For example], it has been asserted that postmodern picture books provide a bridge from the text-based literacies of the traditional middle and high school classroom to the multiliteracies necessary in the future... Therefore, it is important that teachers understand how to take full advantage of multimodal resources in general, and the visual images and design features of complex picture books in particular, to introduce students to the strategies necessary for comprehending these ensembles. (p. 420)

In this task, we will follow Serafini's advice, and we will focus on the analysis of picture books for children aged between 7 and 12 years. You will work in groups of 4–5.

Step 1. With your classmates, find books that are recommended by teachers or think of those you like/you have been using in the classes you might be teaching. Choose one. Here are some of our favorite ones, written by American and British authors:

- *Carmela Full of Wishes.* Author: Matt de la Peña; illustrator: Christian Robinson. Publisher: G. P. Putnam's Sons Books for Young Readers.

- *El Chupacabras: A Bilingual Tale of the Legendary Creature.* Author: Adam Rubin; illustrator: Crash McCreery. Publisher: Dial Books.
- *Gina Kaminski Saves the Wolf.* Author: Craig Barr-Green; illustrator: Francis Martin. Publisher: Little Tiger.
- *Islandborn.* Author: Junot Díaz; illustrator: Leo Espinosa. Publisher: Rock the Boat.
- *Someone Just Like You.* Author: Helen Docherty; illustrator: David Roberts. Publisher: Simon & Schuster UK Children's Books.
- *The Artist.* Author and illustrator: Ed Vere. Publisher: Puffin.
- *The Day You Begin.* Author: Jacqueline Woodson; illustrator: Rafael López. Publisher: Orchard Books.
- *Zoo.* Author and illustrator: Anthony Browne. Publisher: Red Fox.

Step 2. With the members of your group, read the book you have chosen and answer the following questions. Distribute questions among group members.

1. **Book Title**:
2. **Author**:
3. **Intended Audience**:
4. **Summary of the Story:** Provide a brief overview of the book. Highlight the main plot and themes in 2–3 sentences.
5. **Analysis of Multimodal Communication:** Examine how meaning is conveyed through different meaning forms in the picture book. Use the questions below to guide your work. Provide examples to support your answers.
   (a) Text:
      1. What type of language is used (e.g., formal, conversational)? How does it support the story? How is it related to the audience of focus?
      2. Are any typographical features (e.g., font size, style) used to emphasize certain aspects of the story? How do these features convey meaning/relate to the audience?

(b) **Image**:
   1. How do illustrations and color convey mood or symbolism? How do they relate to the audience of focus?
   2. How do visuals support or expand the text? Is the relationship between text and image coherent? Explain.

(c) **Space**:
   1. How are elements arranged on a page? Do they guide the reader's eye?
   2. Does the use of space enhance storytelling? Is the relationship between text, image, and space coherent? Explain.

(d) **Body**:
   1. What meaning do characters' gestures, facial expressions, body language, and clothing convey in the illustrations?
   2. Do these elements complement or contrast with the text? What actions are emphasized in the illustrations, and how do they drive the narrative?

6. **Interaction Among Meaning Forms**: Summarize your insights about the effectiveness of multimodal communication in this book. What worked well, and what could be improved? Is the book appropriate for the intended audience and its sociocultural context?

Step 3. Now present your book and analysis to another group. Identify similarities and differences in your books. What is needed in terms of multimodal literacy to fully engage with your texts?
Step 4. Employ a GenAI tool of your preference (e.g., ChatGPT, Gemini) to create a possible blueprint grounded on LbyD's knowledge processes (see Chapter 4, pages 144–145) to guide elementary/primary school learners' work with the book you have

analyzed. Once you have done so, with your groupmates do the following:

1. **Analyze GenAI's Output**:
   1. Is it appropriate for your students? How close is it to the instructional ideas you had in mind?
   2. Does the AI "understand" the kind of learning involved in each knowledge process?
   3. Do you notice any problems with the created content? If so, of what type?
2. Modify the output to better answer your students' personal and academic needs.
3. Reflect on your use of GenAI to complete this task:
   1. What are the positive aspects? Think of workload, creativity, etc.
   2. Did you have any difficulties? If so, describe what you did to overcome them.
   3. What are the drawbacks resulting from your use of GenAI in this activity?
   4. How does this task reflect the affordances and limitations discussed in this chapter?
   5. Do you believe that this use of GenAI is a good example of cyber-social learning? Explain.

Task 2: Investigating AI Bias

In this task, you will work in a group of 4–5 to critically examine the ethical challenges of AI bias and its implications for digital citizenship. You will explore real-world cases of algorithmic bias and propose solutions for more equitable AI systems.

Step 1. Each member of the group will select and research an AI bias case and will focus on a different aspect of AI bias:

- bias in facial recognition (e.g., racial misidentifications);
- gender bias in AI recruitment tools (e.g., AI preferring male candidates);
- language and accessibility bias (e.g., AI struggling with dialects);

- bias in news and social media algorithms (e.g., political polarization);
- educational bias (e.g., AI grading systems being unfair to certain students).

Conduct in-depth research on your assigned bias. Find real-world examples, academic articles, and/or expert analyses that explain how this bias occurs, who it affects, and what ethical concerns it raises.

Step 2. Each member of the group summarizes their findings in a one-page report including the following:

- key findings;
- ethical issues;
- real-world consequences;
- potential solutions.

After each person presents their findings, as a group, compile them into an infographic or short video to visually/multimodally explain the impact of AI bias to an audience unfamiliar with the topic.

Step 3. Exchange reports and multimodal artifacts with another group. Compare biases across different AI systems and discuss patterns in connection with who is the most affected and why. Identify which biases overlap and whether the same solutions might apply to multiple problems.

Step 4. As a new team, with the members of the other group, develop a policy proposal to reduce AI bias in education, hiring, or media. Present your findings and proposal to the rest of the class. Can AI truly be unbiased, or is bias inevitable?

Task 3: GenAI as a Creative Partner—Testing GenAI in Content Creation

This task challenges you to collaborate with GenAI while critically evaluating its role in writing and multimodal meaning-making.

Option 1

Step 1. You will work in groups of 5. Each member should generate a different type of written/multimodal content using a GenAI tool (e.g., ChatGPT, Gemini, or DALL·E for visuals):

- Group member 1 generates an essay introduction;
- Group member 2 generates a summary of a research article;
- Group member 3 generates a multimodal representation of one of the concepts introduced in this chapter (e.g., AI literacy, cyber-social learning);
- Group member 4 produces an AI-generated infographic or video script;
- Group member 5 generates a short, creative story.

Step 2. Compare the AI-generated content to similar texts/representations created by humans. As a group, consider the following:

- Does AI enhance creativity or limit it? Explain.
- How accurate and coherent are the AI-generated outputs?
- What biases or inconsistencies do you notice?
- Should AI-generated outputs be considered "authentic"? Explain.

Step 3. Work together to revise the AI-generated written content, ensuring accuracy and coherence. Then, reflect on the following:

- How did AI impact your writing process?
- When should AI be used in writing, and when should it be avoided?
- How should educators approach AI in academic settings?

Support your opinions with the information presented in this chapter.

Step 4. Go back to the personal definition of literacy you developed in Chapter 1 and modified in Chapters 2–4. Considering your work in this task and the concept of AI literacy we introduced in this chapter, what changes would you make to your personal definition? What has changed? What remains the same? Why? Do you feel your definition reflects literacy in the age of GenAI? Are you getting close?

Option 2

Step 1. You will work in pairs. With your partner, decide on one of two options for your GenAI-assisted storytelling project:

1. **Retelling or Hybridizing a Classic Tale**: Select a well-known children's story and modify it using GenAI. You can modernize it, mix two stories together, or change the setting, characters, or theme.
2. **Creating an Original Children's Story**: Use GenAI to help generate an entirely new children's story, brainstorming ideas, themes, and characters.

Step 2. Each of you will use a different GenAI tool to create complementary elements of your story:

- **Partner 1:** Use a GenAI text generator (e.g., ChatGPT, Gemini, etc.) to produce the story at two or more different grade/reading levels, adjusting for vocabulary, sentence complexity, and themes.
- **Partner 2:** Use a GenAI image generator (e.g., DALL·E, Midjourney, etc.) to create illustrations that match the story's tone and style.

Step 3. Together, analyze the GenAI-generated text and images:

- Does the GenAI-generated story feel engaging and appropriate for different reading levels?
- Do the illustrations match the story's tone and content? Are they consistent?
- Are there any biases, inconsistencies, or unexpected patterns in the AI-generated outputs?

Support your opinions with the information presented in this chapter.

Step 4. Work together to refine and edit the GenAI-generated story and visuals. This could involve rewriting sections, adding a personal touch, or modifying GenAI-generated illustrations. Then, reflect on the following:

- How did AI help or hinder the creative process?
- Did GenAI enhance storytelling, or did it limit originality?
- When should GenAI be used as a tool in storytelling, and when is human creativity more valuable?

Step 5. Share your final story and visuals with another pair or the class. Discuss your insights on GenAI's role in creative storytelling and the challenges and benefits of using GenAI tools.

Step 6. Go back to the personal definition of literacy you developed in Chapter 1 and modified in Chapters 2–4. Considering your work in this task and the concept of AI literacy we introduced in this chapter, what changes would you make to your personal definition? What has changed? What remains the same? Why? Do you feel your definition reflects literacy in the age of GenAI? Are you getting close?

References

Abbate, J. (1999). *Inventing the internet*. The MIT Press.

Akgun, S. & Greenhow, C. (2022). Artificial intelligence in education: Addressing ethical challenges in K-12 settings. *AI and Ethics*, *2*, 431–440. https://doi.org/10.1007/s43681-021-00096-7

Baker, R. S. & Hawn, A. (2022). Algorithmic bias in education. *International Journal of Artificial Intelligence in Education*, *32*, 1052–1092. https://doi.org/10.1007/s40593-021-00285-9

Behrens, J. & DiCerbo, K. (2013). Technological implications for assessment ecosystems. In E. W. Gordon (Ed.), *The Gordon Commission on the future of assessment in education: Technical report* (pp. 101–122). The Gordon Commission.

Bereiter, C. (2002). *Education and mind in the knowledge age*. Lawrence Erlbaum.

Bienkowski, M., Feng, M., & Means, B. (2012). *Enhancing teaching and learning through educational data mining and learning analytics: An issue brief*. Office of Educational Technology, U.S: Department of Education.

Black, P. & Wiliam, D. (1998). Assessment and classroom learning. *Assessment in Education*, *5*, 7–74. https://doi.org/10.1080/0969595980050102

Chang, H.-H. (2012). Making computerized adaptive testing diagnostic tools for schools. In R. W. Lissitz & H. Jiao (Eds.), *Computers and their impact on state assessment: Recent history and predictions for the future* (pp. 195–226). Information Age Publishing.

Chang, H. H. (2015). Psychometrics behind computerized adaptive testing. *Psychometrika*, *80*(1), 1–20. https://doi.org/10.1007/s11336-014-9401-5

Coeckelbergh, M. (2023). Democracy, epistemic agency, and AI: Political epistemology in times of artificial intelligence. *AI and Ethics*, *3*(4), 1341–1350. https://doi.org/10.1007/s43681-022-00239-4

Conati, C. & Kardan, S. (2013). Student modeling: Supporting personalized instruction, from problem solving to exploratory open-ended activities. *AI Magazine*, *34*, 13–26. https://doi.org/10.1609/aimag.v34i3.2483

Cope, B. & Kalantzis, M. (2009). Ubiquitous learning: An agenda for educational transformation. In B. Cope & M. Kalantzis (Eds.), *Ubiquitous learning* (pp. 1–19). University of Illinois Press.

Cope, B. & Kalantzis, M. (2015). The things you do to know: An introduction to the pedagogy of multiliteracies. In B. Cope & M. Kalantzis (Eds.), *A pedagogy of multiliteracies: Learning by Design* (pp. 1–36). Palgrave Macmillan.

Cope, B. & Kalantzis, M. (2017). Conceptualizing e-learning. In B. Cope & M. Kalantzis (Eds.), *ELearning ecologies* (pp. 1–45). Routledge.

Cope, B. & Kalantzis, M. (2019). Education 2.0: Artificial intelligence and the end of the test. *Beijing International Review of Education*, *1*(2–3), 528–543. https://brill.com/view/journals/bire/1/2-3/article-p528_528.xml?language=en

Cope, B. & Kalantzis, M. (2022). The cybernetics of learning. *Educational Philosophy and Theory*, *54*(14), 2352–2388. https://doi.org/10.1080/00131857.2022.2033213

Cope, B. & Kalantzis, M. (2023). Towards education justice: Multiliteracies revisited. In G. C. Zapata, M. Kalantzis, & B. Cope (Eds.), *Multiliteracies in international educational contexts: Towards education justice* (pp. 1–33). Routledge.

Cope, B. & Kalantzis, M. (2024a). A multimodal grammar of artificial intelligence: Measuring the gains and losses in generative AI. *Multimodality & Society*, *4*(2), 123–152. https://doi.org/10.1177/26349795231221699

Cope, B. & Kalantzis, M. (2024b). On cyber-social learning: A critique of artificial intelligence in education. In T. Kourkoulou, A. O. Tzirides, B. Cope, & M. Kalantzis (Eds.), *Trust and inclusion in AI-mediated education: Where human learning meets learning machines* (pp. 3–34). Springer. https://doi.org/10.1007/978-3-031-64487-0_1

Cope, B., Kalantzis, M., & Magee, L. (2011a). *Towards a semantic web: Connecting knowledge in academic research*. Woodhead Publishing.

Cope, B., Kalantzis, M., McCarthey, S., Vojak, C., & Kline, S. (2011b). Technology-mediated writing assessments: Paradigms and principles. *Computers and Composition*, *28*, 79–96.

Cope, B., Kalantzis, M., Abd-El-Khalick, F., & Bagley, E. (2013). Science in writing: Learning scientific argument in principle and practice. *E-Learning and Digital Media*, *10*, 420–241. https://newlearningonline.com/_uploads/7_Cope_ELEA_10_4_article2_web.pdf

Dai, W., Lin, J., Jin, F., Li, T., Tsai, Y., Gasevic, D., & Chen, G. (2023, April 13). Can large language models provide feedback to students? A case study on ChatGPT. https://doi.org/10.35542/osf.io/hcgzj

DiCerbo, K. & Behrens, J. (2014). *Impacts of the digital ocean on education*. Pearson.

Driver, R., Newton, P., & Osborne, J. (2000). Establishing the norms of scientific argumentation in classrooms. *Science Education*, *84*, 287–312. https://doi.org/10.1002/(SICI)1098-237X(200005)84:3<287::AID-SCE1>3.0.CO;2-A

Farmer, F. R. & Glass, B. (2010). *Web reputation systems*. O'Reilly.

Gee, J. P. (2007). *What video games have to teach us about learning and literacy*: Revised and expanded edition. Palgrave Macmillan.

Gee, J. P. (2014). *The social mind: Language, ideology, and social practice*. Common Ground.

Gergen, K. J. & Dixon-Román, E. (2013). *Epistemology in measurement: Paradigms and practices*. The Gordon Commission.

Haythornthwaite, C. (2009). Participatory transformations. In B. Cope & M. Kalantzis (Eds.), *Ubiquitous learning* (pp. 32–37). University of Illinois Press.

Jenkins, H. (2006). *Confronting the challenges of participatory culture: Media education for the 21st century*. John D. and Catherine T. MacArthur Foundation.

Kalantzis, M. & Cope, B. (2012). *New learning: Elements of a science of education*. Cambridge University Press.

Kalantzis, M. & Cope, B. (2025). Literacy in the time of artificial intelligence. *Reading Research Quarterly*, *60*, Article e591. https://doi.org/10.1002/rrq.591

Kalantzis, M., Cope, B., & the Learning by Design Project Group. (2005). *Learning by design*. Victorian Schools Innovation Commission and Common Ground Publishing.

Kalantzis-Cope, P. (2016). Whose data? Problematizing the 'gift' of social labor. *Global Media and Communication*, *12*(3), 295–309. https://doi.org/10.1177/1742766516676207

Kalantzis, M. & Cope, B. (2020). Adding sense: Context and interest in a grammar of multimodal meaning. Cambridge University Press.

Knight, S., Buckingham Shum, S., & Littleton, K. (2013, April 8–12). Epistemology, pedagogy, assessment, and learning analytics. In *Proceedings of the Third Conference on Learning Analytics and Knowledge* (LAK 2013) (pp. 75–84). ACM.

Kordzadeh, N. & Ghasemaghaei, M. (2022). Algorithmic bias: Review, synthesis, and future research directions. *European Journal of Information Systems*, *31*(3), 388–409. https://doi.org/10.1080/0960085X.2021.1927212

Laupichler, M. C., Aster, A., Schirch, J., & Raupach, T. (2022). Artificial intelligence literacy in higher and adult education: A scoping literature review. *Computers and Education: Artificial Intelligence*, *3*, Article 100101. https://doi.org/10.1016/j.caeai.2022.100101

Long, D., & Magerko, B. (2020). What is AI literacy? Competencies and design considerations. In *Proceedings of the 2020 CHI Conference on Human Factors in Computing Systems* (pp. 1–16). https://doi.org/10.1145/3313831.3376727

Lessig, L. (2008). *Remix: Making art and commerce thrive in the hybrid economy*. Penguin Press.

Lim, F. V., Cope, B., & Kalantzis, M. (2022). A metalanguage for learning: Rebalancing the cognitive with the socio-material. *Frontiers in Communication*, *7*, Article 830613. https://doi.org/10.3389/fcomm.2022.830613

Mislevy, R., Behrens, J., Dicerbo, K., & Levy, R. (2012). Design and discovery in educational assessment: Evidence-centered design, psychometrics, and educational data mining. *Journal of Educational Data Mining*, *4*(1), 11–48. https://doi.org/10.5281/zenodo.3554641

Mollick, E. R., & Mollick, L. (2023). Assigning AI: Seven approaches for students, with prompts. SSRN. http://dx.doi.org/10.2139/ssrn.4475995

Munford, D., & Zembal-Saul, C. (2002, April 6–10). Learning science through argumentation: Prospective teachers' experiences in an innovative science course. Paper Presented at the *Annual Meeting of the National Association for Research in Science Teaching*, New Orleans, LA.

National Research Council. (2000). *How people learn: Brain, mind, experience, and school* (Expanded ed.). The National Academies Press. https://doi.org/10.17226/9853

Ng, D. T. K., Leung, J. K. L., Chu, S. K. W., & Qiao, M. S. (2021). Conceptualizing AI literacy: An exploratory review. *Computers and Education: Artificial Intelligence*, *2*, Article 100041. https://doi.org/10.1016/j.caeai.2021.100041

O'Reilly, T. (2005). *What is Web 2.0? Design patterns and business models for the next generation of software*. http://www.oreillynet.com/pub/a/oreilly/tim/news/2005/09/30/what-is-web-20.html

Pagano, T. P., Loureiro, R. B., Lisboa, F. V. N., Peixoto, R. M., Guimarães, G. A. S., Cruz, G. O. R., Araujo, M. M., Santos, L. L., Cruz, M. A. S., Oliveira, E. L. S., Winkler, I., & Nascimento, E. G. S. (2023). Bias and unfairness in machine learning models: A systematic review on datasets, tools, fairness metrics, and identification and mitigation methods. *Big Data and Cognitive Computing*, *7*(1), Article 15. https://doi.org/10.3390/bdcc7010015

Paloque-Bergès, C. & Schafer, V. (2019). Arpanet (1969–2019). *Internet Histories*, *3*(1), 1–14. https://doi.org/10.1080/24701475.2018.1560921

Raji, I. D., & Buolamwini, J. (2019). Actionable auditing: Investigating the impact of publicly naming biased performance results of commercial AI products. In *AAAI/ACM Conference on AI, Ethics, and Society (AIES '19)*. ACM. https://doi.org/10.1145/3306618.3314244

Reese, G. (2009). *Cloud application architectures: Building applications and infrastructure in the cloud*. O'Reilly.

Rupp, A. A., Nugent, R., & Nelson, B. (2012). Evidence-centered design for diagnostic assessment within digital learning environments: Integrating modern psychometrics and educational data mining. *Journal of Educational Data Mining*, *4*(1), 1–10. https://doi.org/10.5281/zenodo.3554639

Serafini, F. (2015). Multimodal literacy: From theories to practices. *Language Arts*, *92*(6), 412–423. https://www.jstor.org/stable/24577533

Shute, V. J. & Zapata-Rivera, D. (2012). Adaptive educational systems. In P. J. Durlach & A. M. Lesgold (Eds.), *Adaptive technologies for training and education* (pp. 7–27). Cambridge University Press. https://doi.org/10.1017/CBO9781139049580.004

Steiss, J., Tate, T., Graham, S., Cruz, J., Hebert, M., Wang, J., Moon, Y., Tseng, W., Warschauer, M., & Booth Olson, C. (2024). Comparing the quality of human and ChatGPT feedback of students' writing. *Learning and Instruction*, *91*, Article 101894. https://doi.org/10.1016/j.learninstruc.2024.101894

Surowiecki, J. (2004). *The wisdom of crowds: Why the many are smarter than the few and how collective wisdom shapes business, economies, societies and nations*. Doubleday.

Twidale, M. B. (2009). From ubiquitous computing to ubiquitous learning. In B. Cope & M. Kalantzis (Eds.), *Ubiquitous learning* (pp. 72–89). University of Illinois Press.

Tzirides, A. O., Saini, A., Zapata, G. C., Searsmith, D., Cope, B., Kalantzis, M., Castro, V., Kourkoulou, T., Jones, J., da Silva, R. A., Whiting, J., & Kastania, N. P. (2023). Generative AI: Implications and applications for education. *ArXiv*. https://arxiv.org/abs/2305.07605

Tzirides, A. O., Zapata, G. C., Kastania, N. P., Saini, A. K., Castro, V., Ismael, S. A., You, Y., Afonso dos Santos, T., Searsmith, D., O'Brien, C., Cope, B., & Kalantzis, M. (2024a). Combining human and artificial intelligence for enhanced AI literacy in higher education. *Computers and Education Open*, *6*, Article 100184. https://doi.org/10.1016/j.caeo.2024.100184

Tzirides, A. O., Zapata, G. C., Bolger, P. A., Cope, B., Kalantzis, M., & Searsmith, D. (2024b). Exploring instructors' views on fine-tuned generative AI feedback in higher education. *International Journal on E-Learning*, *23*(3), 319–334. https://www.learntechlib.org/primary/p/225173/

UNESCO. (2023). *Guidance for generative AI in education and research*. UNESCO. https://unesdoc.unesco.org/ark:/48223/pf0000386693

van Leeuwen, T. (2017). Multimodal literacy. *Metaphor*, *4*, 17–23.

Walkington, C. (2013). Using adaptive learning technologies to personalize instruction to student interests: The impact of relevant contexts on performance and learning outcomes. *Journal of Educational Psychology*, *105*, 932–945. https://doi.org/10.1037/a0031882

Weiner, N. (1965). *Cybernetics: Or control and communication in the animal and the machine* (Original work published 1948). MIT Press.

West, D. (2012). *Big data for education: Data mining, data analytics, and web dashboards*. Brookings Institution.

Wiliam, D. (2011). *Embedded formative assessment*. Solution Tree Press.

Wolf, M. A. (2010). Innovate to educate: System [re]design for personalized learning—A report from the 2010 symposium. Software & Information Industry Association, August 4–6.

Zapata, G. C. (2018). A match made in heaven: An introduction to learning by design and its role in heritage language education. In G. C. Zapata & M. Lacorte (Eds.), *Multiliteracies pedagogy and language learning: Teaching Spanish to heritage speakers* (pp. 1–26). Palgrave Macmillan. https://doi.org/10.1007/978-3-319-63103-5_1

Zapata, G. C. (2022). *Learning by design and second language teaching: Theory, research, and practice*. Routledge.

Zapata, G. C. (2025). Reflections and future directions. In G. C. Zapata (Ed.), *Generative AI technologies, multiliteracies, and language education (pp. 136–140)*. Routledge.

Zapata, G. C., Cope, B., Kalantzis, M., Tzirides, A. O, Saini, A., Searsmith, D., Whiting, J., Kastania, N. P., Castro, V., Kourkoulou, T, Jones, J., & Abrantes da Silva, R. (2025a). AI and peer reviews in higher education: Students' multimodal views on benefits, differences, and limitations. *Technology, Pedagogy and Education*, *34*(5), 583–601. https://doi.org/10.1080/1475939X.2025.2480807

Zapata, G. C., Saini, A. K., Tzirides, A. O., Cope, B., & Kalantzis, M. (2024). The role of AI feedback in university students' learning experiences: An exploration grounded in activity theory. *Ubiquitous Learning: An International Journal*, *18*(2), 1–30. https://doi.org/10.18848/1835-9795/CGP/v18i02/1-30

Zapata, G. C., Tzirides, A. O., Cope, B., You, Y.-L., Kalantzis, M., & Searsmith, D. (2025b). A systemic functional linguistics discourse analysis of learner-centered, generative AI feedback in higher education. *EdArXiv Preprints*. https://doi.org/10.35542/osf.io/nuhq2_v1

Zhou, J., Zhang, Y., Luo, Q., Parker, A. G., & De Choudhury, M. (2023). Synthetic lies: Understanding AI-generated misinformation and evaluating algorithmic and human solutions. In *Proceedings of the 2023 CHI Conference on Human Factors in Computing Systems (CHI '23),* April 23–28, 2023, Hamburg, Germany. ACM. https://doi.org/10.1145/3544548.3581318

Chapter 6
Literacies Development Across Levels of Learning

Introduction

In previous chapters, we examined literacy through historical perspectives (Chapter 1), multimodal meaning-making (Chapter 2), the functions and dynamics of literacy practices (Chapter 3), pedagogical approaches to literacy teaching and learning (Chapter 4), and the transformative influence of digital technologies, including generative artificial intelligence (GenAI) (Chapter 5). Building on this comprehensive understanding, in Chapter 6, we focus on how literacy, which we now refer to in the plural (i.e., *literacies*), develops across various stages of learning, starting with the intricate relationship between linguistic, visual, spatial, and symbolic forms of literacy and cognitive development. Drawing upon key theorists, we discuss how children and learners progressively acquire the ability to think abstractly and generalize concepts across different communicative modes. Our discussion then moves to the role of

Literacies in the Age of AI: Teaching and Learning in the Digital Era,
First Edition. Gabriela C. Zapata, Bill Cope, and Mary Kalantzis.

GenAI in reshaping literacy practices within educational contexts, including its potential to enhance individualized learning experiences, support creative and collaborative processes, and foster critical digital literacy. Specifically, we show how literacy instruction can leverage GenAI to accommodate diverse learner needs across educational settings, from early childhood classrooms to higher education, emphasizing both opportunities and challenges in navigating artificial intelligence (AI)-mediated learning environments.

Literacy and Cognition

A significant body of research in cognitive science, psychology, and education has explored the relationship between language learning and cognitive development. However, as we have seen in previous chapters, due to the multimodal nature of communication, it is also important to consider that cognitive abilities similarly emerge through other meaning forms, including visual symbolization. These abilities reflect cognitive processes parallel to those evident in linguistic development.

As children mature and develop language skills, words initially tied to tangible, adjacent items in their immediate environment—like the particular fork and spoon in their toddler cutlery set—gradually evolve into abstract concepts. This shift enables children to generalize and engage in higher-order, adult-level abstract thinking. For instance, the concrete fork or spoon used for meals everyday evolves into a conceptual entity that encapsulates an abstract function. Thus, when encountering forks and spoons that differ in appearance, we can still identify them as belonging to the same general category, linking them further to broader conceptual categories like "cutlery" or "table set." Such abstraction represents cognitive processing mediated through linguistic symbols.

When considering other meaning forms, such as image or space, we can see that similar cognitive abstractions are formed through diagrams, drawings, and plans, which represent elements of the observable world. These linguistic, visual, spatial, and other modes of thinking develop concurrently, each mode complementing the others.

To further investigate the distinctive qualities of these literacies, in the next three sections, we reference the philosopher Charles Sanders Peirce (1998), who distinguished three ways in which representations—or signs—relate to the world: *icon*, *indicator*, and *symbol*.

Icon

The first type of sign identified by Peirce (1998) is an *icon*, which represents something through similarity or resemblance. An icon is thus defined as a signifier representing something in the real world (the signified), established through resemblance between the sign and its referent. For instance:

- A picture is not the actual object; it signifies that object by resembling it.
- The word "meow" does not physically reproduce my cat Nora's voice; rather, it represents the sound she makes by mimicking it. In language, this form of iconic representation is known as *onomatopoeia*.
- A building plan or spatial map is not the actual structure or area; instead, it signifies these by providing a visual resemblance.
- A gesture imitating someone's mannerisms or behavior does not replicate the actual demeanor but conveys its meaning through resemblance.

Thus, an icon connects to its signified meaning through mimicry, imitation, or visual similarity.

Indicator

The second type of sign is an *indicator* (also called an *index*), which establishes meaning through a direct connection or "pointing" toward something specific in the world. Indicators are signs directly linked to the particular thing they represent. For example,

- Smoke indicates the presence of fire, a weathervane points to wind direction, and footprints indicate someone's path.

- The name "Aconcagua" directly refers to a specific mountain in Argentina.
- A nod toward a nearby chair indicates a place to sit.
- Facial expressions such as smiling or frowning are indicative signs of emotions.
- When birds chirp urgently upon sensing danger, they communicate through indicator or indexical signs.

An indicator is therefore defined as a signifier whose meaning is established through directly pointing or referring to something specific.

Symbol

The third type of meaning described by Peirce (1998) involves *symbolic thinking*—a uniquely human capability enabling people to create and transmit meanings across generations, including:

- *Words as symbols*: Words generally offer no immediate or direct connection to their meaning. Consider words like "freedom," "tree," or "friendship." Each word symbolizes an idea or object without physically resembling or directly pointing to what it represents. Peirce (1998) notes that a word such as "tree" neither visually resembles nor directly presents a tree to us; instead, it requires us to mentally associate it with the concept of a tree. A symbolic word does not indicate a specific tree; rather, it signifies an abstract category encompassing millions of different trees that share essential characteristics.
- *Visual symbols*: Examples include national flags that represent countries, symbols in road signage indicating general instructions (such as "stop"), artistic works representing broad human experiences (like a painting symbolizing peace), or traffic-light colors symbolizing stop/go instructions universally.
- *Symbolic objects*: Objects may symbolize abstract ideas, such as national monuments representing patriotism or historical events, or trophies representing achievements. Everyday

functional objects can symbolize actions or concepts, such as a judge's gavel symbolizing authority or decision-making.

- *Symbolic gestures*: Certain gestures express general concepts rather than specific referents, such as giving a thumbs-up to symbolize approval or success, or waving goodbye as a symbolic gesture of farewell.
- *Symbolic sounds*: Sounds like a school bell indicating class transitions, an alarm signaling danger, or background music creating moods symbolically communicate abstract meanings or contexts rather than referring directly to particular objects.

Symbols also function within broader systems, deriving meaning not only from their direct referents but also from relationships with other symbols within a system. For instance, "fork + knife + spoon" collectively symbolize "cutlery" or "dinner setting" (Figure 6.1).

The meanings associated with symbols rely entirely upon convention, social consensus, or collective agreement. They emerge from shared rules, habits, or societal customs. For instance, we have

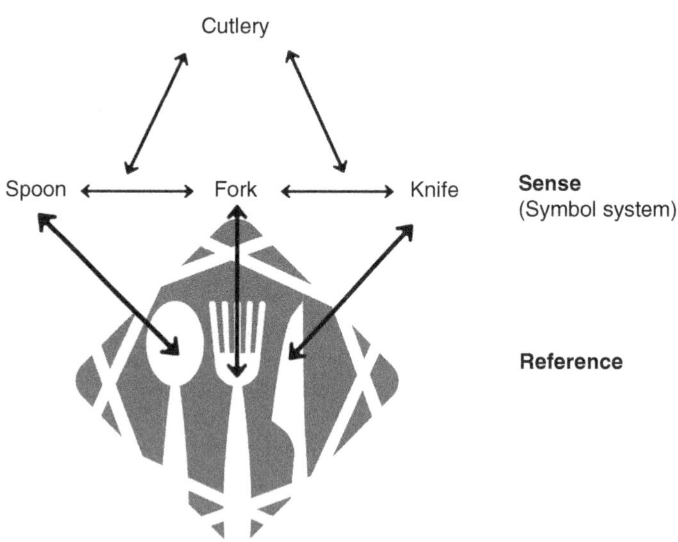

Figure 6.1 Connecting concepts.

collectively learned the symbolic meaning of words and depend upon these meanings in daily communication. Thus, encountering someone who speaks an unfamiliar language forces us to revert to iconic or indicative methods of communication to convey basic information.

Much of human language is symbolic, as words often represent general categories ("cat") rather than specific entities ("Nora"). Visual images also function symbolically—examples include brand logos, heraldic symbols on a shield, or the symbols in a weather forecast diagram. Similarly, physical objects (like birthday candles symbolizing celebration), spaces (such as courtroom layouts symbolizing authority and justice or the contrasting decoration of kitchens versus offices), and gestures (a salute symbolizing respect or a handshake symbolizing agreement) all operate symbolically within human societies.

The meaning associated with a symbol is called a *concept*. Symbols have general meanings, as they refer to types or categories rather than specific entities. The cognitive processes involved in using symbols are known as *generalization*, *abstraction*, or *conceptualization*. A sign communicates an idea about something to the mind. To mean something involves thought. Animals are capable of meaning and thinking, but they cannot independently create or effectively utilize symbols, since animal cognition relies primarily on manipulating icons and indicators. In contrast, human thinking integrates icons, indicators, and symbols.

Symbols thus connect to reality in a unique cognitive manner because they refer to the world through processes of conceptualization. Moreover, symbols do not exist in isolation; instead, they form interconnected systems of meaning. Within these symbolic systems, meanings emerge from relationships between symbols themselves. For example, people learn to identify trees and differentiate them from bushes—a task more complex than it initially appears. This dimension of conceptualization relates to something external to the symbol system (identifying real-world referents).

However, conceptualization also involves building internal, systematic relationships among concepts within the symbol system itself. For instance, people learn not only that trees belong to a broader category called plants, but that plants themselves are a category of living organisms. Furthermore, we learn that there are numerous varieties of trees, and that certain characteristics shared among trees are also shared with other plants, grouping them as part of a broader classification known as vegetation. Thus, this conceptualization process involves symbols being linked to one another in a hierarchical and relational structure. These interrelationships help us understand, for example, how apple trees and oak trees differ yet share fundamental properties as members of the plant kingdom.

Such conceptualization involves symbols being interconnected within structured systems, where meaning arises through the relationships between symbols (e.g., apples and bananas as fruits; fruits as edible plants; edible plants as a type of food). This interplay between symbols is central to disciplines such as science, mathematics, and everyday classification systems, where meaning and understanding are derived from symbolic connections within broader meaning systems.

Designing Meaning

Human infants enter the world profoundly reliant upon their social surroundings. No other animal is born as helpless. Yet, unlike any other species, humans inherit complex symbolic systems from their community, enabling them to interpret the world (self-representation) and communicate with each other (interpersonal meaning-making) (see Chapter 3, pp. 90–91). For instance, infants in Argentina learn Spanish, those in Brazil learn Portuguese, and hearing-impaired infants adopt the symbolic structures of sign language. These symbolic systems function by categorizing, grouping, classifying, generalizing, and abstracting everyday experiences, thus rendering the world understandable. Additionally, infants form internal connections between symbols or concepts, illustrating two closely intertwined aspects of symbolization: symbol-to-symbol connections and symbol-to-world references.

These inherited interpretative frameworks are shaped by the literacy practices or symbolic systems developed by preceding generations. Human conceptual capabilities are extraordinary in their ability to engage with these sophisticated systems of meaning-making (i.e., meaning as design, discussed in Chapter 3). Nevertheless, this inheritance is dynamic rather than static. It involves more than mere assimilation and accommodation—terms borrowed from Swiss psychologist and philosopher Jean Piaget (1971)—of culturally pre-existing knowledge. Rather, it is a potent system allowing the continual recombination and reinterpretation of meanings, always generating new variations.

Language exemplifies this capacity. Utilizing just a few thousand significant words and several hundred logical and grammatical connectives, humans can create limitless meanings. Cultures provide us with extensive symbolic resources, a repertoire of design elements, from which individuals continually generate novel meanings through recombination or redesign. Such recombinations, as we saw in Chapter 3, consistently produce originality. Therefore, humans do not merely inherit established symbolic systems; they actively contribute to their ongoing development. This capacity for innovation further distinguishes humanity as a unique species. Humans possess the remarkable ability to forge novel meanings, thus gaining significant control over their destinies. Consequently, we bear a unique responsibility, both individually and collectively, for shaping our futures and the ecological contexts we inhabit.

Cognitive Development in Children

The Russian psychologist Lev Vygotsky (2012) explored the dynamic processes involved in children's language acquisition, learning, and conceptual thinking. He began with language, identifying the word as "the [most basic] unit of verbal thought" (p. 6). Vygotsky was particularly concerned with words that, using Peirce's terminology, possess symbolic characteristics. Such words "do not refer to a single object, but to a group or to a class of objects. Each word is therefore already a generalization. Generalization is a verbal act of thought and reflects reality in quite another way than sensation and perception reflect it" (Vygotsky, 2012, p. 6). For instance, "cat" serves as a generalization, while "Nora" does not. Moreover, when the word "cat" refers exclusively to one specific cat (*my cat* or *that cat*), it ceases to function symbolically and does not necessitate the type of conceptual thinking that Vygotsky emphasized.

How then do children develop conceptual thinking through symbolic words? Vygotsky (2012) described the initial phase of a child's linguistic-cognitive development as involving an undirected extension of symbols toward inherently unrelated objects, connected only by subjective and chance associations within the child's perception. This stage of language and thought is characterized by unstable, "unorganized *congeries*," or "heaps"—"inherently unrelated objects linked by chance in the child's perception" (Vygotsky, pp. 117–118). For instance, tables become associated with chairs simply due to proximity. Although children's words match adult language in terms of reference, they initially lack the conceptual quality found in adult speech. When a young child uses the word "table," they specifically mean "this table," whereas an adult browsing a furniture website applies the broader concept of a "table" as a category of furniture. Despite using identical words, adults and children differ significantly in cognitive operations.

The subsequent phase identified by Vygotsky (2012) involves children's formation of *complexes*, a critical intermediate stage toward genuine conceptual thinking. Here, children begin making logical associations. However, "in a complex, the bonds between its components are concrete and factual rather than abstract and logical" (Vygotsky, 2012, p. 120). Complex meanings emerge from aggregating objects and associating them with particular words. Vygotsky emphasized that "a complex does not rise above its elements as does a concept; it merges with concrete objects that compose it" (p. 125). For example, a child may use "dog" to denote an animal based on specific personal associations.

Vygotsky (2012) also outlined several sub-stages within this period, representing different forms of complexes that typically occur sequentially. Initially, children form *associative complexes*, analogous to assigning a "family" name to individuals frequently linked through experience. Later, children engage in complexes based on shared practical functions, such as grouping various animals together in a toy farm or zoo. Subsequently, they construct *chain complexes*, linking objects like differently shaped colored blocks, but with constantly changing criteria for association. A vivid example given by Vygotsky involves the term "quah," which initially describes a duck swimming in a pond, then extends to a coin with a duck-like image, and ultimately to any round, coin-like item—demonstrating the continually shifting nature of chain complexes.

Following chain complexes, children reach a stage called *diffuse complexes*, where attributes linking items continue to shift indefinitely. Eventually, children start using words that coincide operationally with adult concepts—a phenomenon Vygotsky (2012) described as achieving an operational concept through complex associations. For instance, a child might group triangles together, using the same word as adults for the geometric concept "triangle," although their cognitive basis differs significantly.

Vygotsky (2012) emphasized that these "complexes corresponding to word meanings are not spontaneously developed by the child: The lines along which a complex develops are predetermined by the meaning a given word already has in the language of adults" (p. 135). This overlap between child and adult language ensures mutual understanding, even though children and adults conceptualize differently. Adults may conceptualize "cat" abstractly as an animal distinct from a dog, whereas children specifically reference "this cat, Nora" or "that dog, Fido."

Nonetheless, this linguistic overlap is pedagogically effective. Children learn because words are introduced to them, shaping their perceptions and experiences. Vygotsky (2012) believed that "at the complex stage, word meanings as perceived by the child refer to the same objects that the adult has in mind, which ensures understanding between child and adult, but that the child thinks the same thing in a different way, by means of different mental operations" (pp. 134–135).

After the stage of complexes, evidence emerges of a subsequent significant phase in children's cognitive development characterized by the use of words as fully developed concepts. *Conceptual thinking* encompasses the ability to use words to abstract meaning, to identify essential features that classify events, people, or objects under a single term, and to unite as well as distinguish, analyze, and synthesize. For instance, understanding that Nora is a cat, cats are mammals, mammals are vertebrates, vertebrates belong to animals, and animals differ from plants illustrates conceptual thinking clearly.

While complex thinking initiates the process of unifying disparate impressions by grouping distinct experiential elements, thereby laying a foundation for future generalizations, advanced conceptual thinking demands more than simple unification. Forming an advanced concept requires the ability to abstract, isolating elements and examining these abstracted features separately from the comprehensive concrete experience from which they originate. In the developmental trajectory of children's thinking, the processes of generalization and abstraction are notably intertwined (Vygotsky, 2012).

Initially, children demonstrate their understanding of concepts by translating abstract concepts into concrete language. Vygotsky (2012, p. 148) illustrated this phenomenon by noting that "even [the most] abstract concepts are often translated into the language of concrete action: 'Reasonable means when I am hot and don't stand in a draught." During these early stages, children may accurately form and use concepts within concrete contexts but find articulating the same concepts verbally challenging. The greatest difficulty arises when a child must apply an abstract concept they have grasped to a new, distinct concrete situation.

Concepts function not only to describe the world abstractly or generally—for example, recognizing a previously unseen breed as a cat after encountering multiple cats—but also to interact symbolically with each other within a conceptual system. This includes knowing that cats and dogs are mammals, whereas fish, though also animals, are not mammals. Vygotsky (2012) provided another illustrative example:

> A child learns the word flower, and shortly afterwards the word rose; for a long time the concept 'flower', though more widely applicable than 'rose', cannot be said to be more general for the

> child. It does not include and subordinate 'rose' – the two are interchangeable and juxtaposed. When 'flower' becomes generalized, the relationship of 'flower' and 'rose', as well as of 'flower' and other subordinate concepts, also changes in the child's mind. A system is taking shape. (pp. 183–184)

Consequently, although children might grasp the meanings of words like "rose" and "flower" sufficiently to interact with adults, these terms initially lack the full conceptual depth they acquire in mature cognition. This understanding has significant pedagogical implications. According to Vygotsky (2012, p. 159), directly teaching concepts through merely passing on established generalizations is "impossible and fruitless." He elaborated further by stating that "a teacher who tries to do this usually accomplishes nothing but empty verbalism, a parrot-like repetition of words by the child, simulating a knowledge of the corresponding concepts but actually covering up a vacuum."

This issue represents a common pitfall in didactic instruction (see Chapter 4)—training children to mechanically repeat abstract definitions and rules without genuinely internalizing their meaning. Instead, Vygotsky (1978, 2012) highlights the developmental significance of play, learning through action guided by adults, negotiated adult–child interactions, and connecting acquired generalizations to practical, experiential learning. Effective learning strategies should therefore guide children through complex thought toward full conceptualization, gradually transforming complex thinking into conceptual thinking. In Table 6.1, we summarize the stages of cognitive development discussed in this section.

Table 6.1 Vygotsky's stages of cognitive development

Stages	Description
Congeries	Heaps of inherently unrelated objects linked by chance in the child's perception
Complexes	When the child begins to make logical connections between the particular things they perceive
Concepts	Words that can generalize about kinds of things in the child's experience

Literacies for Learning

Learning in the Zone of Proximal Development

According to Vygotsky (1978), learning takes place within an area he defined as *the zone of proximal development* (ZPD)—"the distance between the actual development level as determined by independent problem solving and the level of potential development as determined through problem solving under adult guidance or in collaboration with more capable peers" (p. 86; Figure 6.2).

Learning in the ZPD depends on teacher guidance that provides *scaffolding*, defined as a process that "enables a child or novice to solve a task or achieve a goal that would be beyond [their] unassisted efforts" (Wood et al., 1976, p. 90). That is, scaffolding is the provision of sufficient support to promote learning when concepts and skills are being first introduced to students. Wood et al. state that, through this process (visually represented in Figure 6.3), educators can not only capture learner interest and control frustration while maintaining the pursuit of instructional goals, but they can

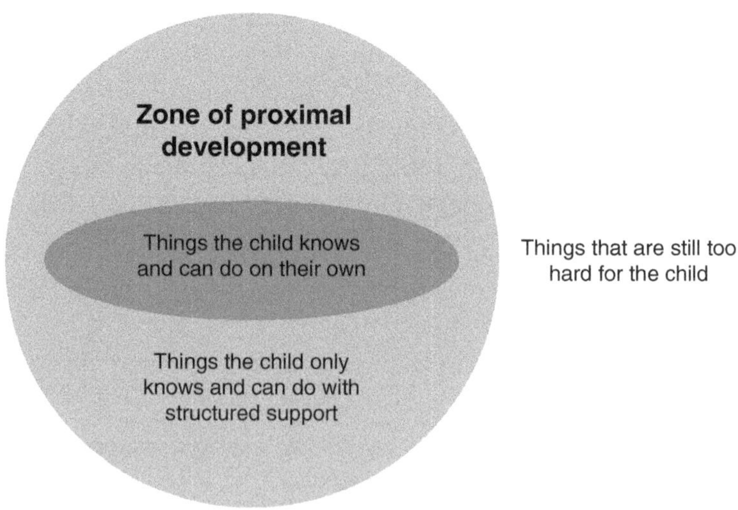

Figure 6.2 The zone of proximal development.

Figure 6.3 Instructional scaffolding (SOURCE: SHARE Multi Academy Trust/https://www.lilyparkprimary.org.uk/attachments/download.asp?file=598&type=pdf).

also simplify tasks by offering students examples and information about steps to achieve expected results and outcomes.

Cognitively, this developmental process is reflected in the interaction between pseudo-concepts and genuine concepts. Although a child may not yet possess fully developed conceptual thinking, they construct their understanding of the world using language and cognitive structures "borrowed" from adults. This borrowed language is not merely imitative; it serves as a bridge between the child's current cognitive limitations and future conceptual development by aligning with adult conceptual structures. Over time, repeated engagement in scaffolded activities helps learners internalize these structures, eventually leading to independent, higher-order thinking.

Inherited systems of symbols play a significant role in this process. Intellectual scaffolding points children toward conceptual understanding through the very symbols that envelop them, despite their continued use of these symbols in more complex, rather than fully conceptual, forms of thought. The ZPD thus outlines the set of functions that are not yet fully developed but are actively developing, i.e., functions that will mature in the near future but presently exist in an early, formative state (Vygotsky, 1978).

Vygotsky (1978, 2012) differentiated his perspective on learning from the *constructivist theory* proposed by his contemporary, Jean

Piaget (1971). According to the constructivist perspective, the learning mind is viewed as a self-organizing system. At certain developmental stages, linked to biological maturation, children's minds actively "construct" meanings that align with their developmental level. Children integrate their constructed meanings into their understanding of the world by either assimilating new experiences into their existing conceptual frameworks or accommodating and altering these frameworks to fit new experiences.

Piaget (1971) emphasized that biological development creates the conditions necessary for learning from experiences. He posited that

> [T]here are biological factors linked to the ... maturation of the nervous system. These factors, which doubtless owe nothing to society ... [are] decisive in the development of cognitive functions ... [F]rom the biological point of view, the stages ... show a 'sequential' character (each being necessary to the following one in a constant order). ... [T]his would naturally suppose a certain constancy or uniformity of development regardless of the social milieu within which individuals are formed. (pp. 46–47).

This viewpoint generally situates the individual, self-constructing child as central to cognitive development. In contrast, Vygotsky (1978, 2012) assigned considerably greater significance to social influences on learning. He observed that children often speak aloud to themselves, imitating adult speech, before gradually internalizing these spoken thoughts as *inner speech* or silent self-dialogue. Consequently, language—and symbolic thinking across various meaning forms such as image, space, and body—significantly shapes thinking processes. That is, thinking capabilities are largely acquired through culturally developed tools for representation and communication, rather than solely through biological maturation or each child independently constructing meaning. This is essentially a process of cognitive sharing, transferring culturally embedded collective memories and understandings across generations.

The Role of Literacies in Learning

Literacies learning takes place during a critical phase in a child's internalization of adult symbolic-conceptual frameworks for learning. This transition from complex to conceptual thinking occurs concurrently across oral language, written language, visual imagery, and other forms of meaning-making—hence our use of *literacies* in the plural instead of *literacy*, associated, as we saw in Chapters 1 and 2, solely with reading and writing.

Contrary to the theories underlying authentic pedagogy about learning to write, Vygotsky (2012, pp. 191–192) argued that "the development of writing does not repeat the developmental history of speaking," as even the most basic forms of writing involve "a high level of abstraction." For instance, children must "disengage themselves from the sensory aspect of speech and replace words by images of words," as well as "take cognizance of the sound structure of each word, dissect it, and reproduce it in alphabetical symbols," which implies that writing "requires deliberate analytical action on the part of the child" (Vygotsky, 2012, p. 192).

Furthermore, the motivations for writing are considerably removed from being "authentic" or "natural," even if these terms correctly describe how children use oral language to express immediate needs and interests in their early years. Writing, in contrast, is "more abstract, more intellectualized, further removed from immediate needs" (Vygotsky 2012, p. 192). Indeed, this abstraction extends to the difference between thinking through *inner speech*—a tool for thinking derived from early oral language—and the language of writing. Inner speech is predominantly predicative, as the thinker already knows the context or subject. In contrast, written speech must explicitly and comprehensively describe situations to ensure intelligibility. This shift from highly condensed inner speech to extensively detailed written language necessitates what Vygotsky (2012) referred to as *deliberate semantics*, the intentional structuring of meaning.

Clearly, children begin writing before their cognitive capabilities are sufficiently developed to fully utilize this form of deliberate semantics, which, at its most advanced level, involves activities such as planning and drafting. Yet, the initiation of writing instruction at a stage when the cognitive abilities underpinning writing are still elementary demonstrates that cognitive capacity "does not precede instruction"; instead, it "unfolds in a continuous interaction with the contributions of instruction" (Vygotsky, 2012, p. 195). Consequently, "grammar" assumes "paramount importance for the mental development of a child" by fostering deliberate, abstract, and analytical thinking specific to writing (Vygotsky, 2012, p. 194). These sophisticated thinking patterns subsequently permeate adult speech, particularly in forms of speech resembling writing, as explored in Chapter 2 (see sound and speech).

We propose extending Vygotsky's concept of *deliberate semantics* beyond writing alone to include *literacies* involving multiple meaning forms. We believe this is necessary since learners also engage in abstract and conceptual thinking through visual images, gestures, and spatial representations. As discussed in previous chapters, we inherently think multimodally, and frequently, representing meanings in multiple meaning forms can enhance our thinking capacity. That is, representing knowledge through text, image, speech, or any sequence or combination of these meaning forms can facilitate more effective and efficient thinking, tailored to the particular content or, in educational contexts, the learner's preferred approach. As shown in Chapter 2, different meaning forms enable parallel yet distinct ways of thinking, highlighting the inherent multimodality of our cognitive processes. However, literacy, in the singular, in the narrow sense of reading and writing alone, does not necessarily imply enhanced cognitive ability.

Scribner and Cole's (1981) research on West African Vai script readers and writers underscores this point. Their comparative study found no significant cognitive differences between Vai who could write in their native language and those who could not. However, significant cognitive differences did emerge among those who acquired literacy through formal education, with its uniquely generalizing conceptual frameworks characteristic of disciplinary learning. It was, therefore, formal schooling rather than literacy per se that influenced cognition.

Developing "Metarepresentations"

Historically, as we saw in Chapters 3 and 4, traditional didactic literacy instruction incorporated teaching grammar as a metalanguage to describe the logic underlying language. Although we have already acknowledged the limitations of this traditional approach, there remains value in preserving the concept of what we refer to as *metarepresentations*—essentially, meanings about meaning or symbols that describe symbol systems, such as grammar, visual keys, and musical notation. For instance, the word "cat" symbolizes a specific type of animal, whereas labeling "cat" as a *noun* involves using one symbol to categorize another symbol. Here, a *noun* serves as a *metasymbol* or *metarepresentation* (Figure 6.4).

We advocate using the concept of *metarepresentations* as practical learning tools to help learners identify and understand design elements within representations (used to facilitate thinking) and communications (used to convey messages). The primary goal of engaging with metarepresentations is therefore not to memorize definitions or adhere rigidly to conventional grammar rules. Instead, it involves learning to dissect or "unpack" texts by developing and applying conceptual frameworks—expressed through language, diagrams, or other symbolic means—to elucidate the structure and design of texts. For example, when analyzing a website, you could construct a metarepresentation detailing the site's visual, textual,

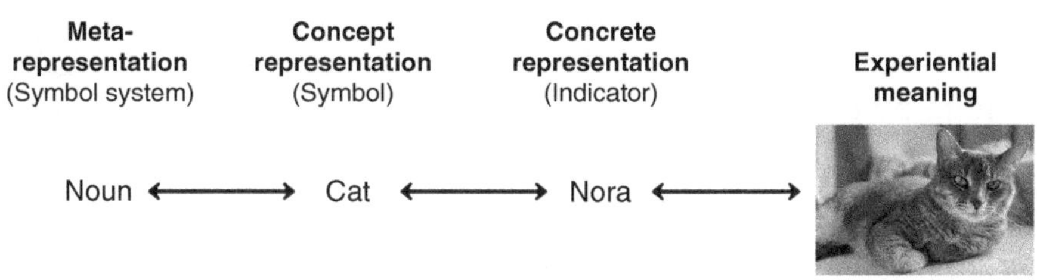

Figure 6.4 From experience to metarepresentation.

and possibly auditory elements. This representation might take the form of written descriptions, system diagrams, or network maps.

Also, another compelling rationale for employing metarepresentations as a learning strategy is their inherent efficiency. By the time children enter formal education, they already possess rich resources for meaning-making through sophisticated interactions with words, images, gestures, and spatial relationships. Leveraging and expanding these existing foundations is the most effective way to support students' gradual, multi-step transition from complex to conceptual thinking. Since children arrive at school already equipped with emerging conceptual abilities, it is logical and efficient to nurture and further develop these skills rather than relying solely on immersion-based methods.

Given the vast intellectual terrain schools must cover with increasingly limited resources, employing conceptualization, generalization, and abstraction provides a valuable shortcut. These cognitive strategies concentrate reality into identifiable patterns, allowing students to master broader, generally applicable concepts rather than numerous isolated specifics. And, as we will see later in this chapter, GenAI can facilitate and expand these strategies in today's classrooms.

The Strangeness of School

Schooling presents us with a peculiar strangeness—a distinctive and somewhat unnatural way of speaking about the world. Vygotsky (2012) emphasized this difference, noting that the mind encounters unique challenges when it assimilates concepts in school compared to when concepts are acquired independently. For instance, he highlighted the distinctive nature of school-based learning by emphasizing the idea of *scientific concepts*—abstract terms such as "nouns," "integers," or "atoms." Unlike everyday language, which typically references tangible, immediate objects within a child's personal experience, scientific concepts rely heavily on language itself, utilizing words as tools to deliberately focus and structure thought.

Thought built upon scientific concepts involves abstract references that typically distance the learner from direct, immediate experience. Classroom discourse often embodies what Courtney Cazden (2001) described as *schoolishness*, distinctively unlike the other forms of communication encountered by a child in daily life. Cazden also introduced the idea of *exophoric reference*—communication referencing objects or concepts external and distant from the immediate school context. Importantly, she argued that the challenges students face are less about losing the immediacy of everyday contexts and more about grappling with implied but frequently unstated references to other texts, both spoken and written.

We expand upon this by noting the role of complex visual representations in scientific diagrams and the audio representations utilized in music or recorded speech. This phenomenon, Cazden (2001) believes, culminates in academic discourse—the special ways of talking expected in school. Because classroom discourse is so different from the child's common sense, it is the role of the teacher to help students to recontextualize, to construct contexts actively in the mind. This unique character of classroom discourse parallels, in linguistic and intellectual terms, the peculiarity of literacies in general. Recording and re-presentation of non-present meanings can occur in writing, but also today in various other readily available digital forms of recording: speech, music, video recordings of gesture, photographs, drawings, graphs, diagrams, and the like. Classrooms can use these expanded literacies to refer to an outside world. The representation of the world by schooling is intrinsically the stuff of literacies.

Toward the "Reflective Consciousness" of Adult Cognition

Extending this argument further, the progression into conceptual thinking described by Vygotsky (2012) involves more than merely understanding abstract terms; it involves moving toward what he calls *reflective consciousness*. According to Vygotsky, children's journey into conceptual thought eventually leads them to a higher cognitive stage, characterized by an "awareness of the activity of the mind—the consciousness of being conscious" (p. 180). Thus, the acquisition of scientific concepts such as "nouns," "integers," or "atoms" not only refers to abstract ideas but also creates a new cognitive space, where concepts gain meaning through structured systems within disciplines—grammar in language, numbers in mathematics, and atomic structures in chemistry.

From a cognitive perspective, Vygotsky (1978) posited that children's memory becomes increasingly logical and structured as they mature, ultimately reducing memory processes to the establishment of logical relationships. Young learners move from recognizing objects based on simple, sensory familiarity to identifying concepts through logical connections indicated by the context of tasks.

In this sense, literacies support new modes of thinking—characteristic modes of adult cognition. Literacies provide frameworks for adult-like conceptual thinking, enabling individuals to interpret and understand their world differently. These literacies are embedded within and communicated through tangible objects (such as tables or computers), spatial arrangements (parks or classrooms), gestures (such as nodding or shrugging), language (naming and conceptually linking actions or entities), and visual imagery. The answers children discover through these literacies are inherently embedded in the meanings already constructed around them.

Leontyev (2009) argued that individuals do not discover the world independently; instead, they internalize the accumulated experiences of previous generations. That is, we assimilate cultural experiences through the conceptual meanings prevalent in our environments, whether these involve physical tools or symbolic representations like language and imagery (see also Wertsch 1991, 1998). Thus, literacies form a foundational means by which learners internalize and utilize their culture's conceptual and symbolic resources.

Literacies as Extensions of Mind

We end this section by positing that literacies are not merely a medium through which we think; they also serve as constant extensions of memory and individual cognition, transcending inherent limitations. They function as social mnemonics or aides-memoire—forms of collective memory external to our individual minds, which become increasingly crucial supplements as children mature into adults. Literacies provide access to knowledge even when it cannot be immediately recalled, enabling us to "look up" information by consulting someone who already knows, reading written texts, reviewing recorded images, triggering memory through spatial cues (such as recalling items when walking supermarket aisles or navigating complicated routes), or replaying audio clips (such as hearing a familiar piece of music or the sound of a doorbell). Thus, literacies serve as conceptual artifacts that significantly extend our capacities for thinking and action beyond the confines of our own brains.

Moreover, literacies embody a cumulative, collective, and distributed intelligence that is fundamentally human. Created and sustained within communities, literacies represent the connective tissue that holds these communities together. They persistently serve as indispensable social expansions of our individual cognitive capacities.

The intricate process of symbolization, conceptual thinking, and literacies development we have examined so far in this chapter underscores a fundamental aspect of human cognition: Our unique ability to construct, internalize, and critically engage with complex symbolic systems. In this chapter and previous ones, we have seen how we continuously inherit, reshape, and expand symbolic resources, actively designing and redesigning meanings across generations. Today, however, these human-driven processes face a profound shift due to the rise of GenAI, a form of technology capable of autonomously producing texts, images, audio, and other symbolic representations. Even though, as discussed in Chapter 3 (see pages 101–103), humans and GenAI "think" and communicate in fundamentally different ways, as GenAI-generated symbols become increasingly embedded within educational practices, everyday communication, and even early childhood learning environments, it is crucial that learners not only understand the generated outputs but also critically engage with the processes by which these meanings are algorithmically constructed. This implies the need for students' in-depth understanding of the differences between human and machine meaning-making.

Indeed, the integration of GenAI into education introduces new dimensions to traditional literacies, necessitating a nuanced understanding that we now term AI literacy (a concept we introduced in Chapter 5 [see pages 192–194)—the new kid on the block. Just as Vygotsky (1978, 2012) emphasized guided learning through scaffolding within a learner's ZPD, AI literacy requires educators to scaffold students' comprehension of how AI systems work, their ethical implications, and their potential biases. Learners across all ages—from early childhood through adulthood—must now be equipped to critically assess, creatively utilize, and ethically navigate AI-generated texts, images, and symbolic representations. The following sections explore this new aspect of human literacies in greater depth, addressing how educational approaches must evolve to prepare learners to interact effectively, critically, and ethically in increasingly AI-enriched contexts. We start by examining the concept of AI literacy in more depth, focusing on conceptualizations and principles developed in the last two years.

Conceptualizing and Developing AI Literacy in Educational Contexts

As discussed in Chapter 5, the development of AI literacy has recently emerged as a significant focus in all educational contexts, part of our literacies repertoire, due to the profound implications for society, economy, and individual agency resulting from the wide availability and use of GenAI technologies (Cope & Kalantzis, 2024; Kalantzis & Cope, 2025). In Chapter 5, we posited that AI literacy broadly encompasses the competencies required to critically and effectively engage with AI technologies, including GenAI, across various sociocultural contexts, enabling both teachers and students to understand, utilize, and create with AI responsibly and ethically. Since November 2022, multiple frameworks have emerged to provide educators, including those in teacher-education programs, with guidance on ways in which GenAI technologies can be incorporated in the classroom and AI literacy can be developed.

One of the most important existing approaches is UNESCO's *AI Competency Framework for Students* (UNESCO, 2024). This document systematically integrates AI education into curricula, emphasizing ethically conscious, responsible, and innovative engagement with AI. The model is based on 12 competencies structured into four dimensions—*Human-Centered Mindset*, *Ethics of AI*, *AI Techniques and Applications*, and *AI System Design*. These competencies progress through three levels: *Understand*, *Apply*, and *Create*, reflecting learners' development from foundational knowledge to advanced creative and innovative skills and ensuring that they acquire a comprehensive, age-appropriate understanding of AI concepts and their societal implications (Table 6.2).

Embedded in UNESCO's (2024) framework, we can identify both Vygotsky's (1978, 2012) conceptualizations and the reflexive pedagogy practices we described in Chapter 4, as well as the definition of cyber-social learning and principles of digital citizenship we brought forward in Chapter 5. For instance, the UNESCO's model emphasizes scaffolded, spiral learning sequences to progressively deepen students' understanding and skills. At the foundational *Understand* level, learners across all educational stages

Table 6.2 UNESCO's AI competency framework for students

Stages	Description		
	Understand	Apply	Create
Human-centered mindset	Human agency	Human accountability	Citizenship in the era of AI
Ethics of AI	Embodied ethics	Safe and responsible use	Ethics by design
AI techniques and applications	AI foundations	Application skills	Creating AI tools
AI system design	Problem scoping	Architectural design	Iteration and feedback loops

Source: UNESCO, 2024 / CC BY-SA.

gain essential cognitive and practical knowledge, enabling them to explain fundamental AI concepts, relate these concepts to real-life contexts, and interpret relevant issues appropriately. Advancing to the *Apply* level, students critically examine AI methodologies, responsibly employ ethical considerations, and practically apply their learning to diverse scenarios. The *Create* level, targeted at learners with a strong interest in AI, promotes advanced competencies, empowering them to design, implement, and ethically evaluate AI solutions to address real-world challenges.

To facilitate effective implementation, UNESCO (2024) provides strategic recommendations for integrating the AI competency framework into educational systems, some of which clearly align with the principles and tenets of *Learning by Design* (LbyD) and reflexive pedagogy discussed in Chapter 4 (see pages 134–142; also, you will explore these connections in more depth in Task 1 on page 142). For example, recommendations include the employment of interactive, collaborative instructional practices, materials, and assessments grounded in authentic tasks, relying on available resources and connected to students' lifeworlds, communities, and personal/academic needs. Additionally, the approach emphasizes the need to align competencies with national AI strategies for cohesive and monitored development, as well as creating interdisciplinary curricula that integrate AI seamlessly with existing STEAM (science, technology, engineering, arts, mathematics) subjects. Further recommendations highlight the establishment of robust digital infrastructure and professional development for educators. Collectively, these measures aim to nurture a human-centered, ethically grounded approach to AI education, preparing students to engage critically and creatively with GenAI technologies. These objectives are clearly parallel to our model for cyber-social learning (see pages 178–183 in Chapter 5) and are reflective of the principles of digital citizenship we introduced in the last section of Chapter 5 (see pages 194–197).

Overall, as posited in Chapter 5 and UNESCO's (2024) framework, AI literacy in education involves the development of technical competencies, critical thinking, ethical reasoning, and practical applications, structured through progressive learning stages and pedagogies that are responsive to learners' lifeworld differences. In the next sections, by examining existing works, we address knowledge and practices that the development of AI literacy might entail, considering learners' developmental pathways discussed in the first two sections of this chapter. We start with early childhood education.

Early Childhood Education

Early childhood literacy has traditionally emphasized print awareness, phonemic knowledge, and oral language development as foundational skills necessary for later reading and writing proficiency (Snow et al., 1998). However, with the emergence of digital technologies, as we saw in the previous chapter, literacy now extends beyond conventional boundaries, encompassing interactions with digital tools such as touchscreen tablets, voice-activated assistants, and interactive e-books (Cope & Kalantzis, 2017). These digital interactions offer multimodal literacies experiences by blending spoken narration, animated visuals, interactive text, and tactile engagement. Such experiences foster vocabulary acquisition, narrative comprehension, and intuitive interactions with technology. As these digital tools, including those relying on GenAI technologies, become more prevalent, early literacy education must also focus on the development of students' AI literacy.

Research on this type of literacy in early childhood (e.g., Su & Yang, 2022; Su & Zhong, 2022) has posited that it involves primarily the development of three competencies: *AI knowledge*, *AI skill*, and *AI attitude*. *AI knowledge* involves an understanding of foundational AI concepts, including basic principles of machine learning, perception, and algorithmic decision-making. *AI skill* encompasses practical abilities such as computational thinking, problem-solving with AI tools, and basic programming activities, enabling children to engage with AI through hands-on experiences. *AI attitude* pertains to children's awareness and critical perspectives on AI technologies, including ethical implications, potential biases, and privacy concerns.

Several effective pedagogical approaches for developing these competencies have been proposed. For example, AI-driven toys or interactive platforms, such as *PopBots* (Williams et al., 2019) and *Zhorai* (Lin et al., 2020), have been shown to provide children with engaging and developmentally appropriate ways to explore AI-related concepts like supervised machine learning and GenAI through play-based learning. Inquiry-based and problem-solving pedagogies, such as our reflexive pedagogy and UNESCO's, (2024) framework, have proven to be particularly effective, as they align with young children's natural curiosity and learning preferences (Kewalramani et al., 2021). Hands-on activities, including sorting algorithms, problem-solving exercises, and supervised learning tasks, have also revealed positive outcomes in building AI literacy (Chen et al., 2020). Additionally, Su and Yang (2022) suggest that incorporating digital enhancements into traditional literacy activities can further strengthen early literacy experiences. For instance, interactive story time sessions involving both physical picture books and digital projections or AI-enhanced voice interactions can effectively scaffold emergent literacy skills.

Despite the promising benefits of AI integration in early childhood education, several challenges persist. Concerns regarding data privacy, commercialization of children's digital experiences, and the need to establish appropriate screen time guidelines necessitate careful curriculum design (Su & Yang, 2022). Additionally, a lack of standardized AI curricula for early learners and insufficient research on the long-term impact of AI literacy further complicate implementation efforts (Chen et al., 2020). Research also indicates a shortage of rigorous validation of assessment tools used to measure children's AI literacy, highlighting the need for robust evaluation frameworks (Su et al., 2023).

To overcome these challenges, AI literacy education must incorporate a structured curriculum framework with well-defined objectives, subject matter, teaching methods, and assessment strategies (UNESCO, 2024). The use of pre-test and post-test assessments, classroom observations, and self-assessment questionnaires can provide valuable insights into children's learning outcomes and the effectiveness of AI interventions (Su & Zhong, 2022). Additionally, the development of age-appropriate AI teaching systems, such as conversational agents and intelligent tutoring systems, can support personalized learning and cognitive development in young children (Su et al., 2023). Furthermore, curriculum developers should explore embodied AI approaches, including AI-enabled robotic toys, to make AI learning more tangible and engaging for early learners. Scaffolded problem-based learning remains a recommended instructional method, fostering children's critical thinking, problem-solving, and cooperation skills through group activities in the ZPD (Vygotsky, 1978, 2012).

In sum, embedding AI literacy in early childhood education requires thoughtfully designed curricular frameworks, effective pedagogical strategies, and continuous educator support. By integrating AI knowledge, skills, and attitudes into early literacy experiences, young learners can develop a foundational understanding of AI technologies and their societal implications. Addressing barriers related to teacher preparedness, equitable access, and curriculum standardization is essential to ensure that AI literacy initiatives benefit all children (Druga et al., 2019, 2022). As AI continues to shape the future of education and society, early childhood AI literacy development will play a crucial role in preparing young learners to become informed, ethical, and adaptive users of GenAI technologies throughout their educational journeys and beyond.

Elementary/Primary School Education

Building on foundational emergent literacy skills developed in early childhood, elementary/primary school contexts (ages 6–11/12) consolidate basic reading, writing, and numeracy while introducing more complex language structures and diverse text types. At this stage, children move beyond decoding simple texts, refining comprehension strategies, developing fluency, and engaging in more sophisticated forms of critical thinking (Strickland et al., 2002). In today's digital age, these traditional literacy skills integrate closely with digital media and interactive platforms, substantially enriching the educational environment and transforming it into a *literacies* environment. The emergence of GenAI technologies further expands this landscape, providing new ways for students to engage with various meaning forms and develop advanced cognitive skills (Kalantzis & Cope, 2025). AI literacy, therefore, is now an essential component of primary education (Simbeck & Kalf, 2024).

The cultivation of AI literacy at the elementary/primary school level involves both conceptual learning and hands-on experiences with AI technologies. At this educational stage, students begin to grasp basic machine learning processes—such as data collection, model training, and iterative refinement—distinguishing these from more explicit instructional programming approaches. Practical engagement with AI fosters technical comprehension while enhancing children's ability to critically evaluate digital content (Simbeck & Kalf, 2024). Existing studies have focused on different ways in which AI technologies can be integrated into literacy instruction.

For instance, Ng et al. (2022) have shown that digital storytelling (DS) can offer students opportunities to create multimodal narratives using text, images, audio recordings, and GenAI tools that generate supportive elements such as transitions, music, and text overlays. In their work with 82 primary school students in Hong Kong, these scholars reported that learners were able to acquire AI knowledge by engaging with basic AI functionalities, including automation and voice recognition. Additionally, the participants successfully applied AI concepts in their digital stories, designing GenAI-driven solutions for real-world problems such as healthcare and environmental protection. Ethical considerations also emerged as a key aspect of AI literacy development, as children integrated discussions about GenAI fairness and bias into their narratives. These findings highlight the potential of DS as an effective pedagogical tool for AI literacy, encouraging students to explore, evaluate, and create GenAI-driven narratives in meaningful ways.

Another emerging trend in AI literacy education is the integration of artificial intelligence of things (AIoT) education programs.

AIoT involves the integration of AI with the internet of things (IoT) to enable smart, autonomous decision-making and enhanced data-driven insights in connected devices and systems. The IoT can be defined as a network of interconnected physical devices embedded with sensors, software, and technologies that enable them to collect, exchange, and act on data over the internet. Research assessing the impact of AIoT on elementary/primary school curricula suggests that these programs can significantly improve students' digital literacy, AI understanding, and problem-solving abilities.

For example, in a study measuring the effectiveness of an AIoT education program, Hong and Kim (2025) found that students demonstrated notable growth in digital literacy skills, including awareness of digital society, problem-solving competencies, and content creation. Additionally, learners exhibited improved comprehension of AI concepts, particularly in relation to AI's societal role and ethical considerations. The hands-on nature of AIoT education was particularly beneficial, as children engaged in assembling IoT devices and applying AI-driven solutions to real-world scenarios.

The findings from these studies align with Vygotsky's (1978, 2012) emphasis on the role of social interaction and scaffolding in cognitive development. That is, AIoT education, much like DS, provides students with structured guidance, collaborative learning experiences, and technological tools that enhance their cognitive growth. Through teacher support and peer collaboration in the ZPD, children can gradually internalize AI concepts, building on their existing knowledge and advancing their problem-solving skills in AI-driven contexts.

Despite the opportunities presented by AI literacy integration in elementary/primary school classrooms, however, several challenges must be addressed to ensure effective implementation. Infrastructure limitations pose a significant barrier, as many schools lack the technological resources necessary to facilitate GenAI-based learning experiences. Concerns regarding data privacy and security also require careful consideration, particularly as AI technologies collect and analyze student-generated content (Han et al., 2024). Another critical issue involves the commercialization of education, as the growing presence of AI-driven learning tools introduces corporate influences into the classroom (Yeter et al., 2024). These challenges highlight the importance of establishing policies and ethical guidelines that ensure AI is integrated in a manner that supports student learning while safeguarding their digital rights.

Middle and High School/Secondary Education

In middle and high school/secondary education (ages 11/12–18), literacies instruction expands significantly beyond foundational skills to incorporate critical interpretation, multimodal composition, and disciplinary literacy (Shanahan & Shanahan, 2008). During these years, students engage with increasingly complex texts across multiple subject areas, such as historical documents in social studies, laboratory reports in science, and literary analyses in English classes, while simultaneously producing writing that adheres to varying disciplinary conventions. Concurrently, they navigate digital environments, including social media, online forums, and more recently, GenAI tools, shaping both their personal and academic lives (Higgs & Stornaiuolo, 2024).

The integration of AI literacy into secondary education is becoming increasingly important, not only for fostering students' engagement with technology but also for equipping them with the critical and ethical skills necessary to navigate a rapidly evolving technological landscape. AI literacy initiatives, such as the Developing AI Literacy (DAILy) workshop designed for middle school students in the United States, have demonstrated that structured AI education can enhance learners' understanding of AI concepts, career awareness, and adaptability skills (Lee et al., 2021). These programs introduce students to AI ethics and applications through interactive projects, fostering engagement with critical discussions about bias, fairness, and the societal implications of AI technologies.

Indeed, critical literacy is particularly central at this educational level, as adolescents learn to interrogate how multimodal artifacts and/or texts—including those generated by AI—may reflect, perpetuate, or challenge cultural values, biases, and societal power structures (Luke, 2012). For example, Cortez et al. (2024) documented how Chicanx youth actively engaged in digital gaming contexts, creatively rewriting AI scripts to authentically represent their cultural narratives and critique embedded ideological assumptions. Such practices underscore how secondary school literacy involves not only technical reading and writing proficiency but also the ability to critically and creatively "re/design" digital environments (Cope & Kalantzis, 2017, 2019; Kalantzis & Cope, 2012; New London Group, 1996).

To support these advanced literacies practices, educators can employ a variety of classroom tasks and pedagogical approaches, such as LbyD's reflexive pedagogy, that actively integrate GenAI. Inquiry-based research projects are one example, where students investigate pressing community issues such as climate change or civic activism using GenAI tools for preliminary data synthesis, sentiment analysis, or literature summary/exploration. In these tasks, teachers can facilitate critical discussions regarding the reliability, potential biases, and ethical considerations of AI-generated information, thereby fostering critical data literacy and media literacy skills (Cope & Kalantzis, 2024; Cope et al., 2025; Kalantzis & Cope, 2025; McBride et al., 2024).

Additionally, educators can engage students in structured debates about algorithmic ethics, drawing from frameworks such as Higgs and Stornaiuolo's (2024) exploration of youth as philosophers of technology. In these debates, learners can critically examine the ethical dimensions of GenAI, including some of the issues discussed in Chapter 5 (see pages 183–186), such as misinformation, deepfakes, and surveillance, as well as digital echo chambers (i.e., online environments where individuals are exposed primarily to information and opinions that reinforce their existing beliefs, limiting diverse perspectives and critical discourse). Such activities can enrich reading, writing, and argumentative skills as students analyze real-world case studies, gather evidence, and craft persuasive and ethically informed arguments.

Multimodal composition further expands secondary school literacies, with students producing podcasts, video essays, interactive hypertexts, and digital stories combining textual analysis, visual imagery, and audio elements, as well as teacher-supervised, GenAI-generated content such as automatic subtitling or musical scores. This approach can not only develop students' technical skills but can also enhance their creative and critical competencies in articulating complex ideas through multiple modalities (Kalantzis & Cope, 2025). The concept of Humanizing Data Expression further supports this approach, emphasizing youth engagement in contextualizing GenAI, unveiling authorship, grappling with ethical questions, and playfully manipulating AI tools to enhance their storytelling and critical inquiry skills (for more on the application of this conceptualization, see McBride et al., 2024).

In these contexts, teachers act as critical facilitators of advanced literacies, bridging traditional academic discourse with contemporary multimodal, media, and digital literacies, including the use of GenAI technologies. Their roles include modeling critical and reflective GenAI usage, demonstrating how GenAI platforms construct texts, and highlighting possible omissions, biases, or ethical concerns. Educators can also design collaborative tasks that facilitate students' work in the ZPD (Vygotsky, 1978, 2012), allowing them to engage collectively in critical sense-making and knowledge construction, thus fostering their capacities for critical reflection and collective knowledge production.

Students, meanwhile, take on increasingly autonomous roles, actively integrating diverse sources, assessing the credibility of GenAI-generated suggestions, and critiquing digital platforms' content filtering and recommendation systems. Their identities as "authors" thus span multiple contexts, including academic essays, multimodal artifacts, social media contributions, and even the re-scripting of GenAI-driven narratives within digital gaming environments (Cortez et al., 2024). These types of engagement illustrate how learners can develop critical and creative agency in digital literacies practices, allowing them to reshape narratives and challenge dominant ideologies.

Addressing diverse educational needs and equity concerns is also critical in middle and high school contexts. While adaptive GenAI-driven platforms can provide differentiated instructional support, effective pedagogies sensitive to learner differences are essential, as students from disadvantaged backgrounds often bring unique critical perspectives to discussions on GenAI's role in either reinforcing or challenging systemic inequities (Cortez et al., 2024; Kalantzis & Cope, 2025; Zapata, 2025). Higgs and Stornaiuolo (2024) further caution educators that not all learners passively embrace AI technologies, as many express concerns regarding authenticity, the erosion of personal voice, or ethical considerations surrounding AI-generated content. Recognizing and validating these ethical reservations can empower students to question the underlying structures of digital knowledge production critically.

Academic Literacies for College and University

In college and university settings, literacies instruction significantly broadens to include advanced disciplinary literacy, specialized critical analysis, and sophisticated multimodal composition practices tailored explicitly to academic and professional contexts. Students at this stage engage deeply with scholarly journals, intricate theoretical frameworks, and domain-specific texts—ranging from literary criticism in the humanities to empirical reports in the sciences (Lea & Street, 1998). Within these diverse academic contexts, AI literacy is increasingly essential, as students encounter sophisticated GenAI tools integral to contemporary academic practice (Higgs & Stornaiuolo, 2024). This importance is underscored by recent studies highlighting significant improvements in learners' conceptual understanding, self-perceived AI literacy, and empowerment after participating in structured AI literacy courses designed for university students with diverse academic backgrounds (Kong et al., 2021; Tzirides et al., 2024a).

AI literacy at the collegiate level involves multidimensional engagement with digital tools, encompassing cognitive, affective, ethical, and sociocultural competencies. Cognitively, students require a robust understanding of advanced AI concepts such as machine learning, neural networks, and large language models, enabling them to critically and effectively utilize AI tools for academic tasks like research synthesis, data analysis, and multimodal composition (Tzirides et al., 2024a).

Educational initiatives aimed at developing AI literacy, such as the program described by Southworth et al., (2023), have focused on integrating AI across the curriculum, preparing students comprehensively for diverse professional and civic roles. For example, these initiatives have entailed the development of interdisciplinary courses, structured pathways, and experiential learning opportunities to create an AI-ready workforce. Additionally, pedagogical approaches, such as flipped classroom models, have been shown to be effective in fostering deeper conceptual understanding, enhancing student empowerment, and increasing classroom interaction (Kong et al., 2021; Southworth et al., 2023).

In our work with postgraduate students at the University of Illinois (e.g., Tzirides et al., 2023, 2024a, 2024b; Zapata et al., 202 4a, 2024b, 2025a, 2025b), we have shown that GenAI can also significantly contribute to enhancing writing instruction by offering real-time, formative feedback on grammar, coherence, style, and rhetorical effectiveness, as well as recommendations for content improvement. Our AI-supported instructional model (grounded in LbyD) has also enabled learners to critically compare GenAI-generated feedback with peer critiques, thereby enhancing their metacognitive awareness of rhetorical and compositional choices (Zapata et al., 2024a, 2024b, 2025a). Our research has highlighted the complementary and contrasting strengths of GenAI and human feedback, ultimately enriching university students' academic writing practices and sophisticated self-regulatory strategies.

Equity considerations are also critical in higher education's GenAI integration. Adaptive AI platforms, providing personalized scaffolding, such as language translation and varied reading complexity levels, can effectively support international and linguistically diverse students. Nonetheless, educators must remain vigilant about potential algorithmic biases, employing effective pedagogies to ensure positive outcomes for all learners (Benjamin, 2019; Cope & Kalantzis, 2024). Institutions carry the responsibility of ensuring AI-driven systems do not inadvertently perpetuate exclusionary or biased practices, thus necessitating an active, carefully calibrated approach to curriculum design.

Moreover, AI technologies catalyze significant transformations in scholarly communication, creating new possibilities for knowledge dissemination and collaborative analysis. While these developments foster academic rigor and creativity, they simultaneously present challenges regarding authenticity, intellectual ownership, and rigorous critical scholarship (Cope & Kalantzis, 2024). Thus, institutions of higher education must strategically manage these tensions through clear guidelines on academic integrity specific to GenAI-enhanced practices, fostering environments supportive of both innovation and critical reflection.

In sum, embedding robust AI literacy throughout college and university curricula offers considerable potential for enriching academic rigor, creativity, and critical engagement. Institutions that effectively integrate comprehensive AI literacy initiatives, accommodating diverse backgrounds and disciplines, will prepare students not merely as consumers of technology but as informed creators, critics, and ethical participants shaping digital futures (Cope & Kalantzis, 2024; Kong et al., 2021; Southworth et al., 2023).

AI Literacy in Educational Contexts: Summary

As posited in Chapter 5 and the previous sections, the integration of AI literacy into educational curricula is increasingly vital as GenAI technologies become pervasive in society. Our discussion has shown that developing AI literacy involves cultivating foundational knowledge, practical skills, and ethical attitudes across all educational levels, from early childhood through higher education. In Table 6.3, we summarize the information previously presented, outlining targeted instructional focuses for each educational stage

Table 6.3 AI literacy in education

Educational level	AI literacy: instructional focus	Sample instructional interventions
Early childhood education	• Emphasis on foundational AI literacy through interactive, inquiry-driven, and play-based activities. • Focus includes foundational AI knowledge (basic concepts), AI skills (computational thinking and problem-solving), and AI attitude (ethical awareness, biases, and privacy).	• Interactive AI toys (e.g., *PopBots*, *Zhorai*) teaching supervised learning concepts. • AI-enhanced interactive story time sessions using digital narration, animations, and projections. • Sorting algorithm games and supervised learning tasks (e.g., categorizing objects using AI-based robots). Hands-on exploration of basic algorithms using physical manipulatives. • Problem-solving activities involving basic machine learning through tangible experiences. • Guided discussions about fairness, biases, and ethical implications of GenAI. • Family co-use of digital tools to foster AI literacy and digital fluency. • Collaborative play scenarios using voice-activated devices and touchscreen technologies.
Elementary/ Primary School Education	• Instructional focus broadens to conceptual understanding of AI and practical engagement with GenAI tools. • It encourages critical evaluation, foundational machine learning processes, collaborative problem-solving, and ethical considerations.	• Digital storytelling activities leveraging GenAI to produce multimedia narratives. • Practical tasks involving data collection, model training, and iterative refinement. • AIoT educational programs combining AI with IoT through interactive tasks and devices. • Group projects using GenAI to tackle real-world issues (e.g., environmental, health, community challenges). • Hands-on tasks with voice recognition, automation, and data-driven decision-making. • Critical analysis activities exploring ethical issues, biases, and privacy in AI contexts. • Interactive tasks utilizing AI-based educational games for problem-solving and computational thinking. • Simulations and role-playing activities demonstrating the applications and limitations of GenAI technologies.

Middle and High School/Secondary Education	• Students engage in deeper critical literacies, multimodal composition, disciplinary literacy applications, and ethical reasoning related to AI/GenAI. • Instruction prioritizes critical evaluation, ethical reasoning, and active creation of AI-informed projects (including the use of GenAI).	• Multimodal composition projects utilizing GenAI tools (e.g., podcasts, digital storytelling, video essays). • Inquiry-based research projects critically evaluating GenAI-generated content (e.g., focus on misinformation, deepfakes). • Structured debates and discussions on algorithmic ethics, surveillance, and biases. • Case studies analyzing GenAI's impact on social and cultural contexts. • Collaborative design of AI-based applications addressing local community issues. • Simulation tasks demonstrating GenAI-driven recommendation systems, evaluating ethical implications. • Digital literacies projects incorporating AI tools for sentiment analysis and to summarize diverse perspectives. • Project-based learning tasks using AI simulation tools to address real-world scenarios. • Opportunities for personalized, GenAI-generated feedback/instructional support.
College and University Education	• Advanced integration of AI literacy across disciplines, emphasizing critical engagement, sophisticated analytical abilities, and complex multimodal composition tailored to academic, professional, and civic contexts. • Strong emphasis on ethics, metacognition, and interdisciplinary application of GenAI technologies	• Integration of GenAI into academic research methodologies, multimodal projects, and knowledge synthesis. • Structured AI literacy courses covering technical, ethical, and critical dimensions of AI technologies. • Flipped classroom practices and collaborative inquiry tasks to foster interactive and critical AI discussions. • Real-world scenario analyses involving ethical implications, biases, and accountability in GenAI. • Development and implementation of GenAI-driven solutions addressing academic, professional, or civic challenges. • GenAI-supported idea generation for academic tasks, including multimodal projects, presentations, essays, and interactive digital artifacts. • Employment of GenAI for personalized, formative feedback/instructional support, and peer collaboration. • Metacognitive tasks comparing human-generated and GenAI-generated feedback on academic writing and other instructional tasks. • Exploration and critique of digital recommendation and filtering systems through student-led projects. • Advanced research and design tasks for developing innovative AI/GenAI systems and applications. • Collaborative interdisciplinary projects addressing complex societal and ethical challenges involving AI/GenAI. • Critical evaluation tasks examining the socio-economic and environmental impacts of GenAI technologies.

and offering diverse, detailed examples of classroom interventions designed to equip learners with the critical, creative, and responsible use of GenAI technologies. This summary reflects both evidence from existing literature (including our research with university students) as well as UNESCO's (2024) AI competency framework. The suggested foci and practices are also reflective of the developmental stages we discussed in the first two sections of the chapter.

Conclusion

In this chapter, we have explored the multifaceted processes through which literacies develop across various stages of learning, emphasizing the integral relationship between cognition and multimodal forms of meaning-making such as linguistic, visual, spatial, and other symbolic representations. Drawing on theoretical insights from Peirce and Vygotsky, we discussed how learners navigate the complex transition from concrete experiences to abstract and symbolic thinking, illustrating how educational scaffolding and symbolic systems significantly influence cognitive development. Additionally, we have investigated the transformative role of GenAI in reshaping literacies practices, highlighting both its potential to personalize learning experiences and the necessity for critical engagement with AI-generated content.

Reflecting upon lifelong literacies, we underscore the need for educators and learners alike to continuously adapt their practices in response to evolving technologies and multimodal literacies. Literacies development, as we have seen in this chapter and previous ones, is an ongoing process that requires not only the mastery of conventional language skills but also proficiency in navigating diverse symbolic systems and critically evaluating the outputs of emerging technologies such as GenAI. As literacies practices increasingly incorporate digital and AI-mediated contexts, the capacity for critical thinking, creative innovation, and ethical engagement becomes indispensable in empowering learners to thrive in an interconnected, rapidly evolving world.

Moving forward, in Chapter 7, we will go deeper into access and inclusion in technology-supported educational contexts, addressing critical themes such as learner identities from a singularities-in-pluralities perspective, strategies for empowering learners of all backgrounds through differentiated instruction, and the importance of nurturing learner agency and self-efficacy. Furthermore, the chapter will examine literacies practices aimed at enhancing outcomes and ensuring appropriate teaching and assessment, demonstrating how embracing productive diversity can enrich learning environments, foster inclusive educational experiences, and enhance learning outcomes for all students.

Consolidate, Explore, Reflect, Do

We end this chapter with activities that will allow you to apply the concepts discussed in novel ways. Our goal is that these tasks will facilitate further exploration and reflection and will inspire your present and/or future teaching practice.

Task 1: Aligning UNESCO's (2024) AI Competency Framework with LbyD

In this task, you will work in a group of 3–4 to critically align UNESCO's pedagogical recommendations with Learning by Design's reflexive pedagogy as detailed in Chapter 4 (see pages 134–140).

Step 1. Read UNESCO's *AI Competency Framework for Students.* Identify the key recommendations for AI in educational contexts. Focus on suggested classroom practices. Divide the task among group members.

Step 2. Map the identified practices recommendations onto the principles and tenets of *LbyD,* as well as the instructional practices in our reflexive pedagogy (including work in the knowledge processes). This information can be found in Chapter 4 (see pages 134–140). Prepare a comparative chart or matrix.

Step 3. Discuss your alignment as a group, highlighting synergies, gaps, or tensions, considering applications for the development of students' AI literacy. Produce a short reflective report discussing how *LbyD* aligns with or diverges from UNESCO's framework.
Step 4. Exchange reports with another group. Compare your work. Are there any differences between your works? Why? Are these differences connected to conceptualizations and/or your interpretation of the information? Or are differences connected to your educational experiences?

Task 2: UNESCO's (2024) AI Competency Levels and Instructional Practices

In this task, you will work in groups of 4 students. You will focus on the information in Table 6.3 to identify instructional practices appropriate for the different stages and dimensions in UNESCO's framework.

Step 1. Assign an educational level to each member of the group (e.g., Student 1: Early childhood education; Student 2: Elementary/ Primary School; etc.).
Step 2. Each member of the group revises the information in Table 6.3 (pp. 37–38), focusing on the instructional interventions column in the educational level assigned to them. Each student then needs to consider what stages and dimensions in UNESCO's framework the interventions might reflect. Record your work in the following table (Table 6.4). Each person should use a separate table.
Step 3. Share your table with the members of your group. Explain your choices. Also, using one or two examples, consider how these interventions reflect Vygotsky's developmental stages.
Step 4. Consolidate your tables. Propose other possible interventions for each educational level and share your work with the rest of the class. Based on the new proposed interventions, the class can expand Table 6.3.

Table 6.4 Table for UNESCO's AI competency task

Stages	Description					
	Understand	**Educational level and intervention**	**Apply**	**Educational level and intervention**	**Create**	**Educational level and intervention**
Human-centered mindset	Human agency		Human accountability		Citizenship in the era of AI	
Ethics of AI	Embodied ethics		Safe and responsible use		Ethics by design	
AI techniques and applications	AI foundations		Application skills		Creating AI tools	
AI system design	Problem scoping		Architectural design		Iteration and feedback loops	

Source: Adapted from UNESCO (2024).

Task 3: Designing a Multimodal and AI Literacy Activity

In this task, you will work in pairs. You will use GenAI tools to design a multimodal literacy activity for primary school students that also develops their AI literacy.

Step 1. Select a specific educational objective (e.g., teaching abstract concepts, vocabulary expansion, conceptual categorization). Choose at least two meaning forms to integrate into your activity (e.g., text, image, etc.).

Step 2. Incorporate specific AI literacy objectives into your activity, such as understanding how AI tools generate content, evaluating AI-generated materials, or critically reflecting on AI use in educational contexts. Use GenAI (e.g., ChatGPT, Gemini, etc.) to help brainstorm, develop, or refine detailed instructions, ensuring the activity is clear and engaging. Your plan should include:

- Clearly defined educational objectives and outcomes
- Step-by-step teacher guidelines
- Required materials (physical and/or digital resources, including AI tools)
- Explanation of cognitive benefits tied to each meaning form
- Explanation of how the activity might develop students' AI literacy

We suggest you ground your activity in *LbyD* and reflexive pedagogy (see pages 134–140 in Chapter 4).

Step 3. Exchange your activity plan with another pair for peer feedback. Once you have received your feedback, employ GenAI to further refine your activity based on your peers' comments. Submit the final version along with a reflection detailing the use of GenAI tools throughout your design process and the AI literacy outcomes targeted by your activity.

Step 4. Go back to the personal definition of literacy you developed in Chapter 1 and revised in Chapters 2, 3, 4, and 5. Considering your work in this task and the discussion on AI literacy included in Chapter 5 and this chapter, what changes would you make to your personal definition? What has changed? What remains the same? Why? Do you feel your definition reflects literacy in the age of GenAI? Are you ready to move to literacies in the plural? What aspects of UNESCO's (2024) *AI Competency Framework* are reflected in your definition?

References

Benjamin, R. (2019). *Race after technology: Abolitionist tools for the new Jim Code*. Polity.

Cazden, C. B. (2001). *Classroom discourse: The language of teaching and learning*. Heinemann

Chen, X., Xie, H., Zou, D., & Hwang, G. J. (2020). Application and theory gaps during the rise of artificial intelligence in education. *Computers and Education: Artificial Intelligence*, *1*, Article 100002. https://doi.org/10.1016/j.caeai.2020.100002

Cope, B. & Kalantzis, M. (2017). Conceptualizing e-learning. In B. Cope & M. Kalantzis (Eds.), *ELearning ecologies* (pp. 1–45). Routledge.

Cope, B. & Kalantzis, M. (2019). Education 2.0: Artificial intelligence and the end of the test. *Beijing International Review of Education*, *1*(2–3), 528–543. https://brill.com/view/journals/bire/1/2-3/article-p528_528.xml?language=en

Cope, B. & Kalantzis, M. (2024). On cyber-social learning: A critique of artificial intelligence in education. In T. Kourkoulou, A. O. Tzirides, B. Cope, & M. Kalantzis (Eds.), *Trust and inclusion in AI-mediated education: Where human learning meets learning machines* (pp. 3–34). Springer. https://doi.org/10.1007/978-3-031-64487-0_1

Cope, B., Kalantzis, M., & Zapata, G. C. (2025). Language learning after generative AI. In G. C. Zapata (Ed.)., *Generative AI technologies, multiliteracies, and language education* (pp. 14–29). Routledge. https://doi.org/10.4324/9781003531685-2

Cortez, A., Lizárraga, J. R., & Rivero, E. (2024). AlgoRitmo literacies in gaming: Leveraging Chicanx praxis to reimagine AI systems. *Reading Research Quarterly*, *59*(4), 609–623. https://doi.org/10.1002/rrq.539

Druga, S., Vu, S. T., Likhith, E., & Qiu, T. (2019). Inclusive AI literacy for kids around the world. In *Proceedings of ACM Fablearn Conference (Fablearn '19)*. ACM. https://doi.org/10.1145/3311890.3311904

Druga, S., Christoph, F., & Ko, A. J. (2022). Family as a third space for AI literacies: How do children and parents learn about AI together?*Proceeding CHI Conference on Human Factors in Computing Systems*. ACM. https://doi.org/10.1145/3491102.3502031

Han, A., Zhou, X., Cai, Z., Han, S., Ko, R., Corrigan, S., & Peppler, K. (2024). Teachers, parents, and students' perspectives on integrating generative AI into elementary literacy education. In *Proceedings of the CHI Conference on Human Factors in Computing Systems*. AMC. https://doi.org/10.1145/3613904.3642438

Higgs, J. M. & Stornaiuolo, A. (2024). Being human in the age of generative AI: Young people's ethical concerns about writing and living with machines. *Reading Research Quarterly*, *59*(4), 632–650. https://doi.org/10.1002/rrq.552

Hong, J. & Kim, K. (2025). Impact of AIoT education program on digital and AI literacy of elementary school students. *Education and Information Technologies*, *30*, 107–130. https://doi.org/10.1007/s10639-024-12758-0

Kalantzis, M. & Cope, B. (2012). *New learning: Elements of a science of education*. Cambridge University Press.

Kalantzis, M. & Cope, B. (2025). Literacy in the time of artificial intelligence. *Reading Research Quarterly*, *60*, Article e591. https://doi.org/10.1002/rrq.591

Kewalramani, S., Kidman, G., & Palaiologou, I. (2021). Using Artificial Intelligence (AI)-interfaced robotic toys in early childhood settings: a case for children's inquiry literacy. *European Early Childhood Education Research Journal*, *29*(5), 652–668. https://doi.org/10.1080/1350293X.2021.1968458

Kong, S.-C., Cheung, W. M.-Y., & Zhang, G. (2021). Evaluation of an artificial intelligence literacy course for university students with diverse study backgrounds. *Computers and Education: Artificial Intelligence*, *2*, Article 100026. https://doi.org/10.1016/j.caeai.2021.100026

Lea, M. R. & Street, B. V. (1998). Student writing in higher education: An academic literacies approach. *Studies in Higher Education*, *23*(2), 157–172. https://doi.org/10.1080/03075079812331380364

Lee, I., Ali, S., Zhang, H., DiPaola, D., & Breazeal, C. (2021). Developing middle school students' AI literacy. In *Proceedings of the 52nd ACM Technical Symposium on Computer Science Education (SIGCSE '21) (pp. 1–7)*. ACM. https://doi.org/10.1145/3408877.3432513

Leontyev, A. N. (2009). An outline of the evolution of the psyche. In M. Cole (Ed.), *The development of mind* (pp. 137–244). Marxists Internet Archive.

Lin, P., Van Brummelen, J., Lukin, G., Williams, R., & Breazeal, C. (2020). Zhorai: Designing a conversational agent for children to explore ML concepts. In *Symposium on Educational Advances in Artificial Intelligence (EAAI)*. https://uploads-ssl.webflow.com/5e388f0cc3c41617d66719d8/5e432a7280e474409a4c2e83_EAAI-LinP.27.pdf

Luke, A. (2012). Critical literacy: Foundational notes. *Theory into Practice, 51*(1), 4–11. https://doi.org/10.1080/00405841.2012.636324

McBride, C., Lee, C. H., & Soep, E. (2024). "Gotta love some human connection": Humanizing data expression in an age of AI. *Reading Research Quarterly, 59*(4), 678–689. https://doi.org/10.1002/rrq.550

New London Group. (1996). A pedagogy of multiliteracies: Designing social futures. *Harvard Educational Review, 66*, 60–92. https://doi.org/10.17763/haer.66.1.17370n67v22j160u

Ng, D. T. K., Luo, W., Chan, H. M. Y., & Chu, S. K. W. (2022). Using digital story writing as a pedagogy to develop AI literacy among primary students. *Computers and Education Artificial Intelligence, 3*, 100054. https://doi.org/10.1016/j.caeai.2022.100054

Peirce, C. S. (1998). What is a sign? In The Peirce Edition Project. In *Selected philosophical writings, volume 2 (1893–1913)* (pp. 5–10). Indiana University Press.

Piaget, J. (1971). *Biology and knowledge: An essay on the relations between organic regulations and cognitive processes*. University of Chicago Press.

Scribner, S. & Cole, M. (1981). *The psychology of literacy*. Harvard University Press.

Shanahan, T. & Shanahan, C. (2008). Teaching disciplinary literacy to adolescents: Rethinking content-area literacy. *Harvard Educational Review, 78*(1), 40–59. https://dpi.wi.gov/sites/default/files/imce/cal/pdf/teaching-dl.pdf

Simbeck, K., & Kalf, Y. (2024). Understanding how computers learn: AI literacy for elementary school learners. In *Proceedings of Mensch und Computer 2024*. ACM. https://doi.org/10.1145/3670653.3677511

Snow, C. E., Burns, S. M., & Griffin, P. (1998). *Preventing reading difficulties in young children*. National Academy Press.

Southworth, J., Migliaccio, K., Glover, J., Southworth, J., Glover, J. N., Reed, D., McCarty, C., Brendemuhl, J., & Thomas, A. (2023). Developing a model for AI across the curriculum: Transforming higher education via innovation in AI literacy. *Computers and Education: Artificial Intelligence, 4*, Article 100127. https://doi.org/10.1016/j.caeai.2023.100127

Strickland, D., Snow, C., Griffin, P., Burns, M. S., & McNamara, P. (2002). *Preparing our teachers: Opportunities for better reading instruction*. Joseph Henry Press. https://doi.org/10.17226/10130

Su, J. & Yang, S. (2022). Artificial intelligence in early childhood education: A scoping review. *Computers and Education. Artificial Intelligence, 3*, Article 100049. https://doi.org/10.1016/j.caeai.2022.100049

Su, J. & Zhong, Y. (2022). Artificial Intelligence (AI) in early childhood education: Curriculum design and future directions. *Computers and Education. Artificial Intelligence*, *3*, Article 100072. https://doi.org/10.1016/j.caeai.2022.100072

Su, J., Ng, D. T. K., & Chu, S. K. W. (2023). Artificial intelligence (AI) literacy in early childhood education: The challenges and opportunities. *Computers and Education. Artificial Intelligence*, *4*, Article 100124. https://doi.org/10.1016/j.caeai.2023.100124

Tzirides, A. O., Saini, A., Zapata, G. C., Searsmith, D., Cope, B., Kalantzis, M., Castro, V., Kourkoulou, T., Jones, J., da Silva, R. A., Whiting, J., & Kastania, N. P. (2023). Generative AI: Implications and applications for education. *arXiv*. https://arxiv.org/abs/2305.07605

Tzirides, A. O., Zapata, G. C., Kastania, N. P., Saini, A. K., Castro, V., Ismael, S. A., You, Y. L., dos Santos, T. A., Searsmith, D., O'Brien, C., & Cope, B. (2024a). Combining human and artificial intelligence for enhanced AI literacy in higher education. *Computers and Education Open*, *6*, Article 100184. https://doi.org/10.1016/j.caeo.2024.100184

Tzirides, A. O., Zapata, G. C., Bolger, P. A., Cope, B., Kalantzis, M., & Searsmith, D. (2024b). Exploring instructors' views on fine-tuned Generative AI feedback in higher education. *International Journal on E-Learning*, *23*(3), 319–334. https://www.learntechlib.org/primary/p/225173/

UNESCO. (2024). *AI competency framework for students*. UNESCO. https://doi.org/10.54675/JKJB9835

Vygotsky, L. S. (1978). *Mind in society: The development of higher psychological processes*. Harvard University Press.

Vygotsky, L. S. (2012). *Thought and language*. MIT Press.

Wertsch, J. V. (1991). *Voices of the mind*. Harvard University Press.

Wertsch, J. V. (1998). *Mind as action*. Oxford University Press.

Williams, R., Park, H. W., & Breazeal, C. (2019). A is for artificial intelligence: The impact of artificial intelligence activities on young children's perceptions of robots. In *Proceedings of the CHI Conference on Human factors in Computing Systems (CHI 2019)*. Association for Computing Machinery (ACM). https://doi.org/10.1145/3290605.3300677

Wood, D., Bruner, J. S., & Ross, G. (1976). The role of tutoring in problem solving. *Journal of Child Psychology and Psychiatry*, *17*(2), 89–100. https://doi.org/10.1111/j.1469-7610.1976.tb00381.x

Yeter, I. H., Yang, W., & Sturgess, J. B. (2024). Global initiatives and challenges in integrating AI literacy in elementary education. *Future in Educational Research*, *2*(4), 382–402. https://doi.org/10.1002/fer3.59

Zapata, G. C. (2025). Reflection and future directions. In G. C. Zapata (Ed.), *Generative AI technologies, multiliteracies, and language education* (pp. 136–140). Routledge.

Zapata, G. C., Cope, B., Kalantzis, M., Tzirides, A. O., Saini, A., Searsmith, D., Whiting, J., Kastania, N. P., Castro, V., Kourkoulou, T., Jones, J., & Abrantes da Silva, R. (2025a). AI and peer reviews in higher education: Students' multimodal views on benefits, differences, and limitations. *Technology, Pedagogy and Education* 34(5), 583–601. https://doi.org/10.1080/1475939X.2025.2480807

Zapata, G. C., Saini, A. K., Cope, B., Kalantzis, M., & Searsmith, D. (2024a). Peer-reviews and AI feedback compared: University students' preferences. *EdArXiv*. https://doi.org/10.35542/osf.io/uy8qp

Zapata, G. C., Saini, A. K., Tzirides, A. O., Cope, B., & Kalantzis, M. (2024b). The role of AI feedback in university students' learning experiences: An exploration grounded in Activity Theory. *Ubiquitous Learning: An International Journal, 18*(2), 1–30. https://doi.org/10.18848/1835-9795/CGP/v18i02/1-30

Zapata, G. C., Tzirides, A. O., Cope, B., You, Y.-L., Kalantzis, M., & Searsmith, D. (2025b). A systemic functional linguistics discourse analysis of learner-centered, generative AI feedback in higher education. *EdArXiv*. https://doi.org/10.35542/osf.io/nuhq2_v1

Chapter 7
Learner Differences in Teaching and Assessment

Introduction

In Chapters 1–5, we traced literacy's multifaceted evolution, examining how human communication has evolved across historical periods, social practices, technological developments, and multimodal expressions as well as discussing pedagogical approaches that have mirrored diverse societal trends, changes, and ideologies. Chapter 6 marked an important conceptual shift, when we transitioned from the singular notion of *literacy* to the plural *literacies*, a more adequate conceptualization to reflect learners' needs to effectively communicate and function in contemporary society. This plural conceptualization does not only make reference to multimodal meaning making, but also entails aspects connected to both digital and artificial intelligence (AI) literacy.

Literacies in the Age of AI: Teaching and Learning in the Digital Era,
First Edition. Gabriela C. Zapata, Bill Cope, and Mary Kalantzis.

Building upon this expanded understanding, Chapter 7 addresses the key importance of integrating rigorous performance goals and inclusivity within literacies education, in connection with both teaching and assessment. We begin by examining the impact of learner differences, emphasizing the unique strengths and challenges that characterize their singularities. This leads us to discuss literacies which aim to empower all students by aligning educational practices with their unique identities, including their lifeworlds, lived experiences, and the communities to which they belong. Reflecting on the integration of Generative AI (GenAI) in contemporary pedagogy, we also explore how instruction can be effectively differentiated to accommodate and enhance learning for all students.

In the second part of the chapter, we address the crucial role of assessment in literacies education, detailing first various types and objectives. We then investigate how GenAI technologies can facilitate personalized assessment practices, catering to learners' individual personal and academic needs and supporting educators in crafting effective and appropriate assessment experiences. Our discussion culminates with our proposal for inclusive assessment practices grounded in *Learning by Design*'s (LbyD) reflexive pedagogy and the seven principles of e-learning affordances presented in Chapter 6.

Dimensions of Learner Difference

The recognition and celebration of learners' different backgrounds and the rapid expansion of digital media and AI technologies, including GenAI, present both wonderful instructional opportunities as well as pressing challenges for education today. Students arrive at school with manifold life experiences, linguistic and cultural backgrounds, and differing physical and cognitive realities; yet, institutional practices often fail to fully accommodate these realities. Many schools continue to rely on an architecture of sameness, in which standardized curricula, tests, and pedagogical methods overlook the singularities that each learner brings to the classroom. In response, education scholars and practitioners have increasingly called for a "singularities in pluralities" approach, one that recognizes and legitimizes "the singularity of the individual experiences that make up... the plurality of experiences in the classroom" (García & Sylvan, 2011, p. 391). This implies embracing each learner's unique identities and backgrounds by identifying their *material*, *embodied*, and *symbolic* differences, all of which might influence their sense of belonging to instruction and their learning process, and must guide the pedagogical practices implemented in the classroom (Kalantzis & Cope, 2012; New London Group, 1996; Tzirides et al., 2023).

The first aspect of learner differences we need to consider is to be cognizant of *material differences*, related to issues of access to resources and social capital (Piketty, 2014). These might include disparities in income, family wealth, neighborhood infrastructure, and school funding. For instance, material conditions might result in some students having ample opportunities for high-quality education, private tutoring, and robust digital tools, while others might experience underfunded schools, crowded classrooms, and limited access to technology (e.g., hardware and software, Wi-Fi infrastructure, etc.) (Case & Deaton, 2020). And even in nations that profess commitment to equality of opportunity, such unequal distribution of material resources might perpetuate cycles of privilege and disadvantage.

Embodied differences encompass a range of physical and cognitive attributes, including age, sex, sexuality, and those that are identified as neurodiverse or neurotypical traits. These categories/conceptualizations continue to evolve as societies redefine the nature of childhood, adolescence, adulthood, and old age. Additionally, although "race" lacks biological validity, it remains a powerful social construct that can trigger prejudicial practices and institutional biases, bringing questions of fairness to the forefront of education (Miles, 1989; Roberts, 2011). Understandings of sex and sexuality have also expanded beyond heteronormative assumptions to include those learners that profess identities that include lesbian, gay, bisexual, transgender, and queer or questioning (LGBTQ), cisgender, non-binary, and more—challenging schools to address issues long overlooked (Mayo, 2022). Similarly, diverse physical and cognitive manifestations are now embraced as expressions of embodied potential and neurodiversity, prompting the need for inclusive design and differentiated strategies so that all learners' strengths are supported, and their needs are effectively addressed (Bowe, 1978; Tzirides et al., 2023).

Symbolic differences refer to the cultural, linguistic, and ideological dimensions of personhood, including community values, languages and dialects, religion (or lack of), and ethnicity (Anderson, 1991; Kalantzis & Cope, 2012; Tzirides et al., 2023). This dimension also encompasses personal identities—those that are chosen by an individual for themselves (i.e., traits, characteristics, and behaviors that an individual uses to describe themselves and differentiate themselves from others) (Reid & Deaux, 1996). These attributes are self-selected and reflect how a person views their own personality and unique qualities. In educational contexts, symbolic differences might shape how students learn and how they interpret curriculum content (Cope & Kalantzis, 1997).

When these three domains of learner difference intersect in unique, context-dependent ways, each learner emerges as a singularity. At the same time, students embody broader pluralities reflecting class, race, language, religion, or other shared identifications. To engage with these complexities, schools must move beyond narrow assimilation or superficial celebrations of difference, adopting instead an approach that sees learner differences as a collective, productive resource. This entails dealing with entrenched inequalities by developing transformative pedagogies, and bringing digital technologies into alignment with outcome-oriented goals (Figure 7.1). We will discuss how this objective might be achieved in the classroom later in the chapter. Before we do so, we will examine one more important concept connected with learners' different backgrounds—their *lifeworld*.

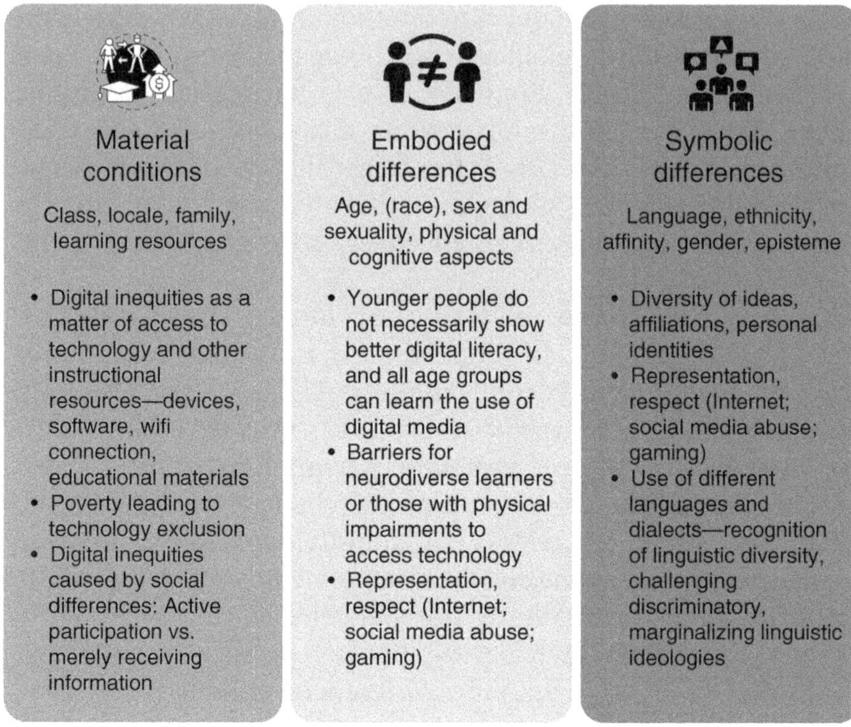

Figure 7.1 Dimensions of learner difference and instructional needs.

Learners' Lifeworld

The concept of *lifeworld* encompasses knowledge acquired effortlessly, without consciously considering how this knowledge was gained. It reflects the implicit rather than explicitly articulated habitual actions, behaviors, values, and interests that seem inherently understood within specific contexts. It remains unspoken precisely because it has never required articulation. Lifeworld knowledge is not typically conveyed through formal instruction; instead, individuals absorb how to exist within their lifeworld through everyday experiences, frequently without even recognizing this process as learning.

Lifeworld, in other words, forms the basis of human existence—comprising both previously learned and continuously emerging experiences of daily life. It is also integral to an individual's identity, subjectivity, and motivational foundations, operating intuitively, instinctively, and profoundly. Students enter educational settings carrying their lifeworld with them; it shapes their learning and influences the ways in which they interact with instruction, mirroring behaviors, and values found in their family, community, peers, and specific segments of popular or domestic culture. Luis Moll and his colleagues (Moll et al., 1992) have described these aspects as a learner's *funds of knowledge* (we introduced this concept in Chapter 4; see p. 135).

An individual's lifeworld also shapes their likes and dislikes, inherently forming their identities and influencing their interactions across various sociocultural experiences, including those found in the classroom. Key attributes of a person's lifeworld include *narrative*, *persona*, *affinity*, and *orientation*, which are summarized as follows:

- *Narrative*
  - Personal life stories, background, and life histories
  - Family cultures
  - Life experiences
- *Persona*
  - Identity informed by personality traits and social-historical experiences
  - Personal identities: How individuals perceive and present themselves
  - Can be intentional or implicit, conscious or unconscious
  - Might be expressed through gestures, fashion, speech patterns, and interaction styles
  - Interpersonal styles
  - Languages/dialects spoken
- *Affinity*
  - Associations with groups, worldviews, religious or non-religious affiliations, and political or non-political alignments
  - Can extend to products, objects, games, sports, aesthetics, or styles
  - Reflects personal beliefs, attitudes, group memberships, or formal affiliations

    - Includes personal values, interests, political positions, and social values
    - Contacts and networks (local, regional, national, international)
    - Employment sectors
- *Orientation*
    - Preferred ways of engaging with new or unfamiliar contexts based on ways of learning (e.g., experiential versus conceptual), ways of knowing (e.g., fact immersion versus abstraction), modes of communication (e.g., technical or applied language), and relational styles
    - Thinking and communication styles
    - Dispositions and sensibilities
    - Demeanors and intersubjective styles

Narrative, persona, affinity, and orientation provide categories to complement the dimensions of learner differences examined in the previous section. Together, these conceptualizations can offer support to educators for exploring individual learner differences, focusing explicitly on the distinctiveness of personal life experiences, to identify variations within groups and highlight unique intersections of each individual's social and historical position. When we focus on all students individually, we move beyond superficial demographic categorizations, truly incorporating all learners into our practice.

In the following section, we examine a fundamental aspect of symbolic differences and learners' lifeworld—their languages (and dialects), crucial in today's translingual society, where half of the world speaks more than one language (Grosjean, 2021). We do so through a *translanguaging* lens.

Translanguaging

Pedagogical literacies approaches inclusive of learners' varied translingual practices (i.e., involving two or more languages and/or dialects) take the position that linguistic boundaries are fluid and creative (García & Kleifgen, 2020). These practices have been explored under the umbrella of the concept of *translanguaging*. This term was first introduced by Cen Williams as *trawysieithu* in Welsh in his untranslated doctoral dissertation from 1994 (Williams, 2012), and subsequently translated into English by Baker (2003). Translanguaging can be defined as an integrated approach that transcends traditional boundaries of separate languages, recognizing multilingual learners' racial, ethnic, and linguistic identities as inherently interconnected (Wei, 2024; for a history of this concept, see Lewis et al., 2012a, 2012b). That is, unlike conventional monolingual ideologies or the "two solitudes" model (Cummins, 2019) present in traditional bilingual education programs, instruction embracing translanguaging acknowledges students' complete linguistic repertoires and lived experiences, viewing multilingualism as holistic rather than compartmentalized (Cope et al., 2024; Wei & García, 2022).

Pedagogically, translanguaging is deemed as a fundamental aspect of instruction to support and maintain the linguistic and cultural practices of students from diverse backgrounds. Rather than viewing these practices as deficits or merely as starting points for learning standardized academic language, the incorporation of translanguaging into the classroom recognizes and values them as integral components of learners' identities, lifeworld, and educational experiences, as well as legitimate and valuable in their own right. This perspective shifts the educational focus from assimilation to affirmation, challenging deficit perspectives, and thus moving away from approaches that stigmatize students' home languages and cultural practices (Wei, 2024). By promoting an awareness of how language practices are marginalized, translanguaging thus enables educators and learners to critically examine and resist the reproduction of harmful linguistic ideologies in educational contexts.

Inclusive Classroom Practices

The main objectives of inclusive (and, in turn, culturally sustaining) pedagogical practices must be to actively ensure that all students have access to productive, meaningful, and affirming educational experiences. These practices must also help learners cultivate a positive sense of self and of their cultural backgrounds. This dimension is essential for fostering resilience, confidence, and a strong connection to one's classroom and community. Educators can create learning environments that not only respect and affirm students' varied lifeworlds but also empower them to express their voices confidently.

Key aspects of academic and culturally sustaining practices include several foundational principles, already reflected in LbyD and reflexive pedagogy (see Chapters 4 and 5), as well as in the syncretic approaches we discussed in Chapter 4. The first principle of action is to know who our learners are. Schools commonly rely on a few demographic markers—age, grade level, ethnicity, or test scores—to categorize students, but, as we saw in the previous sections, these are only a starting point. By creating open and dialogical processes, educators can continually refine their understanding of each student's background—not only aspects connected to material conditions, embodied and symbolic differences, and but also with their lifeworld, including linguistic repertoires and translingual practices, family circumstances, personal interests, and future aspirations. This aligns with LbyD's processes of *experiencing the known* and *applying creatively*, where learners bring lifeworld experiences into the curriculum and, in turn, apply new knowledge to real-life contexts connected to their personal lives and the communities they live in (Cope & Kalantzis, 2015a; Kalantzis et al., 2016; Zapata, 2022). In this way, schools become living communities of mutual exchange, rather than static institutions that simply sort students according to broad demographic labels.

The second principle is to create a differentiated, inclusive curriculum. The old one-size-fits-all approach, in which every student sits through the same lecture or reads the same textbook chapter at the same pace, no longer suits digitally connected, diverse classrooms (Cope & Kalantzis, 2019; Kalantzis & Cope, 2012). Learners can now pursue shared goals in varied ways or at different speeds, supported by personalized learning platforms, adaptive software, and collaborative projects (Cope & Kalantzis, 2017, 2019). This does not mean lowering expectations but recalibrating them so that learning remains comparably rigorous for all. Digital media, and specially GenAI technologies, as we will see in the following sections, can make such differentiation more feasible, allowing teachers to track progress, facilitate peer interaction, and tailor learning materials to individual strengths and needs.

The third principle is to provide recursive feedback. Learner differences demand ongoing, formative assessments that offer students the guidance they need to improve in real time (Black & Wiliam, 1998; Wiliam, 2011). Machine-based systems, including GenAI tools, and peer feedback loops can help teachers deliver input at scale (Cope et al., 2011). Students can revise, refine, and reflect on their work in iterative cycles, a process that recognizes their evolving capacities and contextual needs. This recursive element also validates the multiple languages/dialects, cultural references, and interpretive frameworks learners bring, offering individualized responses to the singularities that characterize each classroom (more on this later in the chapter).

The fourth principle is to foster and instructionally facilitate learner agency. Rather than confining students to textbook content or rote memorization, inclusive education treats them as active creators of knowledge. For instance, they research topics, evaluate sources, and generate artifacts showing their knowledge growth and understanding, effectively becoming designers of their own learning experiences and conveying their personal/academic uniqueness (Cope & Kalantzis, 2015a; Kalantzis et al., 2016; Zapata, 2022). This is a radical shift from teacher-centered instruction; it acknowledges that when students integrate their personal diversity and lifeworld into schoolwork, they deepen both individual engagement and collective insight (Kalantzis & Cope, 2012). In this sense, learner agency is the energy that drives an inclusive, dynamic classroom, characterized by what we describe as *productive diversity*.

Also, when recognized and harnessed, the variety of viewpoints in any group of learners can lead to richer debates, more creative problem-solving, and stronger empathy among classmates

(Cope & Kalantzis, 1997). Learner differences become productive when participants see these not as a barrier but as a mutual resource. This collective synergy is especially relevant in societies that need citizens capable of navigating intercultural communication, negotiating conflicts, and building common ground across social divides. Schools thus evolve into spaces where students learn not merely from teachers but also from each other's unique perspectives and life histories.

In tandem with these steps, measuring comparabilities remains central to an inclusive agenda. Inclusive education asks how learners might demonstrate mastery or growth in ways that do not simply re-enact standard exams. Portfolio evaluations, project-based interventions, peer and self-reviews, and ongoing data analytics can provide nuanced evidence of academic development (Cope & Kalantzis, 2015a; Zapata, 2022). The concept of comparabilities thus recognizes that learners can produce different types of work—whether essays, multimodal projects supported by diverse technologies, or collaborative investigations—that still meet equivalent standards of intellectual rigor. This focus moves away from homogenizing achievement and toward cultivating each learner's capacity to transform and expand their horizons without discarding their personal diversity and lifeworld.

Taken together, these principles articulate a vision of schools that take seriously learners' singularities in pluralities: Each learner's individual profile emerges from a confluence of material, embodied, and symbolic differences as well as the experiences, views, and identities reflective of their lifeworld. Far from treating difference as a deficit or a problem to be managed, inclusive pedagogy recasts it as a productive force. The result is a learning environment designed to expand each learner's horizons, foster high-order literacies and intellectual rigor, and strengthen civic capacities such as empathy and ethical responsibility.

In this way, the promise of digital technologies, including GenAI, combined with thoughtful pedagogical design, can realize a new architecture of productive diversity, one that benefits learners as they confront the complex challenges of our rapidly changing world (Cope & Kalantzis, 2017; Tzirides et al., 2023).

GenAI and Inclusive Classroom Practices

GenAI presents significant opportunities to enhance inclusive classroom practices by addressing learner differences through personalized and adaptive approaches. For example, GenAI can tailor educational content dynamically, responding in real time to individual personal and academic needs and learning preferences. This personalized approach aligns seamlessly with differentiated instruction methodologies, enabling students to access content multimodally, through their preferred meaning forms—be they textual, visual, auditory—or featuring a combination of various forms.

Moreover, GenAI technologies can facilitate alternative navigation paths by creating adaptive learning sequences tailored to individual strengths, interests, and challenges. For instance, students who require additional support due to embodied differences can benefit significantly from AI-driven interventions, which can offer customized scaffolding, continuous feedback, and targeted progress monitoring. Early identification of challenges and real-time adaptations can dramatically improve educational outcomes for these learners.

GenAI, as discussed in Chapters 3–5, also promotes multimodal literacies practices, allowing learners to engage and produce content using diverse meaning forms such as text, image, sound, space, and speech. For instance, GenAI-driven platforms can assist learners in transforming their ideas from one modality into another—such as turning spoken narratives into written text or generating visual illustrations from textual descriptions—thus fostering cross-form communication skills and expanding learner repertoires.

Additionally, AI-based systems support the integration of diverse learner lifeworlds by recognizing and leveraging the varied knowledge, narratives, and perspectives students bring into the classroom. GenAI tools can curate personalized learning resources drawn from diverse cultural and experiential backgrounds, thereby validating and enriching the unique identities of learners. These affordances also entail student work supported by GenAI in connection with idea generation, research, and the consideration of diverse viewpoints. These practices contribute to creating productive diversity, nurturing inclusive dialogs, and enhancing collaborative meaning-making processes as well as facilitating connections between classroom work and real-life knowledge applications that might not only enhance students' understanding of issues affecting their communities, but also result in the development of artefacts or actions that benefit those communities.

Included within these affordances are those in which GenAI technologies can support translingual/second language education. For instance, in their work with Chinese EFL students, Yang and Lin (2025) identified extensive translanguaging behaviors when students employed GenAI in writing tasks. The participants in this work were university students with beginning to intermediate levels of English proficiency, who consistently utilized their first language for preliminary idea conceptualization, subsequently translating these ideas into English with iterative GenAI assistance. GenAI not only offered linguistic support but also facilitated learners' cognitive engagement through translanguaging practices as well as enhanced their confidence and autonomy in their writing process.

Godwin-Jones (2025) also discusses the promise of GenAI within less commonly taught languages (LCTLs), especially in creating inclusive and diverse multilingual educational environments that open up translingual communication opportunities for LCTLs speakers. This application, however, presents unique challenges, particularly concerning linguistic and cultural authenticity, since GenAI models typically prioritize high-resource languages, thereby marginalizing minority and Indigenous languages. This digital marginalization risks exacerbating existing linguistic hierarchies and underscores the importance of culturally sensitive and linguistically equitable GenAI systems—a topic that we address in Chapter 8.

Nonetheless, as we suggested in Chapter 1 and other recent work (Cope et al., 2025), GenAI can significantly benefit non-dominant languages, offering unprecedented possibilities for revitalizing languages with smaller populations of native speakers. GenAI's multilingual language models have the potential to support linguistic diversity by leveraging patterns from higher-resource languages to enhance performance in lower-resource languages, thus fostering inclusive, translingual communication environments and reducing linguistic inequalities.

To help you visualize the kind of tasks that inclusive, GenAI supported practices could incorporate, we offer an example in Appendix 2. The activities shown were developed for a Spanish Language Arts class for Latinx secondary school students in California, USA (years 6–8 in middle school), whose lifeworld is characterized by translingual practices (Spanish [various dialects] and/or other Indigenous languages of the Americas and English). The samples are reflective of the curriculum for Spanish language literacies development in that state.

In Figure 7.2, we summarize some of the ways in which GenAI can support inclusive, personalized literacies learning. We will revisit this information in the final sections of the chapter, after our discussion on assessment.

Literacies Assessment

The Types and Purposes of Assessment

Assessments can be conducted through various methods, perspectives, and at different stages of the learning process (Pellegrino et al., 2001; Wiliam, 2011). Traditionally, assessment has relied on three specific types, presented as follows:

1. **Diagnostic Assessment:** Employed to identify students' existing knowledge and highlight areas requiring further learning. It occurs prior to instruction and informs educators' planning.
2. **Formative Assessment:** It provides continuous feedback to students about their learning during the instructional process. It is embedded within instruction, primarily benefiting learners

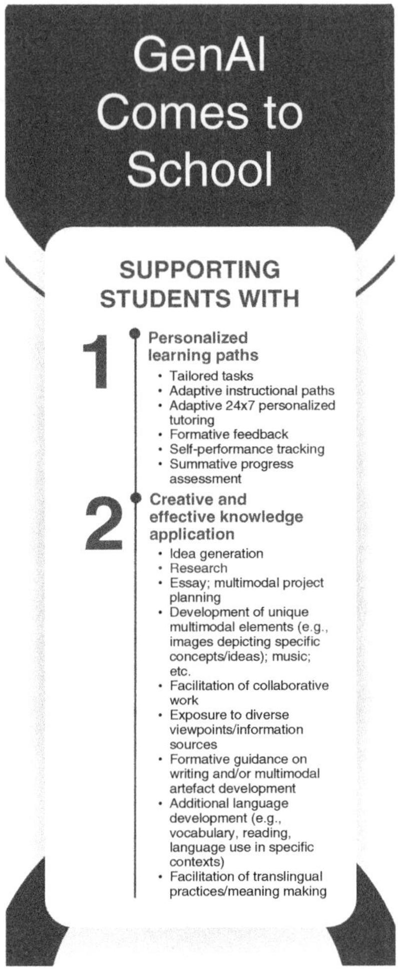

Figure 7.2 Summary of ways in which GenAI can support inclusive learning.

(though it also has benefits for teachers' practice, guiding the adaptation of instructional interventions based on assessment results). Formative assessments are forward-looking (aiming at ongoing learning within current curricular content) and constructive (offering specific guidance on how students can extend their understanding or complete tasks).

3. **Summative Assessment:** Used to evaluate student learning after instructional activities have concluded. It serves the purpose of reviewing completed learning for learners, educators, and parents. Summative assessments adopt a retrospective perspective, assessing past learning activities, and provide generalized evaluations (e.g., assigning grades such as B+ or percentages like 68%).

These diverse assessment approaches might serve multiple purposes. For instance, they can

- Support student learning through valuable information provided before, during, and after instructional activities
- Inform parents and other stakeholders about student learning progress and outcomes
- Help teachers determine instructional effectiveness and identify areas needing further attention
- Offer detailed insights into individual student performance to enable personalized learning programs tailored to diverse student needs
- Identify performance disparities among diverse student groups to address patterns of underachievement and potential discrimination
- Supply school systems with metrics to evaluate overall school effectiveness, thus rewarding schools achieving or progressing towards improved student outcomes, or intervening in schools not meeting expectations
- Serve political agendas by facilitating public discourse around the effective allocation and use of educational resources

Literacy instruction grounded in traditional didactic approaches has mostly relied on summative assessments serving only as retrospective views of student progress and achievement. In such scenarios, tests represent unique artifacts, fundamentally distinct from typical learning processes—students must close their books, cease collaboration, and complete tasks within strictly allocated timeframes. After completing a defined segment of instruction, learners respond to questions devised by teachers or assessment experts, who subsequently evaluate the results to gauge learning outcomes. Assessment artifacts traditionally include selected-response (item-based) tests and constructed-response assessments, such as short-answer questions or essays. Though technological advancements have significantly influenced these two forms of assessment over recent decades, their summative orientation has remained mostly unchanged.

Selected-response tests became machine-readable with the advent of pencil-and-paper "bubble tests" in the late 20th century, later transitioning to online platforms in the 21st century, allowing secure access through personal computers and laptops. The relative affordability and ease of automating such assessments led test creators and administrators to significantly shape the content and focus of assessments, often prioritizing measurable elements like item-based reading comprehension as proxies for overall literacies skills. However, such tests typically emphasized the recall of isolated factual information rather than interpretative skills (e.g., emotional connections with characters or evaluating argumentative strength).

In parallel, in the early 2010s, psychometric methodologies became increasingly sophisticated (and statistically complex) to accurately measure comparative student performances on standardized assessments. Computer-adaptive tests dynamically adjusted question difficulty based on student responses: Correct answers led to more challenging questions, while incorrect answers prompted easier questions (Chang, 2015). Beyond reading comprehension, adaptive assessments could also evaluate certain aspects of writing that involved clear-cut correctness, such as grammar and vocabulary, thus narrowing the conceptual scope of literacy for assessment purposes.

Concurrently, advancements in supply-response assessments incorporated natural language processing (NLP) technology, particularly for grading short-answer and extended essay responses. NLP functions by first analyzing a corpus of human-graded texts (e.g., 500 essays from a specific educational level) rated on a predefined scale. The NLP algorithm then statistically compares new submissions to these benchmark texts, assigning grades accordingly. Research showed that NLP grading accuracy could rival human grading capabilities (e.g., see McNamara & Graesser, 2012; Shermis, 2014; Vojak et al., 2011).

Nevertheless, these advanced assessment technologies remained largely retrospective and evaluative, offering limited actionable feedback. For instance, they provided generalized evaluations (implying praise or improvement suggestions) without detailed, actionable guidance, thereby positioning students within comparative cohorts without necessarily enhancing individual learning trajectories. Also, although these automated assessments may have been more cost-effective than traditional tests, they perpetuated the existing didactic assessment logic, often resulting in increased frequency and volume of testing.

Big Data and Assessment

Despite the limitations of the technology-based assessments discussed in the previous section, some technological advancements have answered the unique demands of contemporary social learning environments, notably through "big data" and cloud computing (Cope & Kalantzis, 2015b, 2015c). One especially promising application of these technologies has been formative assessment; i.e., emerging computer-mediated formative assessments have offered the opportunity to redress the imbalance between this type of assessment and summative evaluations, potentially eliminating traditional distinctions between them altogether (Behrens & DiCerbo, 2013; Pea & Jacks, 2014).

"Big data" in education entails systematically collecting incidental data on learning actions and interactions within digitally integrated environments, enabling detailed tracing of learning processes, microdynamics, and artifact development. Cloud computing logistically facilitates simultaneous collaborative input, rapid iterative revisions, and progress tracking, shifting assessment emphasis from endpoint outcomes to continuous progress evaluation. Furthermore, collaborative, computer-mediated peer assessment practices can harness collective insights, demonstrating that aggregated evaluations from non-expert raters can approximate expert ratings, offering learners timely qualitative feedback from multiple perspectives. Clear rating criteria can also be employed to enhance peer assessment reliability (Kline et al., 2013; McCarthey et al., 2014; Woodard et al., 2013).

A More Inclusive Path to Assessment Practices

In the era of big data, cloud computing, and, as we will see in the following section, GenAI, we propose that, in educational contexts, all assessments might become formative, with summative assessments serving only as retrospective views of student progress and achievement. In such scenarios, assessments could encompass all activities learners have undertaken throughout their learning process. Based on our extensive research in this area (e.g., Cope & Kalantzis, 2015b, 2015c, 2017, 2019), we posit that embedding assessment within ongoing learning activities (including complex tasks like disciplinary writing) blurs traditional distinctions between instruction and assessment, creating numerous, detailed teachable moments accessible through both human and automated feedback.

Our work also leads us to believe that the distinction between formative and summative assessment will become obsolete as semantically meaningful datapoints will simultaneously serve formative purposes and retrospectively aggregate into summative insights. Ultimately, new conceptual frameworks—such as "prospective" and "retrospective" learning analytics—might better represent this evolving assessment paradigm. Additionally, we argue that rich multimodal artefact creation might represent the optimal method for demonstrating student knowledge across diverse subject areas, instead of the traditional tests grounded in didactic pedagogy we discussed in previous sections.

Let's consider different academic disciplines—all of which demand what we term "complex epistemic performance." For instance, the activity most closely resembling authentic scientific practice for students is producing scientific reports, typically enhanced with images, diagrams, videos, or data compiled from observational studies. Scientific inquiry itself constitutes a complex performance, and a scientific report serves as a comprehensive representation of that performance. The report can capture and convey the entirety of the learner's cognitive processes (i.e., representation and communication) to various stakeholders, including peers, parents, subject experts, or teachers. In contrast, traditional ABCD-style selected-response tests that merely assess isolated scientific facts provide only a limited perspective on students' understanding. Such assessments primarily evaluate learners' memory of fragmented information, definitions, or theories, often resulting in fleeting retention despite their nominal entry into long-term memory.

In contrast, multimodal science writing authentically mirrors scientific practice. The representation and communication of complex epistemic performance constitute the true nature of scientific engagement. Assessing scientific writing, complemented by other appropriate meaning forms, thus brings students closer to actual scientific practices, particularly the critical processes of interpreting and reporting scientific findings. Science truly materializes only through its representation in written forms such as journal articles or books, often combining text with image, space, and/or object. Consequently, engaging authentically with scientific practice involves developing and contributing to scientific texts in a multimodal fashion.

Similarly, in history education, the closest students come to authentic historical practice involves activities such as interviewing elderly individuals, examining historical newspapers, consulting source documents, evaluating diverse historical interpretations, and developing their own historical arguments supported by evidence. Learners might incorporate multimedia elements such as audio or video excerpts from interviews, archival images, and hyperlinks to sources. Previously, assessments of students' understanding of events like the French Revolution relied upon simple factual recall, such as correctly identifying "D. The year was 1789," or writing a timed examination essay without access to external resources, citations, or visual aids. Conversely, multimodal historical writing authentically represents historical practice. Reasoning from evidence and citing historical sources constitute core historian tasks. Today's multimodal tools allow students to present such evidence vividly, making historical reasoning and evidence-based arguments more authentically assessable.

In sum, instead of testing memory recall in traditional examinations, we propose assessing knowledge representation (critical analysis in scientific reports or historical arguments) and knowledge communication (the clear articulation of created knowledge to others). Rather than inferring understanding from temporary memory retention during examinations, we need to assess authentic disciplinary practices, such as engaging in scientific or historical reasoning. Writing, especially multimodal writing widely accessible today, effectively represents knowledge across multiple subject areas.

More importantly, inclusive assessment practices, particularly formative assessments, are essential for addressing learner diversity, personalizing instruction, and integrating students' diversity and lifeworld. Effective feedback is crucial in this context, as learners must clearly understand how their performance aligns with expected outcomes, recognizing both what they have accomplished and what they need to work on, thus enabling them to set relevant goals and move closer to established learning expectations. To enhance this effectiveness, teachers "should focus on success... rather than deficits," and provide feedback that is "immediate, specific, and actionable" (Chan et al., 2014, p. 97). Furthermore, formative assessments inform instructors' practices, allowing them to adapt pedagogical interventions to diverse student experiences, identities, and cultural backgrounds, thereby enriching the learning process.

Adopting a comprehensive and carefully calibrated assessment framework requires educators to take "a holistic and integrated approach to assessment" (Kalantzis et al., 2005, p. 94). This involves assessing literacies appropriate for the disciplinary content of focus, along with competencies such as collaboration, problem-solving, and creativity. Formative assessment, as previously stated, should also span a whole instructional sequence, incorporating holistic methods like project-based, multimodal tasks, and ePortfolios, which can capture multimodal representation and communication as well as experiential, conceptual, analytical, and applied disciplinary dimensions. Additionally, assessment should occur within collaborative contexts, and in the zone of proximal development (Vygotsky, 1978), through learner participation in co-operative instructional tasks and peer assessment. In the following section, we explore how GenAI can contribute to these assessment practices.

GenAI-Supported Assessment

GenAI has emerged as a powerful force in reshaping not only teaching and learning but also assessment practices, offering new formats and affordances that can foster greater personalization and inclusion. For example, our research on GenAI formative feedback in university classes (e.g., Tzirides et al., 2024a, 2024b; Zapata et al., 2024, 2025a, 2025b) has shown the benefits of real-time, tailored GenAI suggestions and guidance on multimodal student work, and when combined with self and peer reviews, this type of feedback can in turn result in richer, personalized learning experiences.

Additionally, in academic and disciplinary literacies, GenAI is particularly adept at identifying "genre signals," and can track how much help it provides by capturing keystrokes, thus offering insights into the degree of student autonomy present in the task as well as the extent to which their work has been created independently. This affordance addresses one of the main concerns of GenAI in educational contexts—academic misconduct (Cope & Kalantzis, 2024; Hart-Davidson, 2024; Kalantzis & Cope, 2025).

Furthermore, by working in concert with Contextual AI, GenAI can monitor students' progress as they evolve into progressively more independent writers, and can calibrate learning activities and assessments for different learners, encompassing not only literacies capacities but also the broader experiences that shape each learner's lifeworld. GenAI can also offer feedback tailored to different linguistic needs (including those of second language learners; e.g., see Wang, 2024; Zapata, 2025) and assess student work through automated grading offering more context-sensitive responses than the older automated writing assessments we discussed in the previous sections (Steiss et al., 2024; Tang et al., 2024; Tate et al., 2024).

In reading, GenAI can engage students in dialogs that explore how they interpret texts, acknowledging that individual backgrounds, life histories, and interests shape unique perspectives rather than converging on a single correct answer. This aligns with the idea that AI platforms are active participants in learning ecologies (Stornaiuolo et al., 2023) and underscores the importance of examining how learners interact with user interfaces (Monea, 2020). GenAI thus enables new and improved literacies assessments, addressing the flaws of older methods that rely on small samples in time, offer narrow measures of comprehension, produce variable judgments, and provide limited feedback.

Further evidence of GenAI's transformative role also comes from cross-national higher education research. For instance, Kizilcec et al.'s (2024) work involving both educators and students' views in institutions of higher education in Australia, Cyprus, and USA has shown that essay writing, project-based tasks, and coding exercises are particularly appropriate for GenAI support, which has led educators to rethink these types of assessments to accommodate these technologies. For example, this can involve enhancing prompts to prioritize critical thinking and problem-solving, shifting focus away from mere knowledge recall and toward higher-order skills.

From existing work on GenAI and assessment, several recommended practices emerge for strengthening formative and summative assessments. The first one involves adopting guided AI-literacy training for both instructors and students so they can understand the capabilities, limitations, and ethics of GenAI and learn to generate meaningful prompts, interpret AI suggestions, and critique AI outputs (Kalantzis & Cope, 2025; Tzirides et al., 2024a; UNESCO, 2024; Zapata et al., 2024). The second one is to align AI feedback with institutional course rubrics by fine-tuning systems to reflect specific standards and styles, supplementing AI-based scoring with human reviews or oral interviews for summative tasks (Tzirides et al., 2024b; Zapata et al., 2024, 2025a, 2025b).

Also, as shown in our work, blending peer and AI feedback offers layered perspectives that combine speed and consistency with the nuance of human insights, prompting students to analyze differences among reviews (Tzirides et al., 2024a; Zapata et al., 2025a). Collaborative GenAI tools and platforms can also further promote teamwork, allowing GenAI, teachers, and learners to engage in iterative dialog that stimulates constructive thinking and extends the classroom's community of practice (Zapata et al., 2024, 2025b). Using staged, multiphase assignments is also important, since breaking larger projects into iterative segments encourages students to consider multiple perspectives, including GenAI-suggested revisions, throughout their workflow.

When examined through the lens of the seven principles of e-learning ecologies, we introduced in Chapter 5 as well as the concept of cyber-social learning grounded in the principles of reflexive pedagogy, GenAI has the capacity to strengthen inclusive assessment by supporting ubiquitous learning, recursive feedback, multimodal meaning, active knowledge making, collaborative intelligence, metacognition, and differentiated learning. For instance, GenAI can contribute by offering on-demand explanations, examples, and prompts accessible anytime, anywhere, making learning resources highly flexible and reinforcing the principle of "learning everywhere."

A commitment to recursive feedback places continuous assessment at the center of instruction and integrates formative and summative evaluations, so that learners can receive real-time, data-informed insights into their work. GenAI fits this model by quickly analyzing drafts or conceptual understandings of new knowledge, and, in turn, suggesting improvements and adapting content difficulty in a cycle of ongoing refinement.

An emphasis on multimodal meaning underscores the use of diverse tools and meaning forms—text, image, sound, etc.—to represent knowledge, distinguish one's own ideas from cited sources, and foster remixing and integration of varied content. GenAI can assist by automatically generating relevant images, designs, or interactive simulations from written input, or by flagging potential overlaps in references, helping learners develop unique multimodal presentations and/or artefacts.

Active knowledge making positions students as producers, not consumers, of knowledge, favoring authentic investigation and the creative application of newly learned concepts over memorization. GenAI can spur creativity by proposing ideas, simulating scenarios, and even co-authoring content, challenging learners to refine their own thinking. At the same time, collaborative intelligence encourages collective sense-making in a digitally connected environment. GenAI can support group work by synthesizing or summarizing multiple perspectives, matching learners with complementary skill sets, and spurring deeper inquiry through AI-driven prompts.

Metacognition emphasizes that learners share responsibility for assessment, fostering a culture of self- and peer-assessment and reciprocal knowledge exchange. GenAI can promote this by offering reflective prompts tailored to a student's current level of thinking and providing diagnostic feedback to guide improvements in strategies such as planning or evaluating. Finally, differentiated learning calls for tailoring instruction to meet each learner's needs, incorporating the diversity dimensions discussed in the first section of this chapter as well as their lifeworld. For instance, GenAI can customize reading levels or offer alternative project ideas, providing varied curricular pathways. These technologies can also help form equitable, engaging collaborations by grouping students whose skills and interests complement one another. By integrating all these principles into assessment design, GenAI becomes not just a tool for automated grading or content generation but a catalyst for more inclusive, equitable, and personalized educational experiences. In Figure 7.3, we illustrate the relationship among LbyD, reflexive pedagogy, the seven principles of e-learning ecologies, and GenAI-supported instruction and assessment.

We end this chapter with a table that highlights keyways in which GenAI can foster more inclusive and personalized assessment practices, as discussed in this section. Each row addresses a different aspect of assessment, the specific GenAI contribution, and how it enhances inclusivity and personalization (Table 7.1).

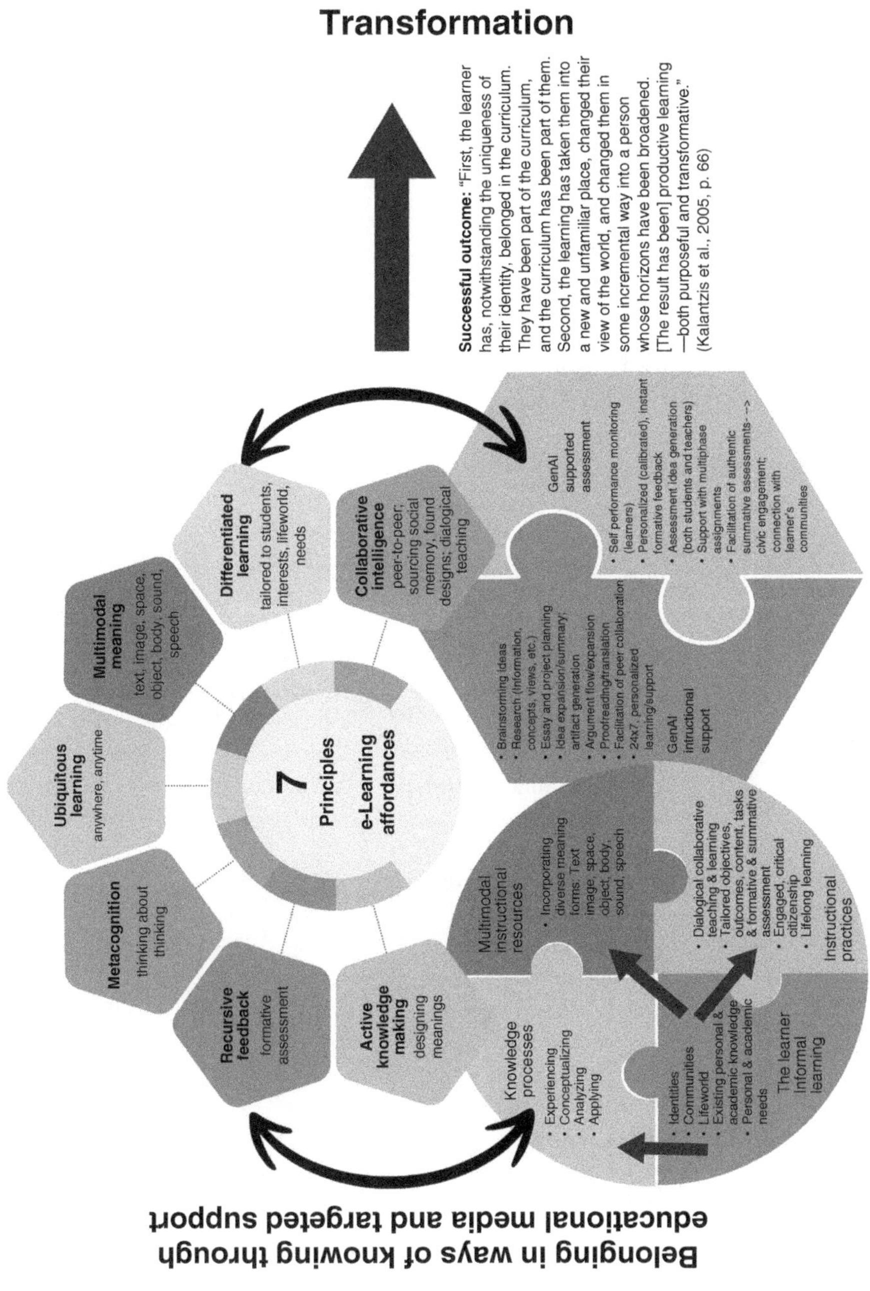

Figure 7.3 Inclusive, GenAI-supported instruction and assessment.

Table 7.1 GenAI supported assessment

Aspect of assessment	GenAI contribution	Inclusion and personalization
Real-time formative feedback	Can generate immediate, criterion-based guidance on writing or other diverse instructional tasks	Provides on-the-spot support tailored to individual needs, facilitating diverse learners' progress and reducing dependence on a single feedback source.
Progressive independent learning tracking	Can monitor students' evolving skills through keystroke capture and adaptive feedback	Helps differentiate between GenAI input and student-generated work, ensuring that learners receive personalized scaffolding as they grow more autonomous, but also assessing to what extent an assignment has been completed by the learner independently.
Active, critical reading, and meaning interpretation	• Can engage students in interactive dialogs, probing unique perspectives shaped by life histories and interests • Can monitor missing aspects in learners' interpretations and can offer guidance to reach expected instructional levels/outcomes • Can adjust reading levels, pace, and content difficulty based on individual learner profiles, performance, and contexts	Moves beyond one-size-fits-all comprehension checks, acknowledging students' diversity and individual backgrounds and providing targeted support.

Table 7.1 (Continued)

Aspect of assessment	**GenAI contribution**	**Inclusion and personalization**
Automated grading and summative assessment	Can offer consistent, real-time scoring of essays, projects, and coding assignments, as well as holistically consider a student's work during the academic year to offer data on performance, growth, and outcome achievement	Reduces educator workload and speeds turnaround, freeing instructors to focus on higher-order cognitive and metacognitive teaching—an especially important factor for diverse classrooms. Also, summative assessment becomes a holistic record of student learning instead of an isolated assessment event such as a final, cumulative exam.
Formative adaptive learning tools	Can identify misconceptions and knowledge gaps, delivering individualized guidance and remediation actions	Creates tailored learning pathways, ensuring students with varying skill levels and backgrounds receive support at the exact point of need.
Fine-tuned GenAI and peer feedback blends	Can combine automated, criterion-based suggestions with human commentary, relying on the same formative assessment criteria	Merges the speed and consistency of GenAI with the nuanced understanding of peers, providing multi-layered perspectives and accommodating diverse student voices.
Focus on higher-order skills	Can help teachers shift assessment designs toward critical thinking and problem-solving tasks rather than rote knowledge recall	Ensures that learners engage with deeper cognitive processes in a personalized manner, promoting creativity and originality while leveraging GenAI's assistive functionalities.

Conclusion

In this chapter, we explored the imperative for academic rigor and inclusivity in literacies education, advocating for the meaningful cognizance of learners' lifeworld differences across material, embodied, and symbolic dimensions in today's educational contexts. Embracing these factors requires an active commitment to transforming traditional educational practices, challenging institutional biases, and dismantling systemic barriers. Critical to these changes is also the consideration of students' lifeworld. We believe teachers need to leverage learners' personal narratives, identities, affinities, and orientations to create meaningful, relevant, and affirming educational experiences that resonate deeply with students' lived realities and foster a sense of belonging and empowerment.

This discussion was complemented with the examination of the transformative practice of translanguaging, a conceptualization and approach that transcend traditional monolingual and monoglossic ideologies by incorporating students' complete linguistic repertoires into literacies instruction. Translanguaging not only validates multilingual learners' unique identities but also actively counters linguistic biases prevalent in educational contexts. In the second part of the chapter, we discussed how GenAI technologies can significantly enhance inclusive educational practices, providing educators with dynamic tools for differentiated instruction and assessment.

Next, in Chapter 8, the last chapter of this volume, we build on these foundations and those delineated throughout the book, to present innovative strategies for human-AI collaboration in learning and teaching, examining the evolving role of the teacher as researcher, investigating the potential of GenAI in literacies research, and ultimately envisioning a path toward education justice that seeks equity and inclusivity for all learners.

Consolidate, Explore, Reflect, Do

We end this chapter with activities that will allow you to apply the concepts discussed in novel ways. Our goal is that these tasks will facilitate further exploration and reflection and will inspire your present and/or future teaching practice.

Task 1: Reflecting on Our Lifeworld

Working with a classmate, you will critically reflect on your lifeworld and discuss how your personal narrative, persona, affinity, and orientation have influenced your educational experiences and your present/future teaching practice.

Step 1. Individually, create a multimodal presentation illustrating key aspects of your lifeworld (e.g., those reflecting personal narratives, cultural identities, and orientations towards learning). You can employ different meaning forms and/or include multimodal personal artifacts.
Step 2. Share your presentation with your partner, and discuss similarities and differences, reflecting on how these aspects might have influenced your educational journey, and also, what role they play/might play in your teaching practice.
Step 3. Together, write a short reflection outlining insights gained from similarities/differences identified and consider implications for inclusive teaching practices.
Step 4. If you were to adapt this task for your classroom, what would you change? Considering our discussion of GenAI supported learning and assessment, what role could GenAI play in the task? How would you offer scaffolding for its successful student work? Reflect on these questions with your partner and another student pair.

Task 2: Translanguaging in Action

In this task, you will work in groups of 3. You and your classmates will explore translanguaging practices in real-world educational contexts.

Step 1. Each member selects a different real-world example from academic journals or educational reports. Each person should focus on a different educational context:

- **Group Member 1:** Elementary/Primary school
- **Group Member 2:** Secondary/Middle/High school
- **Group Member 3:** Higher education

We suggest you start with the articles cited in the chapter. You can have a look at them, and find other sources in the reference section of each work. Each person gathers information on the following:

- Implementation—examples of pedagogical interventions, teacher and student roles
- Benefits—personal and academic
- Challenges to implementation—logistical, ideological, etc.

Each member of the group summarizes their findings in a one-page report, and presents them to the rest of the group.
Step 2. After each person presents their findings, as a group, compile them into an infographic, concept map, and/or short video to multimodally explain how translanguaging is implemented in different educational contexts. Focus on similarities and differences across educational contexts, as well as benefits and challenges.
Step 3. Exchange reports and multimodal artifacts with another group. Compare results. Where do the challenges to translanguaging originate?
Step 4. As a new team, with the members of the other group, consider whether GenAI could help mitigate the challenges you have identified. If so, what actions would you suggest? What are other ways in which these challenges could be addressed? Propose actions for classroom implementation, including teacher training.

Task 3: Inclusive GenAI-Supported Assessment

In this task, you will work in groups of 4. You and your classmates will design GenAI-supported inclusive assessment tasks for the activities in Appendix 2.

Step 1. Together, carefully review Appendix 2, discussing key objectives, skills targeted, and learner profiles.
Step 2. Each member of the group selects a task, and develops GenAI-enhanced assessments (1 or 2 tasks), clearly outlining how GenAI technologies could support personalized, formative feedback and accommodate diverse learning needs. Use the information in this chapter and the previous ones to guide your work.
Step 3. Each person presents their work to the rest of the group, and receives formative feedback, which is then used to refine the original task. Once all revisions have been carried out, combine all members' tasks in a document.
Step 4. Exchange your document with another group. Together, provide detailed constructive feedback to the other group. After you have received feedback, collaboratively refine your assessment ideas for final presentation to the rest of the class.
Step 5. The class compiles all assessment ideas into a document that reflects everyone's work, and identifies the concepts introduced in this chapter that are reflected in all students' products.

Task 4: Creating Inclusive Curricula

In this task, you will work in groups of 4–5. Ideally, you should work with classmates that teach/will teach in the same educational context as you do/will. You and your classmates will develop a comprehensive inclusive curriculum unit leveraging learner diversity and GenAI.

Step 1. As a group, identify and analyze relevant dimensions of learner diversity (material, embodied, symbolic; lifeworld) in your educational context.
Step 2. Create a curricular unit integrating differentiated instruction tasks, grounded in LbyD and reflexive pedagogy (see Appendix 1), translanguaging practices, and GenAI technologies. We suggest you structure learners' work within the knowledge processes. You can also use the design template in (Appendix 1, on pages 321–322). After deciding on an instructional focus, each member of the group can concentrate on one specific

knowledge process (i.e., experiencing, conceptualizing, analyzing, applying).

Step 3. All members' work is combined. As a group, then prepare a detailed presentation explaining your design rationale, instructional strategies, and the anticipated impact of inclusivity, demonstrating practical applications for real-world classrooms.

Step 4. Exchange your presentation with another group. With the members of your group, provide detailed constructive feedback to the other group. After you have received feedback, collaboratively refine your work.

Step 5. Now, each member of the group goes back to the personal definition of literacy/literacies they have developed so far. Considering your work in this task and the concepts we introduced in this chapter, what changes would you make to your personal definition? What has changed? What remains the same? Why?

Step 6. Share your definition with the other members of your group. Together, consider similarities and differences. Create a new group definition. We will revisit your individual and group definitions in Chapter 8.

References

Anderson, B. (1991). *Imagined communities: Reflections on the origin and spread of nationalism*. Verso.

Baker, C. (2003). Biliteracy and transliteracy in Wales: Language planning and the Welsh national curriculum. In N. H. Hornberger (Ed.), *Continua of biliteracy: An ecological framework for educational policy, research, and practice in multilingual settings* (pp. 71–90). Multilingual Matters.

Behrens, J. T. & DiCerbo, K. E. (2013). Technological implications for assessment ecosystems. In E. W. Gordon (Ed.), *The Gordon commission on the future of assessment in education: Technical report* (pp. 101–122). The Gordon Commission.

Black, P. & Wiliam, D. (1998). Assessment and classroom learning. *Assessment in Education*, *5*, 7–74. https://doi.org/10.1080/0969595980050102

Bowe, F. (1978). *Handicapping America: Barriers to disabled people.* Harper & Row.

Caroccio Maldonado, J. (2023). Mixtec pictography and immigrant labor: Resistance in the comic undocumented: A worker's fight. *The New Americanist, 2*(1), 35–55. https://doi.org/10.3366/tna.2023.0004
Case, A. & Deaton, A. (2020). *Deaths of despair and the future of capitalism.* Princeton University Press.
Chan, P. E., Konrad, M., Gonzalez, V., Peters, M. T., & Ressa, V. A. (2014). The critical role of feedback in formative instructional practices. *Intervention in School and Clinic, 50*(2), 96–104. https://doi.org/10.1177/1053451214536044
Chang, H. H. (2015). Psychometrics behind computerized adaptive testing. *Psychometrika, 80*(1), 1–20. https://doi.org/10.1007/s11336-014-9401-5
Cope, B. & Kalantzis, M. (1997). *Productive diversity: A new approach to work and management.* Pluto Press.
Cope, B. & Kalantzis, M. (2015a). The things you do to know: An introduction to the pedagogy of multiliteracies. In B. Cope & M. Kalantzis (Eds.), *A pedagogy of multiliteracies: Learning by Design* (pp. 1–36). Palgrave Macmillan.
Cope, B. & Kalantzis, M. (2015b). Interpreting evidence-of-learning: Educational research in the era of big data. *Open Review of Educational Research, 2*, 218–239. https://doi.org/10.1080/23265507.2015.1074870
Cope, B. & Kalantzis, M. (2015c). Sources of evidence-of-learning: Learning and assessment in the era of big data. *Open Review of Educational Research, 2*, 194–217. https://doi.org/10.1080/23265507.2015.1074869
Cope, B. & Kalantzis, M. (2017). Conceptualizing e-Learning. In B. Cope & M. Kalantzis (Eds.), *ELearning ecologies* (pp. 1–45). Routledge.
Cope, B. & Kalantzis, M. (2019). Education 2.0: Artificial intelligence and the end of the test. *Beijing International Review of Education, 1*(2–3), 528–543. https://brill.com/view/journals/bire/1/2-3/article-p528_528.xml?language=en
Cope, B. & Kalantzis, M. (2024). On cyber-social learning: A critique of artificial intelligence in education. In T. Kourkoulou, A. O. Tzirides, B. Cope, & M. Kalantzis (Eds.), *Trust and inclusion in AI-mediated education: Where human learning meets learning machines* (pp. 3–34). Springer. https://doi.org/10.1007/978-3-031-64487-0_1
Cope, B., Kalantzis, M., McCarthey, S., Vojak, C., & Kline, S. (2011). Technology-mediated writing assessments: Paradigms and principles. *Computers and Composition, 28*, 79–96.
Cope, B., Kalantzis, M., & Tzirides, A. O. (2024). Meaning without borders: From translanguaging to transposition in the era of digitally-mediated meaning. In K. K. Grohmann (Ed.), *Multifaceted multilingualism* (pp. 329–370). John Benjamins. https://doi.org/10.1075/sibil.66.13cop

Cope, B., Kalantzis, M., & Zapata, G. C. (2025). Language learning after generative AI. In G. C. Zapata (Ed.), *Generative AI technologies, multiliteracies, and language education* (pp. 14–29). Routledge. https://doi.org/10.4324/9781003531685-2

Cummins, J. (2019). The emergence of translanguaging pedagogy: A dialogue between theory and practice. *Journal of Multilingual Education Research*, *9*(1), 19–36. https://fordham.bepress.com/jmer/vol9/iss1/13

Delgado Bernal, D., Burciaga, R., & Flores Carmona, J. (2012). Chicana/Latina testimonios: Mapping the methodological, pedagogical, and political. *Equity and Excellence in Education*, *45*(3), 363–372. https://doi.org/10.1080/10665684.2012.698149

García, O. & Kleifgen, J. A. (2020). Translanguaging and literacies. *Reading Research Quarterly*, *55*(4), 553–571. https://doi.org/10.1002/rrq.286

García, O. & Sylvan, C. E. (2011). Pedagogies and practices in multilingual classrooms: Singularities in pluralities. *The Modern Language Journal*, *95*(3), 385–400. https://doi.org/10.1111/j.1540-4781.2011.01208.x

Godwin-Jones, R. (2025). Technology integration for less commonly taught languages: AI and pedagogical translanguaging. *Language Learning & Technology*, *29*(2), 11–34. https://hdl.handle.net/10125/73609

Grosjean, F. (2021). *Life as a bilingual*. Cambridge University Press. https://doi.org/10.1017/9781108975490

Hart-Davidson, W. (2024). Mixing and mastering genre signals: Generative AI, writing, and the near future of writing technologies. Paper presented at the *Global Digital Humanities Symposium*, March 18–20, Michigan State University. https://doi.org/10.17613/ptr6-fj47

Kalantzis, M. & Cope, B. (2012). *New learning: Elements of a science of education*. Cambridge University Press.

Kalantzis, M. & Cope, B. (2025). Literacy in the time of artificial intelligence. *Reading Research Quarterly*, *60*, Article e591. https://doi.org/10.1002/rrq.591

Kalantzis, M., Cope, B., & the Learning by Design Project Group. (2005). *Learning by Design*. Victorian Schools Innovation Commission and Common Ground Publishing.

Kalantzis, M., Cope, B., Chan, E., & Dalley-Trim, L. (2016). *Literacies* (2nd ed). Cambridge University Press.

Kizilcec, R. F., Huber, E., Papanastasiou, E. C., Cram, A., Makridis, C. A., Smolansky, A., Zeivots, S., & Raduescu, C. (2024). Perceived impact of generative AI on assessments: Comparing educator and student perspectives in Australia, Cyprus, and the United States. *Computers and Education: Artificial Intelligence*, *7*, Article 100269. https://doi.org/10.1016/j.caeai.2024.100269

Kline, S., Letofsky, K., & Woodard, B. (2013). Democratizing classroom discourse: The challenge for online writing environments. *e-Learning and Digital Media*, *10*, 379–395. https://doi.org/10.2304/elea.2013.10.4.378

Lewis, G., Jones, B., & Baker, C. (2012a). Translanguaging: Origins and development from school to street and beyond. *Educational Research and Evaluation, 18*(7), 641–654. https://doi.org/10.1080/13803611.2012.718488

Lewis, G., Jones, B., & Baker, C. (2012b). Translanguaging: Developing its conceptualization and contextualization. *Educational Research and Evaluation, 18*(7), 655–670. https://doi.org/10.1080/13803611.2012.718490

Mayo, C. (2022). *LGBTQ youth and education: Policies and practices* (2nd ed). Teachers College Press.

McCarthey, S. J., Magnifico, A., Woodard, R., & Kline, S. (2014). Situating technology facilitated feedback and revision: The case of Tom. In K. E. Pytash & R. E. Ferdig (Eds.), *Exploring technology for writing and writing instruction* (pp. 152–170). IGI Global.

McNamara, D. S. & Graesser, A. C. (2012). Coh-Metrix: An automated tool for theoretical and applied natural language processing. In P. M. McCarthy & C. Boonthum-Denecke (Eds.), *Applied natural language processing: Identification, investigation and resolution* (pp. 188–205). IGI Global.

Miles, R. (1989). *Racism*. Routledge.

Moll, L. C., Amanti, C., Neff, D., & Gonzalez, N. (1992). Funds of knowledge for teaching: Using a qualitative approach to connect homes and classrooms. *Theory into Practice, 31*(2), 132–141. https://www.jstor.org/stable/1476399

Monea, B. (2020). Looking at screens: Examining human-computer interaction and communicative breakdown in an educational online writing community. *Computers and Composition, 59*, Article 102605. https://doi.org/10.1016/j.compcom.2020.102605

New London Group. (1996). A pedagogy of multiliteracies: Designing social futures. *Harvard Educational Review, 66*, 60–92. https://doi.org/10.17763/haer.66.1.17370n67v22j160u

Paiz, C. O., Bedolla, L. G., & Gutiérrez, K. D. (2023). Civics on the move: The politics of Latinx civic integration. *The ANNALS of the American Academy of Political and Social Science, 705*(1), 192–207. https://doi.org/10.1177/00027162231190530

Pea, R. & Jacks, D. (2014). *The Learning Analytics workgroup: A report on building the field of learning analytics for personalized learning at scale.* Stanford University.

Pellegrino, J. W., Chudowsky, N., & Glaser, R. (2001). *Knowing what students know: The science and design of educational assessment.* National Academies Press.

Piketty, T. (2014). *Capital in the twenty-first century*. Harvard University Press.

Reid, A. & Deaux, K. (1996). Relationship between social and personal identities: Segregation or integration. *Journal of Personality and Social Psychology, 71*(6), 1084–1091. https://doi.org/10.1037/0022-3514.71.6.1084

Roberts, D. (2011). *Fatal invention: How science, politics, and big business re-create race in the twenty-first century*. The New Press.

Santiago, M., de los Ríos, C. V., & Gutiérrez, K. (2021). Historicizing Latinx civic agency and contemporary lived civics. In C. D. Lee, G. White, & D. Dong (Eds.), *Civic discourses and reasoning* (pp. 206–224). National Academy of Education.

Shermis, M. D. (2014). State-of-the-art automated essay scoring: Competition, results, and future directions from a United States demonstration. *Assessing Writing*, *20*, 53–76. https://doi.org/10.1016/j.asw.2013.04.001

Stornaiuolo, A., Jennifer Higgs, T., Nichols, P., Leblanc, R. J., & de Roock, R. S. (2023). The platformization of writing instruction: Considering educational equity in new learning ecologies. *Review of Research in Education*, *47*(1), 311–359. https://doi.org/10.3102/0091732X241227431

Steiss, J., Tate, T., Graham, S., Cruz, J., Hebert, M., Wang, J., Moon, Y., Tseng, W., Warschauer, M., & Booth Olson, C. (2024). Comparing the quality of human and ChatGPT feedback of students' writing. *Learning and Instruction*, *91*, Article 101894. https://doi.org/10.1016/j.learninstruc.2024.101894

Tang, X., Chen, H., Lin, D., & Li, K. (2024). Harnessing LLMs for multi-dimensional writing assessment: Reliability and alignment with human judgments. *Heliyon*, *10*. https://doi.org/10.1016/j.heliyon.2024.e34262

Tate, T. P., Steiss, J., Bailey, D., Graham, S., Moon, Y., Ritchie, D., Tseng, W., & Warschauer, M. (2024). Can AI provide useful holistic essay scoring? *Computers and Education: Artificial Intelligence*, *7*, Article 100255. https://doi.org/10.1016/j.caeai.2024.100255

Tonatiuh, D. (2018). *Undocumented: A worker's fight*. Abrams Comic Arts.

Tzirides, A. O., Cope, B., & Kalantzis, M. (2023). Contemporary contexts for learning: An overview. In R. J. Tierney, F. Rizvi, & K. Ercikan (Eds.), *International encyclopaedia of education* (4th ed) (pp. 258–266). Elsevier.

Tzirides, A. O., Zapata, G. C., Kastania, N. P., Saini, A. K., Castro, V., Ismael, S. A., You, Y., Afonso dos Santos, T., Searsmith, D., O'Brien, C., Cope, B., & Kalantzis, M. (2024a). Combining human and artificial intelligence for enhanced AI literacy in higher education. *Computers and Education Open*, *6*, Article 100184. https://doi.org/10.1016/j.caeo.2024.100184

Tzirides, A. O., Zapata, G. C., Bolger, P. A., Cope, B., Kalantzis, M., & Searsmith, D. (2024b). Exploring instructors' views on fine-tuned generative AI feedback in higher education. *International Journal on E-Learning*, *23*(3), 319–334. https://www.learntechlib.org/primary/p/225173/

UNESCO. (2024). *AI competency framework for students*. UNESCO. https://doi.org/10.54675/JKJB9835

Vojak, C., Kline, S., Cope, B., McCarthey, S., & Kalantzis, M. (2011). New spaces and old places: An analysis of writing assessment software. *Computers and Composition*, *28*, 97–111. https://doi.org/10.1016/j.compcom.2011.04.004

Vygotsky, L. S. (1978). *Mind in society: The development of higher psychological processes.* Harvard University Press.

Wang, C. (2024). Exploring students' generative AI-assisted writing processes: Perceptions and experiences from native and nonnative English speakers. *Technology, Knowledge and Learning.* https://doi.org/10.1007/s10758-024-09744-3

Wei, L. (2024). Transformative pedagogy for inclusion and social justice through translanguaging, co-learning, and transpositioning. *Language Teaching, 57*(2), 203–214. https://doi.org/10.1017/S0261444823000186

Wei, L. & García, O. (2022). Not a first language but one repertoire: Translanguaging as a decolonizing project. *RELC Journal, 53*(2), 313–324. https://doi.org/10.1177/00336882221092841

Wiliam, D. (2011). *Embedded formative assessment.* Solution Tree Press.

Williams, C. (2012). *Subject language threshold: Accelerating the process of reaching the threshold: National immersion scheme guidance for teachers.* The Welsh Language Board.

Woodard, R., Magnifico, A., & McCarthey, S. (2013). Supporting teacher metacognition about formative writing assessment in online environments. *e-Learning and Digital Media, 10,* 442–470. https://doi.org/10.2304/elea.2013.10.4.442

Yang, W. & Lin, C. (2025). Translanguaging with generative AI in EFL writing: Students' practices and perceptions. *Journal of Second Language Writing, 67,* Article 101181. https://doi.org/10.1016/j.jslw.2025.101181

Zapata, G. C. (2022). *Learning by design and second language teaching: Theory, research, and practice.* Routledge.

Zapata, G. C. (Ed.). (2025). *Generative AI technologies, multiliteracies, and language education.* Routledge.

Zapata, G. C., Cope, B., Kalantzis, M., Tzirides, A. O., Saini, A., Searsmith, D., Whiting, J., Kastania, N. P., Castro, V., Kourkoulou, T., Jones, J., & Abrantes da Silva, R. (2025a). AI and peer reviews in higher education: Students' multimodal views on benefits, differences, and limitations. *Technology, Pedagogy and Education*, 34(5), 583–601. https://doi.org/10.1080/1475939X.2025.2480807

Zapata, G. C., Saini, A. K., Tzirides, A. O., Cope, B., & Kalantzis, M. (2024). The role of AI feedback in university students' learning experiences: An exploration grounded in activity theory. *Ubiquitous Learning: An International Journal, 18*(2), 1–30. https://doi.org/10.18848/1835-9795/CGP/v18i02/1-30

Zapata, G. C., Tzirides, A. O., Cope, B., You, Y.-L., Kalantzis, M., & Searsmith, D. (2025b). A systemic functional linguistics discourse analysis of learner-centered, generative AI feedback in higher education. *EdArXiv.* https://doi.org/10.35542/osf.io/nuhq2_v1

Chapter 8
Futures for the Discipline of Education and Literacies Research

Introduction

This chapter ushers us into the final phase of our exploration—a forward-looking inquiry into how evolving technologies, especially generative artificial intelligence (GenAI), will continue transforming the landscape of literacies education. Building on previous chapters, we survey a range of contemporary issues and possibilities, from the redefinition of the role of education in research in a digitally infused era to the evolving role of the teacher as a researcher, engaged in a continuous cycle of inquiry and innovation. We also consider the transformative potential of GenAI as a tool for literacies research. Our discussion is framed by a commitment to education justice—an ethos that champions equity and inclusion for all learners. As we envision futures where technology and

Literacies in the Age of AI: Teaching and Learning in the Digital Era,
First Edition. Gabriela C. Zapata, Bill Cope, and Mary Kalantzis.

teaching intersect, we invite readers to reflect on the diverse topics we have explored in this volume and their implications, as well as to consider strategies for fostering more effective, dynamic, and forward-thinking educational contexts.

The Expanded Role of Education and Its Epistemological Imperative

Based on our recent work (e.g., Cope & Kalantzis, 2019, 2024; Kalantzis & Cope, 2025; Zapata et al., 2023) and the issues explored in this volume, we posit that education must assume a crucial role in addressing contemporary anxieties and the emerging meanings that shape our lives and prepare all students as lifelong learners, citizens, and workers. This responsibility extends in the digital age beyond formal educational institutions to include informal contexts—whether in physical communities or virtual spaces—where individuals gather, learn, and share experiences. What is the role of the discipline of education in understanding and navigating the extraordinary changes we experience today? How does literacy research play a part in this?

Historically, philosophy was the discipline uniquely equipped to probe the foundational and expansive questions of knowledge and action. Revered once as the preeminent intellectual endeavor, philosophy's stature diminished after its "language turn" (Jameson, 1972; Rorty, 1992), when it became ensnared in technical explorations of mental processes and was rendered comprehensible only to a select few.

With the abandonment of hierarchical disciplinary structures, education has emerged as the contemporary successor to philosophy (Kalantzis & Cope, 2014). Given the heightened anxieties of our digital times, it is essential to develop a comprehensive reference framework—a model of "coming to know" that spans both the ontogenesis and phylogenesis of all other disciplines, as well as the forms of thinking necessary to engage with every social situation and dilemma. Ontogenesis involves each child developing into a socially aware individual, each adult learning to navigate and respond to changing circumstances, and each expert being initiated into specific social, economic, technical, and political fields of practice. Phylogenesis encompasses the human species' understanding of itself, the stewardship of nature by humans, the role of humans as toolmakers, and our continual transformation through the tools we create. The scope of education is distinctively broad, spanning the full range of natural and human sciences, as well as the arts and technology.

This view of education necessitates an expanded epistemological approach that moves beyond immediate instrumental reasoning by situating our efforts within cohesive social structures, economic prosperity, and environmental sustainability. To fully embrace this expanded role and its meaning in connection with research work, we propose three distinct disciplinary "turns": The *semiotic turn*, the *social turn*, and the *ontological turn* (see also Cope & Kalantzis, 2020a). We explore each of these proposals in the next three sections.

The Semiotic Turn: Reframing Research as a Process of Meaning-Making

The semiotic turn redefines research dynamics as fundamentally about meaning-making rather than merely transmitting observable data. Traditionally, research has been portrayed as the objective communication of observable meanings from participants to a detached researcher. Quantitative methods emphasize faithful data quantification, while qualitative approaches focus on exploring experiences with careful triangulation to maintain objectivity. Ethnographers, for instance, are expected to assume a studied detachment that preserves objectivity, thus positioning the researcher as an explorer of unfamiliar terrain—discovering findings that, though novel to the researcher, might be mundane for the participants, and, as we will suggest below, might not be reflective of their realities and needs. This conventional model—whether framed as empiricism or positivism—presumes that researchers can align their accounts with objectively shared meanings while maintaining impartiality. Yet, this presumed objectivity is largely illusory since researchers inherently are motivated by interests (Cope & Kalantzis, 2015; Kalantzis & Cope, 2014), and has, in most of research history, resulted in the absence and misrepresentation of certain populations (Archibald, 2008; Smith, 2022).

The fundamental flaw in these conventional research models is the notion of communication as the transmission of shared meaning. Umberto Eco's (1976) semiotic model, for example, identifies a sender, a message, and an addressee. Even though Eco acknowledges ambiguities and interpretive failures, successful communication is still conceptualized as message transmission and shared understanding. We challenge this view by reconceptualizing disruptions in communication not as failures but as normative rhetorical occurrences (see Chapter 3, pp. 90–91). Here, differences are not defects to be eliminated but the very basis for meaning. As our rhetorical semiotic theory posits (see Chapter 3, pp. 88–91), meaning emerges from the common ground where differences intersect—whether harmoniously or contentiously. Empathy becomes central in this collaborative construction of meaning, shifting the research challenge from merely validating interpretations to fostering productive, intersubjective relationships.

This approach also reflects our commitment to refocus research methodologies. This would involve interrogating traditional, powerful structures of knowledge and challenging the multitude of biases that dominate knowledge production, thus enabling historically ignored voices and perspectives to resurface (Smith, 2022). For example, indigenous research methodologies, such as *Indigenous Storywork*, highlight culturally meaningful, participatory, and empowering methods (Archibald, 2008). These methodologies emphasize principles of respect, responsibility, reverence, reciprocity, holism, interrelatedness, and synergy, ensuring that research processes are meaningful and beneficial to Indigenous communities and worthy of others' understanding, including those who are students (Archibald, 2008; Archibald et al., 2023). Employing community-based participatory research, incorporating ceremonies and rituals, and using artistic expression or land-based teaching and learning strategies exemplify approaches aligned with inclusive and transparent research (Chilisa, 2015).

An example of the application of such practices in educational research is the TEAM-Learning project (i.e., Transformative Education for Aboriginal Mathematics) described by Archibald et al. (2023). This long-term study (2005–2017) was situated in Haida Gwaii, a semi-isolated Indigenous community in British Columbia, Canada, and brought together a diverse group of participants including teachers, Elders, administrators, and community members. The objectives of this work were to explore and develop culturally responsive methodologies with a specific focus on mathematics teaching and learning. Data were collected through a rich array of qualitative methods, including field notes, teacher journals, interviews, video recordings, and digital photos. In this context, by centering Indigenous knowledges and engaging with community-based participatory practices, the project transcended traditional paradigms and empowered participants to co-create appropriately creative and responsive mathematics pedagogy. The reflective approach adopted by the researchers was sensitive to context, not only validating Indigenous perspectives but also resulting in innovative educational practices that integrated community values and land-based experiences, ultimately benefiting students, educators, and the community as a whole by creating more meaningful and sustainable learning environments.

Another example of this type of work is offered by Tzou et al. (2019), who employed a participatory design research framework that merged Indigenous storytelling with STEM learning. In this study, Native American families from communities such as the Seneca-Cayuga, Lakota, Paiute, and Mayan nations collaborated in a series of workshops where they co-constructed dioramas and engaged with robotics and coding through the lens of their traditional narratives. Participants, including both children and adults, contributed to the research by sharing their family stories, cultural practices, and experiences with materials and technology. Data collection involved extensive video observations, post-workshop interviews, and artifact documentation, while the analysis was guided by coding systems that traced how storytelling catalyzed onto-epistemic navigation between Indigenous and Western knowledge systems. The innovative research practices in this project were central to challenging dominant STEM narratives, as they foregrounded Indigenous cultural values and intergenerational learning as a means of enhancing motivation and performance in STEM learning. Tzou et al.'s work showed that this approach both revitalized traditional storytelling and cultural identity and also fostered transformative learning experiences, enhancing community cohesion and reimagining STEM as a culturally responsive and empowering domain. This more engaged, solid foundation led into higher order outcomes in STEM.

The Social Turn: Emphasizing Learning as a Socially Embedded Process

Our critique of conventional research extends to the cognitive-oriented educational model epitomized by scholars such as Kirschner et al. (2006), who define learning primarily in terms of long-term memory retention. Such a narrow conception privileges testable retention over creative and critical thought and is reinforced by neuroscientific portrayals of the brain as an isolated, individual entity. We argue, as we saw in Chapter 6, that learning is best understood as activity embedded within a social context (Cope & Kalantzis, 2020b; Vygotsky, 1978, 1986).

In this revised perspective, knowledge is not simply an abstract cognitive product but is better observed through differentiated instructional choices and the "works" that learners create. These works are sequences of observable knowledge-actions—encompassing experiential, conceptual, analytical, and applied dimensions—that culminate in a broad range of tangible artifacts. This approach aligns with active, project-based learning (Waks, 1997), defined as "a teaching method in which students gain knowledge and skills by working for an extended period of time to investigate and respond to an authentic, engaging, and complex question, problem, or challenge, and make their work public" (PBLWorks, 2021, p. 9). We have further elaborated on the pedagogical advantages of this approach and the breadth of data it can offer in some of our previous research (e.g., see, Cope & Kalantzis, 2015, 2017; Montebello et al., 2018a, 2018b; Pinheiro, 2020; Zapata, 2022).

Also, as discussed in Chapter 7, digital platforms can now provide data directly related to students' collaborative work and knowledge construction since they allow for the recording of every keystroke and interaction—semantically legible datapoints that capture micro-level learning moments. This also creates an opportunity for significant differentiation as required by differential student needs and capacities. These datapoints can serve both research and formative and summative purposes, blurring traditional distinctions and enabling a more comprehensive view of learning as a socially distributed process. Researchers are encouraged to focus on these collective knowledge ecologies rather than focusing solely on individual cognitive outcomes (Bereiter, 2002; Gee, 2014).

The Ontological Turn: Shifting Focus to Material and Digital Realities

The ontological turn reorients our attention from immaterial cognitive inferences to the social-material artifacts of knowledge production. Digital technologies—particularly AI, GenAI, and big data analytics—have endowed us with unprecedented tools to trace and analyze the learning process in real time. Over the past decade, collaborations between educators and computer scientists (e.g., see Cope et al., 2020) have yielded new pedagogical alternatives that replace outdated didactic-mimetic models with reflexive-ergative approaches. In these environments, every digital interaction, from keystrokes to sensor data, is recorded as "cyberdata," which enables fine-grained analysis of both micro-dynamics and macro-dynamics of learning (Cope & Kalantzis, 2015).

Central to this turn is the challenge of transforming binary computational processes into human meanings. As we saw in

Chapter 3 (see pages 88–100), our transpositional grammar identifies four key dimensions of digital meaning-making—namely, namability, calculability, measurability, and representability (Cope & Kalantzis, 2020b). These dimensions illuminate how AI's capacity to rapidly name, organize, and compute within structured ontologies both exceeds and falls short of human cognitive processes (Kalantzis & Cope, 2025). In practice, AI functions as a cognitive prosthesis that extends our ability to represent and analyze knowledge, while simultaneously introducing gains and losses that researchers must account for when interpreting educational data. In the next section, we will consider how GenAI can complement this and the previously discussed research orientations.

GenAI in Educational Research

As posited in the previous section, AI tools, and particularly GenAI, are rapidly reshaping educational research methodologies by enabling innovative engagement with data as well as transforming traditional research practices. For instance, in literature review and synthesis, GenAI offers capabilities such as rapid summarization, effectively condensing extensive research literature into concise and digestible summaries, and, as a result, researchers can efficiently grasp core findings and relevant insights (Liu et al., 2023; Mozelius & Humble, 2024). Furthermore, GenAI algorithms can facilitate topic modeling and trend analysis, enabling scholars to detect recurrent themes and patterns across vast text corpora, thereby identifying emerging trends and pinpointing research gaps.

Additionally, GenAI can offer support with experiment design and hypothesis generation. For instance, by analyzing existing literature and datasets, GenAI can propose novel research questions and hypotheses, opening new avenues for scholarly inquiry (UNESCO, 2023). Also, GenAI can assist in optimizing study design, by, for example, recommending optimal parameters, appropriate control groups, and other critical changes to bolster both efficiency and validity in research studies (Stremersch, 2024), regardless of whether the proposed work features a quantitative, qualitative, or mixed methods design.

Another pivotal affordance of GenAI lies in its contributions to data collection and analysis. For instance, in scenarios where collecting real-world data is either impractical or prohibitively costly, GenAI can generate synthetic datasets that closely mimic authentic data, thus enabling hypothesis testing and facilitating model development or the assessment of existing ones (Douzas & Bacao, 2018). GenAI can also enhance data analysis through advanced pattern recognition, anomaly detection, and visualization, identifying subtle correlations and inconsistencies within complex datasets that may not be readily apparent to human analysts. Additionally, GenAI can transform raw data into interactive visualizations, significantly aiding scholars to comprehend and communicate their findings effectively (Curry et al., 2024).

With GenAI support, therefore, we can now design studies that leverage its capabilities to examine both the fine-grained details of individual learning moments, the overall learning process, and the broader patterns that emerge across student cohorts and collaborative knowledge construction. Within this new research environment, it is important to carefully calibrate our research questions to account for dynamic, recursive intervention cycles, and the employment of adaptive analytical tools that can accommodate continuously collected, large-scale data. We summarize the possible roles that GenAI can play in educational research in Figure 8.1.

Of course, our reliance on big data and the application of GenAI for research purposes require the creation of novel research infrastructures to support the collection, curation, and analysis of vast, heterogeneous datasets. As noted in our previous work (Cope & Kalantzis, 2015), the future of educational research also depends on the development of platforms that facilitate the publication of datasets alongside traditional scholarly articles. Such infrastructures can enable replication, extension studies, and meta-analyses that provide deeper insights into learning processes. Furthermore, these infrastructures must ensure that data are collected in a

Figure 8.1 Possible GenAI's roles in educational research.

self-describing manner, with robust metadata, provenance tracking, and version control to support auditability and reproducibility.

Clearly, GenAI's participation in research design and data collection and analysis processes underscores the shift toward treating machines as collaborative research partners rather than mere instruments. This cybersocial research approach recognizes that machine learning systems not only collect data but also refine their algorithms based on continuous input, thereby enhancing the overall resolution of learning analytics (Woolf et al., 2013). Interdisciplinary teams that combine expertise in education, data science, and digital humanities can fully leverage these emerging infrastructures, as well as take advantage of their affordances for scholarly work spanning a variety of aspects in teaching and learning.

To end this section, we propose several practical recommendations reflective of the possible transformative potential of GenAI and big data in educational research. We believe in the need for researchers to

- **Design for Multiscalar Data Collection:** Researchers should integrate embedded data collection mechanisms that capture fine-grained learning interactions while also allowing for long-term, retrospective analyses. This requires developing digital environments where every learner action becomes a semantically legible datapoint, useful also for both formative feedback and summative assessment.
- **Embrace Mixed Methods:** With the boundaries between qualitative and quantitative research blurring, investigators should deploy hybrid methodologies that leverage GenAI-powered tools (e.g., natural language processing image recognition) to analyze both structured and unstructured data. This approach enables the extraction of nuanced insights from large-scale datasets, accommodating both general trends as well as individual variations and personal experiences.
- **Establish New Collaborative Research Environments:** Building or joining interdisciplinary networks—such as collaborative platforms and data repositories overseen by investigators—is essential for managing, curating, and sharing the vast amounts of data generated by digital learning environments. This type of work must involve infrastructures that support rigorous data provenance, metadata standards, and compliance with privacy regulations.
- **Adopt Cybersocial Research Practices:** Recognize the role of machines as collaborative partners in data collection and analysis.

By engaging with cyberdata and employing agile research cycles, researchers, in collaboration with educators (e.g., in design-based research [Ford et al., 2017]), can more effectively capture the dynamic, evolving nature of learning processes as well as exert iterative, evidence-based changes to teaching practices.

- **Foster Socially Reflective Research Methodologies:** Researchers must integrate frameworks that acknowledge and leverage the diversity of learner experiences. This includes developing a semiotics of empathy in research, employing community-based participatory research methods, and ensuring that the voices of all groups are central to all aspects of research design.

By following these recommendations, educational researchers can harness the transformative potential of big data and GenAI, achieving insights that are as robust as they are responsive to the challenges and opportunities of our times.

Human-AI Collaboration: Educators' and Researchers' Roles

As shown in the chapters of this volume, at the intersection of literacies education and GenAI, transformative possibilities emerge, and we are now compelled to reexamine the roles of educators and researchers. Human-AI collaboration offers dynamic opportunities for enhancing literacies education by integrating different meaning forms and functions into learning experiences. These multimodal affordances challenge traditional, linear conceptions of literacy, pushing educators to leverage AI-generated content—such as images and texts—to enrich classroom interactions and foster deeper student personal and academic engagement. The complexity of these interactions demands that technology be seen as a collaborative partner rather than a replacement for human creativity and critical thought.

We believe this new chapter in education redefines teachers' role, repositioning them as reflective, collaborative practitioners and researchers who design learning environments that promote active participation, co-creation of knowledge, and mastery of a wide range of forms of meaning-making. Moving beyond the role of mere disseminators of standardized content, educators are now called to cultivate spaces where students engage in creative inquiry and critical reflection on their literacies practices. This expanded role requires continuous professional development, collaboration, and the acquisition of new competencies to navigate the pedagogical implications of AI in educational settings. Simultaneously, the potential of GenAI in literacies research opens compelling avenues for exploring the interplay between human cognition and technology-mediated environments, while also demanding vigilant ethical practices regarding AI biases and socio-cultural impacts.

Ultimately, the integration of GenAI into literacies education calls for a renewed commitment to education justice. Historically, literacy has both challenged and perpetuated inequalities; today, as GenAI democratizes access to powerful multimodal tools, it is incumbent upon educators and researchers to design learning experiences that include historically neglected and disadvantaged learners. This involves intentionally addressing biases inherent in AI systems and foregrounding ethical concerns so that these technologies serve as instruments of empowerment rather than exclusion. In doing so, educational research should move toward more holistic, reflective methodologies that validate diverse epistemologies and foster participatory, community-based inquiry (Archibald et al., 2023; Smith 2022), as well as result in educational contexts oriented to educational justice defined by productive diversity.

Towards Education Justice in the GenAI Era: A Pathway Forward

As we conclude our exploration in this volume, we want to reflect on the journey we have undertaken and consider the pathway forward toward education justice in the era of GenAI. Throughout the chapters in this book, we have traced the trajectory of literacy from the diverse and multimodal practices of early human communication, through the standardized conceptualization based on reading and writing, and into our current digitally mediated landscape. We showed how each stage significantly reshaped social structures, the construction and communication of knowledge, as well as meaning-making, highlighting literacy's persistent role as a powerful agent of both societal transformation and social and economic justice.

Our discussion began with the acknowledgment that literacy has historically been more than a mere mechanism of information transmission—it has been integral to shaping lifeworlds, including identities, communities, and cultural values. The evolution from rich, multimodal first languages to standardized writing systems illustrated both literacy's potential to democratize knowledge and its simultaneous role in perpetuating societal inequalities. The critical lens adopted in earlier chapters set the foundation for understanding how literacy practices have historically privileged certain groups while marginalizing others, thus foregrounding our imperative for education justice.

A critical transition in our understanding of literacy, particularly highlighted in Chapter 6, is the shift from viewing literacy in the singular—as a universal and standardized skill grounded only in the development of reading and writing—to recognizing *literacies*, in the plural. This pluralization emphasizes the multiple, multimodal ways in which we convey meaning, and the multiplicity of literacy practices influenced by cultural, economic, technological, and contextual factors. By moving away from the singular conceptualization, we thereby embrace the diverse ways people produce and interpret meaning, emphasizing the need for an inclusive literacies approach that respects and incorporates diverse epistemologies and modes of communication into educational practice.

Moving into contemporary developments, the integration of digital technologies and specifically GenAI marks a revolutionary moment in literacies education. GenAI not only automates and enhances the production of multimodal content, but fundamentally alters traditional understandings of creativity, authorship, and collaboration. These changes may underscore an essential shift in education toward greater democratization of creative tools, thus expanding opportunities for *all* students, including those belonging to historically disadvantaged communities. However, this democratization comes with its own complexities, as biases embedded within AI systems as well as material differences present both in rich and developing countries risk reinforcing historical inequities unless intentionally and critically addressed.

In considering educational research methodologies within this new context, we have highlighted significant paradigm shifts catalyzed by digital technologies. The traditional binaries of formative and summative assessments, qualitative and quantitative methodologies, and researcher-participant roles have blurred, giving rise to agile, inclusive, and ethically responsive approaches. The adoption of big data and cybersocial research methodologies offers unprecedented detail into learning processes, enabling educators and researchers to track both micro-level and macro-level dynamics. Nonetheless, these approaches require critical vigilance to ensure ethical data practices and culturally sensitive research frameworks.

Reflecting on educators' and researchers' evolving roles, it becomes clear that human-AI collaboration has already fundamentally transformed educational landscapes. Educators are now positioned not merely as disseminators of knowledge but as reflective practitioners and co-creators of dynamic learning environments. This expanded role necessitates ongoing professional development and critical engagement with digital tools to foster inclusive, participatory educational experiences. Similarly, researchers are challenged to redefine their methodologies, integrating empathetic, inclusive frameworks that prioritize community-based participatory research and all voices.

Ultimately, achieving education justice in the GenAI era requires a holistic and transformative reimagining of literacies education. It demands active commitment to dismantling biases inherent in

AI systems, employing epistemological frameworks, and creating equitable, culturally responsive learning spaces. By harnessing GenAI's transformative potential alongside critical, inclusive educational practices, educators and researchers can ensure that literacies remain catalysts for positive social transformation, educational equity, and high-performance outcomes for all.

As we look forward, we invite continued critical dialogue and innovative exploration among educators and researchers. Together, through deliberate and ethical engagement with emerging technologies and methodologies, we can cultivate educational environments that empower *all* learners, particularly those historically marginalized. In this collective effort lies the promise of a more just, robust, inclusive, and transformative educational future.

Conclusion

In this concluding chapter, we have explored potential futures for literacies research and teaching, particularly emphasizing the transformative roles that emerging technologies, such as GenAI, may play in educational research. Our examination highlighted the need to reconceptualize research through semiotic, social, and ontological turns, advocating for practices grounded in meaning-making, social embeddedness, and the material-digital realities of contemporary education. We also considered the profound implications of GenAI, underscoring its potential to enhance research methodologies.

As educators and researchers, our challenge now lies in responsibly navigating these new terrains, maintaining a steadfast commitment to high educational outcomes for all, and thus social justice and inclusion. By embracing collaborative human-AI partnerships, fostering reflective and innovative pedagogical practices, and actively addressing systemic inequalities both in teaching/learning and research spaces, we can ensure that literacies education remains a powerful tool for societal well-being, and productive self and social transformation. We conclude with an invitation for continued exploration, reflection, and action, encouraging readers to actively engage in shaping equitable and dynamic educational futures.

Consolidate, Explore, Reflect, Do

We end this chapter with activities that will allow you to apply the concepts discussed in novel ways. Our goal is that these tasks will facilitate further exploration and reflection and will inspire your present and/or future teaching practice.

Task 1: GenAI and Your Teaching Philosophy

In this task, you will explore how your educational philosophy intersects with GenAI in literacies education. You will work individually and with another classmate.

Step 1. Individually, draft a concise teaching philosophy statement articulating your views on the integration and role of GenAI in literacies education. Clearly illustrate your perspective and provide rationale for your views (e.g., make reference to pedagogical principles/frameworks [see Chapter 4] that ground your perspectives).
Step 2. Share your philosophy with a classmate. Identify and discuss similarities and differences in your perspectives, examining underlying reasons for your viewpoints (e.g., consider your educational journey, lifeworld, and professional experiences, etc.).
Step 3. Together, outline practical strategies for integrating GenAI into your present/future practice. Consider both pedagogical affordances and potential challenges/limitations.
Step 4. Collaboratively reflect on ethical considerations involved in integrating GenAI into literacies education. Propose strategies to effectively address and mitigate these concerns.

Task 2: Designing a GenAI-Supported Research Project

In this task, you will work in groups of 3. Your group will design a small-scale research project integrating GenAI.

Step 1. With the members of your group, select a literacy-related issue or challenge of interest (e.g., you can focus on an issue you have experienced in your practice). Clearly articulate why this issue is significant for literacies education.

Step 2. Collaboratively design a proposal for a small-scale research project employing GenAI for data collection, analysis, and literature review. Clearly identify how GenAI could specifically contribute to the research process. Each member of the group can focus on one of these aspects.

Step 3. Develop a detailed outline for your research proposal, explicitly stating the project's objectives, methodology, the specific role of GenAI, and potential ethical considerations.

Step 4. Present your proposal to another group for constructive feedback, then collaboratively discuss ways to refine your project based on received feedback.

Step 5. After you have revised your proposal, share it with GenAI and ask for advice on how to make it more effective. You can use any platform (e.g., Open AI's *ChatGPT* or Google's *Gemini*). Reflect on GenAI's advice. Do you agree with the advice received? What are the strengths? What are the weaknesses? Can GenAI be a productive research partner?

Step 6. Now compare your experience with another group's. Reflect on your views of GenAI. If the other group used a different GenAI platform, consider how differences might have originated in the models chosen.

Task 3: Reflecting Across Chapters

In this task, you will critically reflect on your evolving understanding of literacy education and its practical implications. You will work individually and with another classmate.

Step 1. Individually, create a reflective journal entry capturing how your understanding of literacy has evolved across the eight chapters of the volume, noting significant shifts, insights, and ongoing questions.
Step 2. Pair up with a classmate to discuss your reflections, highlighting significant changes, key insights, and persistent challenges or questions.
Step 3. Together, analyze how these reflections can inform your future teaching practices, specifically regarding multimodal literacies and the integration of GenAI.
Step 4. Collaboratively, create a multimodal presentation/artifact (e.g., an infographics) summarizing your key insights and their implications for teaching practice.
Step 5. Share your presentation/artifact with the rest of your class.

Task 4: Future-Oriented Literacies Education

In this task, you will work in groups of 3–4. You will envision and illustrate a literacies classroom of the future, emphasizing collaboration between humans and GenAI.

Step 1. As a group, conceptualize a future literacies classroom scenario highlighting effective collaboration between educators, students, and GenAI tools. Consider innovative teaching methodologies and learning interactions. Use the information in this volume to support your work. Divide tasks among group members.
Step 2. Create a multimodal presentation that vividly illustrates your envisioned classroom scenario, including examples of classroom interactions, instructional practices, and anticipated student experience. Make reference to the frameworks and theories grounding your vision (see Chapter 4).
Step 3. Present your scenario to your classmates, soliciting feedback on its feasibility, inclusivity, educational effectiveness, and practical implementation.

Step 4. Collaboratively reflect on the feedback received, considering how these insights might inform your vision and practices as future literacy educators.

Step 5. Now, each member of the group goes back to the personal definition of literacy/literacies they have developed so far. Considering your work in this task and your reflections in this chapter, what changes would you make to your personal definition? What has changed? What remains the same? Why?

Step 6. Share your definition with the other members of your group. Together, consider similarities and differences. Create a new group, final definition.

Step 7. All definitions created by the class's groups are shared. Similarities and differences are noted, and they result in a final, class definition of literacy/literacies.

References

Archibald, J.-A. (2008). *Indigenous storywork: Educating the heard, mind, body and spirit.* University of British Columbia Press.

Archibald, J.-A., Xiiem, Q. Q., Nicol, C., & Yovanovich, J. (2023). Transformative education for aboriginal mathematics learning: Indigenous storywork as methodology. In J.-A. Archibald, J. B. J. Lee-Morgan, & J. De Santolo (Eds.), *Decolonizing research: Indigenous storywork as methodology* (pp. 72–88). Bloomsbury.

Bereiter, C. (2002). *Education and mind in the knowledge age.* Lawrence Erlbaum.

Chilisa, B. (2015). Keynote: Equality in diversity: Indigenous research methodologies. Paper Presented *at the American Indigenous Research Association Conference*, Montana, USA.

Cope, B. & Kalantzis, M. (2015). Interpreting evidence-of-learning: Educational research in the era of big data. *Open Review of Educational Research, 2*(1), 218–239. https://doi.org/10.1080/23265507.2015.1074870

Cope, B. & Kalantzis, M. (2017). Conceptualizing e-learning. In B. Cope & M. Kalantzis (Eds.), *ELearning ecologies* (pp. 1–45). Routledge.

Cope, B. & Kalantzis, M. (2019). Education 2.0: Artificial intelligence and the end of the test. *Beijing International Review of Education, 1*(2–3), 528–543. https://brill.com/view/journals/bire/1/2-3/article-p528_528.xml?language=en

Cope, B. & Kalantzis, M. (2020a). Editorial: Futures for research in education. *Educational Philosophy and Theory, 53*, 1–8. https://doi.org/10.1080/00131857.2020.1824781

Cope, B. & Kalantzis, M. (2020b). *Making sense: Reference, agency and structure in a grammar of multimodal meaning*. Cambridge University Press.

Cope, B. & Kalantzis, M. (2024). On cyber-social learning: A critique of artificial intelligence in education. In T. Kourkoulou, A. O. Tzirides, B. Cope, & M. Kalantzis (Eds.), *Trust and inclusion in AI-mediated education: Where human learning meets learning machines* (pp. 3–34). Springer. https://doi.org/10.1007/978-3-031-64487-0_1

Cope, B., Kalantzis, M., & Searsmith, D. (2020). Artificial intelligence for education: Knowledge and its assessment in AI-enabled learning ecologies. *Educational Philosophy and Theory, 52*, 1229–1245. https://doi.org/10.1080/00131857.2020.1728732

Curry, N., Baker, P., & Brookes, G. (2024). Generative AI for corpus approaches to discourse studies: A critical evaluation of ChatGPT. *Applied Corpus Linguistics, 4*(1). https://doi.org/10.1016/j.acorp.2023.100082

Douzas, G. & Bacao, F. (2018). Effective data generation for imbalance learning using conditional generative adversarial networks. *Expert Systems with Applications, 91*, 464–471. https://doi.org/10.1016/j.eswa.2017.09.030

Eco, U. (1976). *A theory of semiotics*. Indiana University Press.

Ford, C., McNally, D., & Ford, K. (2017). Using design-based research in higher education innovation. *Online Learning, 21*(3), 50–67. https://doi.org/10.24059/olj.v21i3.1232

Gee, J. P. (2014). *The social mind: Language, ideology, and social practice*. Common Ground.

Jameson, F. (1972). *The prison-house of language: A critical account of structuralism and Russian formalism*. Princeton University Press.

Kalantzis, M. & Cope, B. (2014). 'Education is the new philosophy', to make a metadisciplinary claim for the learning sciences. In A. D. Reid, E. P. Hart, & M. A. Peters (Eds.), *Companion to research in education* (pp. 101–115). Springer.

Kalantzis, M. & Cope, B. (2025). Literacy in the time of artificial intelligence. *Reading Research Quarterly, 60*, e591. https://doi.org/10.1002/rrq.591

Kirschner, P. A., Sweller, J., & Clark, R. E. (2006). Why minimal guidance during instruction does not work: An analysis of the failure of constructivist, discovery, problem-based, experiential, and inquiry-based teaching. *Educational Psychologist, 41*(2), 75–86. https://doi.org/10.1207/s15326985ep4102_1

Liu, Y., Shi, K., He, K. S., Ye, L., Fabbri, A. R., Liu, P., Radev, D., & Cohan, A. (2023). On learning to summarize with large language models as references. *ArXiv*. https://doi.org/10.48550/arXiv.2305.14239

Montebello, M., Cope, B., Kalantzis, M., Searsmith, D., Amina, T., Tzirides, A. O., Zhao, N., Chen, M., & Haniya, S. (2018a). Deepening e-learning through social collaborative intelligence. In *Proceedings of the 48th IEEE Annual Frontiers in Education (FIE) Conference* (pp. 1–4). IEEE. https://doi.org/10.1109/FIE.2018.8658779

Montebello, M., Pinheiro, P., Cope, B., Kalantzis, M., Amina, T., Searsmith, D., & Cao, D. (2018b). The impact of the peer review process evolution on learner performance in e-learning environments. In *Proceedings of the Fifth Annual ACM Conference on Learning at Scale*. https://doi.org/10.1145/3231644.3231693

Mozelius, P., & Humble, N. (2024, July). On the use of generative AI for literature reviews: An exploration of tools and techniques. In *Proceedings of the 23rd European Conference on Research Methodology for Business and Management Studies* (ECRM 2024). Mid Sweden University, University of Gävle, & Uppsala University. https://www.diva-portal.org/smash/get/diva2:1882472/FULLTEXT01.pdf

PBLWorks. (2021). *Project based learning handbook for elementary schools.* Buck Institute for Education.

Pinheiro, P. (2020). Text revision practices in an e-learning environment: Fostering the learning by design perspective. *Innovation in Language Learning and Teaching, 14*(1), 37–50. https://doi.org/10.1080/17501229.2018.1482902

Rorty, R. (1992). *The linguistic turn: Essays in philosophical method.* Chicago University Press.

Smith, L. T. (2022). *Decolonizing methodologies* ((3rd ed) ed.). Bloomsbury.

Stremersch, S. (2024). How can academics generate great research ideas? Inspiration from ideation practice. *International Journal of Research in Marketing, 41*(1), 1–17. https://doi.org/10.1016/j.ijresmar.2023.10.002

Tzou, C., Enrique Suárez, M., Bell, P., LaBonte, D., Starks, E., & Bang, M. (2019). Storywork in STEM-art: Making, materiality and robotics within everyday acts of indigenous presence and resurgence. *Cognition and Instruction, 37*(3), 306–326. https://doi.org/10.1080/07370008.2019.1624547

UNESCO. (2023). *Guidance for generative AI in education and research.* UNESCO. https://unesdoc.unesco.org/ark:/48223/pf0000386693

Vygotsky, L. S. (1978). *Mind in society: The development of higher psychological processes.* Harvard University Press.

Vygotsky, L. S. (1986). *Thought and language.* MIT Press.

Waks, L. J. (1997). The project method in postindustrial education. *Journal of Curriculum Studies, 29*(4), 391–406. https://doi.org/10.1080/002202797183964

Woolf, B. P., Lane, H. C., Chaudhri, V. K., & Kolodner, J. L. (2013). AI grand challenges for education. *AI Magazine*, *34*(4), 66–84. https://doi.org/10.1609/aimag.v34i4.2490

Zapata, G. C. (2022). *Learning by design and second language teaching: Theory, research, and practice.* Routledge.

Zapata, G. C., Kalantzis, M., & Cope, B. (Eds.). (2023). *Towards education justice: Literacy, multiliteracies, and the design of social futures.* Routledge. https://doi.org/10.4324/9781003349662

Appendix 1
Pedagogical Intervention Planning Tool

Literacies in the Age of AI: Teaching and Learning in the Digital Era,
First Edition. Gabriela C. Zapata, Bill Cope, and Mary Kalantzis.

Experiencing the Known	Experiencing the New	Applying Appropriately	Applying creatively
By being in students' worlds Drawing on learner prior knowledge and experience, community background, personal interests, identities, concrete experiences, individual motivation, students' own lives, and the everyday and familiar.	**By being in new worlds** Introducing learners to new experiences - real (excursions, guest speakers) or virtual (texts, images, information). New is from learner's perspective—to make sense it should refer to/incorporate familiar elements.	By doing things as expected Acting upon knowledge in an expected, predictable, or typical way based on what has been taught. It involves transformation of the learner and requires that they have opportunities to demonstrate their understanding and learning.	By doing things in interesting ways Doing things in interesting ways by taking knowledge and capabilities from one setting and adapting them to a different setting - taking something out of its familiar context and making it work somewhere else. Thinking/creating outside the box.
Possible artifacts, meaning forms: Functions of focus: Pedagogical moves:	Possible artifacts, meaning forms: Functions of focus: Pedagogical moves:	Possible artifacts, meaning forms: Functions of focus: Pedagogical moves:	Possible artifacts, meaning forms: Functions of focus: Pedagogical moves:
Conceptualizing by Classifying **By connecting the same type of thing** Identifying new concepts/ideas/themes, including abstract, generalizing terms, conventions, features, structures, definitions and rules. Naming and classifying is the first step toward understanding.	Conceptualizing with Theory **By connecting different types of things** Generalizing and synthesizing concepts by linking them together, making sense of how they contribute to the whole, generalizing cause and effect relationships. What if. . .?	Analyzing Functionally **By thinking about what something does** Examines the function or rationale of knowledge, action, an object or represented meaning. What is it for? What does it do? How does it work? What is its structure, function or connections? What are its causes/effects?	Analyzing Critically **By thinking about who benefits** Interrogates human purposes, intentions, and interests of knowledge, an action, an object, or represented meaning. What are its individual, social, and environmental consequences? Who gains? Who loses?
Possible artifacts, meaning forms: Functions of focus: Pedagogical moves:	Possible artifacts, meaning forms: Functions of focus: Pedagogical moves:	Possible artifacts, meaning forms: Functions of focus: Pedagogical moves:	Possible artifacts, meaning forms: Functions of focus: Pedagogical moves:

Appendix 2
Sample Materials for Secondary School Students in a Spanish Language Arts Classroom

Population of focus: Students in grades 6–8 in California schools

A2.1 Introduction

In this section, we offer examples of tasks that involve the use of GenAI technologies to support inclusive classroom practices, including idea generation, research, and language development. These samples are based on the short, graphic novel *Undocumented: A Worker's Fight* by Duncan Tonatiuh (2018). These activities reflect

Literacies in the Age of AI: Teaching and Learning in the Digital Era, First Edition. Gabriela C. Zapata, Bill Cope, and Mary Kalantzis.

California's *Spanish Language Development Standards*, and they value and combine different aspects of students' diversity and life-world, including their full linguistic repertoires, personal identities, and community experiences. Additionally, they highlight *Latinx lived civics* by connecting the themes of the book to real-life civic engagement and community experiences. The concept of Latinx lived civics makes reference to civic engagement that is informed by everyday social practices, family experiences, and community activism—particularly in historically marginalized populations (for more information, see Paiz et al., 2023; Santiago et al., 2021).

A2.2 Sample Classroom Tasks

A2.2.1 Task 1: Testimonios

Objective: Students will connect the experiences of the characters in the novel with personal or family narratives, fostering translanguaging, critical reflection, and personal connections.

1. **Reading and Discussion:**
    - Students read and analyze the book (in Spanish and/or English—the English version is translingual) as a class.
    - Students identify keywords or ideas related to migration, labor rights, and the pursuit of dignity.
2. **Personal Connection:**
    - Students write or record a short *testimonio*—personal or from a family member—about migration or work experiences. A *testimonio* can be defined as "critical reflection[s] of...personal experience[s] within particular sociopolitical realities" (Delgado Bernal et al., 2012, p. 364).
    - To complete this task, they resort to their full linguistic repertoire.
3. **GenAI Support:**
    - Students use GenAI for vocabulary suggestions or synonyms that can enrich their testimonios in Spanish.
    - Students may also employ GenAI to create an outline or generate reflective questions on migration and workers' rights that will allow them to identify a particular experience they would like to share.

- GenAI can offer feedback on students' artifacts, suggesting ways in which the story could be expanded so that it offers a more comprehensive or detailed narrative of the experiences described.

4. **Sharing and Reflection:**
   - Students participate in a "story circle" or reading session to share different perspectives, discussing similarities and differences in their experiences.

Learner Diversity: Students' diverse linguistic and cultural backgrounds will be validated by connecting literary content to real-life contexts.

Latinx Lived Civics: Students will learn how their personal stories of migration and labor connect to broader civic issues, empowering them to participate in related community discussions.

A2.2.2 Task 2: Characters, Communities, and Lived Civics

Objective: Students will critically analyze how characters and themes in the novel reflect Latinx community realities and civic struggles for labor rights.

1. **Character Map:**
   - Students create a character map describing the protagonist, *Juan*, and explaining how his actions and experiences reveal social justice issues.
2. **Theme and Context; Personal Connection:**
   - In small groups, students discuss themes like labor exploitation, fair wages, and community organization as they appear in the book.
   - Students reflect on the similarities and differences between the presentation of these themes in the book, and their experiences within their community.
   - Students can gather information on community organizations/events that support members of their community facing issues similar to *Juan's*, the main character.
3. **GenAI Support:**
   - Students use GenAI to generate discussion questions (e.g., "What motivates the character to fight for his rights?") or to

summarize sections of the story. These questions can help with the character map.

- Students may also ask GenAI to find news articles or historical examples related to undocumented workers. Students can then compare these examples to the story presented in the book as well as those issues faced by their communities.

4. **Report or Presentation:**
    - Students present short written reports reflecting on how the protagonist's struggles connect to real-life situations in their local communities.
    - Before the presentation, students use GenAI to gather feedback on possible issues that could have been discussed or ways in which the report could be more effectively organized.

Learner Diversity: Students will combine literary analysis with sociohistorical inquiry, drawing on both Spanish and English materials as needed.

Latinx Lived Civics: Students will relate the protagonist's experiences to community activism, highlighting possibilities for civic participation and collective action.

A2.2.3 Task 3: Collective Poetic Creation—Voices of Struggle

Objective: Students will express themselves creatively and reflect on the themes in the novel by composing collaborative poetry that underscores resistance and empowerment.

1. **Textual Inspiration:**
    - Students read specific passages from the book that depict emotional or impactful moments (e.g., the death of the protagonist's father, his experiences with *la migra* [the US border patrol agency], the power of community).
2. **Brainstorming:**
    - Students will list words or phrases in both Spanish and English representing major themes; e.g., *coyote*, *migra*, *piquete*, *struggle*, *hope*, *justice*, *family*, and *community*.

3. **GenAI Support:**
   - Students use GenAI to find synonyms or poetic phrases in Spanish (and in English) that relate to their brainstormed keywords.
   - Students may also ask GenAI to suggest poetic structures (e.g., haiku, free verse, couplets, etc.) based on the kind of poem they have in mind.
4. **Collaborative Poem:**
   - In small groups, students create a collective poem, blending Spanish and English to reflect their translingual identities.
5. **Presentation:**
   - Students present or display their poem. They may incorporate artwork or illustrations inspired by the book's visuals and themes. They can use GenAI to suggest presentation styles (e.g., colors, typography, images) to complement the textual aspects of the poem.

Learner Diversity: Students will merge literary creativity with their personal linguistic identities, engaging in translanguaging and cultural self-expression.

Latinx Lived Civics: By producing a shared piece of poetry, students will affirm community solidarity and open dialogue on social justice and civic participation.

A2.2.4 Task 4: Youth Labor Rights Campaign

Objective: Students will translate lessons from the novel into a civic--action project by designing a campaign to raise awareness about labor rights.

1. **Initial Research:**
   - Students employ GenAI to investigate labor rights laws in California, focusing on protections for immigrant workers.
   - They may use Spanish and English sources to gather this information.

2. **Campaign Design:**
   - Students determine which audience they aim to inform (e.g., peers, family members, the community).
   - Based on their decision, they select a channel for communication, such as flyers, infographics, posters, or mock social media posts.
3. **Additional GenAI Support:**
   - Students use GenAI to brainstorm slogans, compose text for flyers or posters, and explore examples of successful campaigns.
   - Students may also ask GenAI for assistance with design ideas.
   - Once students have created their artifacts, GenAI offers suggestions for improvements to make meaning-making more effective.
4. **Presentation and Reflection:**
   - Students present their campaigns and explain how these efforts connect to the novel as well as their communities, emphasizing the significance of collective action.
5. **Extending the Project (Optional):**
   - If feasible, students collaborate with local worker or immigrant rights organizations to adapt or share their campaign materials with the community at large/news media.

Learner Diversity: Students will apply research, writing, and creativity in multiple languages/meaning forms (e.g., image, spatial organization, etc.) to develop a clear, impactful campaign connected to issues affecting their local communities.

Latinx Lived Civics: By actively engaging in civic-minded projects, students will see themselves as changemakers, using literary insights and personal experience to advocate for their communities.

A2.2.5 Task 5: Art and Mixtec Codices—Exploring the Visual Dimension

Objective: Students will appreciate the artistic dimension of *Undocumented: A Worker's Fight*, focusing on how the Mixtec codex-like format and illustrations reflect the main character's Mixtec identity as well as how the book's materiality conveys the author's "rejection of drawn borders," and his symbolic "rejection of national borders" (Caroccio Maldonado, 2023, p. 35).

1. **Initial Observation:**
   - Students examine the book's physical format and illustrations, noting the *codex*-inspired layout. Students discuss and record information on the historical role of Mesoamerican codices, such as Mixtec codices, in preserving cultural knowledge. GenAI can support students' work by offering relevant information and guiding them in the organization of their new knowledge.
2. **Visual Analysis:**
   - Students describe the visual elements that stand out (e.g., color, silhouettes, texture, symbolism). They also focus on the continuous presentation of the story (i.e., the codex-like structure).
   - Students relate these features to the character's identity, and they critically analyze the author/illustrator's objective in connection with the book's themes/story.
   - GenAI can guide students' work by pointing out possible sociocultural-design-audience connections.
3. **Historical and Cultural Context:**
   - Students conduct more in-depth research on Mesoamerican codices (e.g., Aztec, Mayan, Mixtec, etc.) and compare these to Duncan Tonatiuh's style.
   - Students' reflect on how the past is reinterpreted to tell a modern story of undocumented workers.
4. **Mini-Codex Creation:**
   - Students create a short, translingual "mini codex" with folded pages, illustrating and textually narrating personal or familial stories about work and migration.
   - Students incorporate symbolic or stylistic elements inspired by both contemporary and pre-Hispanic designs.
5. **Additional GenAI Support:**
   - Students use GenAI to find information on pre-Hispanic symbols or visual formats from historical codices.

- Students may also ask GenAI to outline key points on codices and their cultural relevance.
- Once they have developed their codices, GenAI can offer suggestions for improvements in terms of communicative effectiveness.

6. **Extending the Project (Optional):**
   - If feasible, students' mini codices are presented in an exhibit for members of the school and community at large. The exhibit also incorporates students' reflections on the creative process and the significance of art/cultural artefacts for activism.

Learner Diversity: Students will integrate historical (codex traditions) and contemporary/personal (immigration/labor experiences) perspectives in a creative project.

Latinx Lived Civics: By designing mini codices, students will view themselves as cultural memory keepers/artivists, linking personal stories of migration/labor to broader social and civic narratives as well as community activism/action.

Index

Literacies in the Age of AI: Teaching and Learning in the Digital Era, First Edition. Gabriela C. Zapata, Bill Cope, and Mary Kalantzis.